ARBITRATION
IN A NUTSHELL
SECOND EDITION

By

THOMAS E. CARBONNEAU
Orlando Distinguished Professor of Law
Penn State University
Dickinson School of Law

WEST®

A Thomson Reuters business

Mat #40828923

Nutshell Series, In a Nutshell and the Nutshell Logo are trademarks registered in the U.S. Patent and Trademark Office.

© West, a Thomson business, 2007
© 2009 Thomson Reuters

> 610 Opperman Drive
> St. Paul, MN 55123
> 1–800–313–9378

Printed in the United States of America

ISBN: 978–0–314–91137–7

To my daughter:

"Lou"
Sara L. Carbonneau

*

ACKNOWLEDGEMENT

In writing the present work, I relied upon my treatise, entitled THE LAW AND PRACTICE OF ARBITRATION (3d ed. 2009). Juris Publishing, Inc. (www. jurispub.com) gave me permission to use and adapt the text of the treatise to this enterprise. The treatise is more comprehensive and detailed and is intended as a reference work for law practice. The present volume acts as a supplement to my CASES AND MATERIALS ON ARBITRATION LAW AND PRACTICE (5th ed.), published by Thomson-West.

OUTLINE

*

TABLE OF CASES

References are to Pages

A

B

XI

C

F

G

H

I

In re (see name of party)

J

K

L

M

N

O

P

R

S

T

U

V

TABLE OF CASES

ARBITRATION

IN A NUTSHELL

SECOND EDITION

*

Introduction

Arbitration has become the primary remedy for the resolution of civil disputes in American society and international commerce. Only the foolhardy lawyer would ignore its new significance to the legal process and the vindication of legal rights. It now reaches standard consumer transactions and employment disputes like it once applied to the sale of goods and services between merchants. It addresses controversies arising under regulatory law, like antitrust and securities regulation, and the civil liberty guarantees in civil rights legislation. Subject-matter inarbitrability and public law limits on private adjudication do not play much, if any, role in the contemporary U.S. law of arbitration. Under United States law, nearly all civil disputes are arbitrable.

The United States Supreme Court has been the instrument of the U.S. judicial doctrine on arbitration. In effect, brandishing the text of the Federal Arbitration Act (FAA), 9 U.S.C. §§ 1–16, the work of the Court in this area has been doggedly determined, revolutionary, and—ultimately—quite undemocratic in tenor and implementation. The arbitral remedy is not a muse for the Court; it does not inspire the Court to elaborate visionary constructs of doctrine. Nonetheless, the Court is persuaded that arbitration is the best, and perhaps last, hope for achieving workable civil justice in contemporary American society.

At this stage in the development of the U.S. Supreme Court's decisional law on arbitration, it is clear that the Court is using the FAA as a stepping stone to elaborate a larger judicial doctrine on arbitration. The Court has added significantly to the content of the legislation. For example, FAA § 2—unquestionably the key provision of the Act both historically and doctrinally—establishes that the surrender of judicial remedies by contract does not violate public policy and thereby validates the choice of arbitration as a legitimate exercise of contract freedom.

Be that as it may, in the Court's rulings, arbitration agreements are not simply contracts. In the words of Justice Black, when he reacted critically to the majority's endorsement of the separability doctrine in his dissent in *Prima Paint Corp. v. Flood & Conklin Mfg. Co.*, 388 U.S. 395 (1967), they are "super" contracts, "[e]levate[d] . . . above all other contractual provisions." Glossing the FAA, the Court has made arbitration agreements nothing less than the means for remedying the ineffectiveness of judicial adjudication in American society.

The case law makes clear that arbitration agreements escape the ordinary rules of contract formation and validity. The obligation to arbitrate can be imposed unilaterally by the stronger party on the weaker one because arbitration is, as a matter of law, in the best interests of both parties. Arbitration supplies each side with material benefits. Contractual oppression only occurs when the reference to arbitration denies the weaker party any access to adjudicatory relief. In this setting, the distribution of costs and the availability of remedies are key concerns. Unconscionability always lurks at the periphery of adhesionary arbitration agreements.

The federal preemption doctrine, pieced together by the Court over a number of cases, has been instrumental to the creation and maintenance of the "strong federal policy on arbitration." It guaranteed that a set of uniformly favorable principles to arbitration would apply in all United States—both federal and state—courts. In establishing the doctrine, the Court literally rewrote the express content of the FAA, extending the federal statute's application to state courts and legislatures. Federal preemption also allowed the Court to "promulgate" impliedly a federal right to arbitrate. Moreover, substantive rights protection is not a barrier to the recourse to arbitration. The Court began dismantling the subject-matter inarbitrability defense in 1985 in *Mitsubishi Motors Corp. v. Soler Chrysler-Plymouth, Inc.*, (473 U.S. 614). Subsequent decisions eventually provided that all statutory and regulatory disputes were arbitrable. *14 Penn Plaza v. Pyett*, 129 S.Ct. 1456 (2009), confirms that there is no subject matter barrier to the arbitrability of civil rights claims. As long as the agreement clearly submits the disputes to arbitral resolution, they are arbitrable. Party provision is controlling, unless the statute provides for exclusive judicial recourse. The statement of exclusive judicial recourse in the statute, however, must be free of ambiguity and avoid any confusion.

On the question of arbitrability, as elsewhere in the decisional law, the protection of legal rights cedes to the imperative of erecting a functional adjudicatory process. Even freedom of contract, as indispensable as it is to the law of arbitration, ultimately yields to the necessity of protecting the reference to arbitration. The allegiance to freedom of contract is conditional: Agreements to arbitrate are enforced as written only if they fulfill the objectives of the federal policy on arbitration. The Court has exhibited singular determination in upholding the federal policy on arbitration.

In this regard, the Court is more perspicacious than it is single-minded or arbitrary. It is generally acknowledged that exceptions to rules, once made, progressively swallow up the initial rule. The U.S. law of arbitration would not be as cohesive, viable, or effective were it riddled with the twists and turns of qualification. The campaign for federalization was waged to create a disciplined, uniform, and unambiguous regulation of arbitration. After all, the goal that is contemplated is nothing less than the building of a workable system of civil adjudication and justice in U.S. society.

The Court has asserted that arbitral proceedings are in all respects equivalent to the judicial trial and submission to arbitration has no impact upon legal rights. Arbitration is "a mere form of trial." *See Rodriguez de Quijas v. Shearson/Am. Express, Inc.*, 490 U.S. 477 (1989). By making this statement, the Court delegated to lawyers (to the bar's drafting, negotiation, and representational skills) the definition and implementation of due process in arbitral proceedings. It also sought to reduce litigation about arbitration by investing arbitrators with greater decisional and procedural powers. Once a court determines that a valid contract to arbitrate exists, the arbitrator decides everything else—consolidation, *res judicata*, allowable relief, the availability of classwide arbitration—that might be generated by the arbitral clause, contract, proceedings, and merits.

Under *First Options of Chicago, Inc. v. Kaplan*, 514 U.S. 938 (1995), courts can even be excluded from deciding threshold jurisdictional issues by contract. Courts resurface in the process only to enforce arbitrator rulings and confirm (in rare instances, vacate) the award. The rulings in *Howsam v. Dean Witter Reynolds*, 537 U.S. 79 (2002), and *Green Tree Financial Corp. v. Bazzle*, 539 U.S. 444 (2003), insulated the arbitral process from judicial interference and gave it unfettered autonomy, allowing it to function as an effective vehicle for the provision and management of adjudicatory resources.

In the Court's decisional law on arbitration, there is a lone exception to the regime of uniform support. It originated in an early case, *Commonwealth*

Coatings Corp. v. Continental Casualty Co., 393 U.S. 145 (1968). The case was arguably decided by a plurality and never reconfirmed. Arbitrator impartiality and disclosures are significant issues in contemporary U.S. arbitration law in part because, in 1968, the Court determined that providing parties with information about prospective arbitrators was necessary to protect their rights as consumers of arbitration services. As a result, designated arbitrators have a duty to disclose relevant information about likely conflicts of interest that might impair their ability to decide disputes in a disinterested fashion. According to the Court, the appointment or conduct of an arbitrator cannot create the appearance of bias, much less amount to actual bias. Otherwise, the award can be vacated for "evident partiality" under FAA § 10.

Current arbitral practice seeks to institute tribunal-wide arbitrator neutrality. That standard is at odds with the tradition associated with three-member tribunals and party-appointed arbitrators. The *quid pro quo* had been that the parties would designate sympathetic arbitrators whom they expected to advocate for them in the tribunal's deliberations, allowing the neutral presiding arbitrator to cast the deciding vote. Although the practice never resulted in any reported abuse or corruption, arbitral institutions and other organizations concluded that partisan arbitrators were not in the best interests of arbitral process and needed to be discontinued— unless the parties provided otherwise in their agreement.

The convergence between the ruling in *Commonwealth Coatings* and the present-day institutional push for tribunal-wide neutrality emphasized the importance of arbitrator disclosures. The practical implementation of the standard, however, has proven to be challenging. It is difficult to establish what should be disclosed and the extent of disclosure. Any failure in disclosure—no matter how small or seemingly innocuous—can make an award vulnerable to vacatur. As a result, some courts apply stringent disclosure standards only to the neutral arbitrator and refuse to vacate awards on the basis of the mere appearance of bias, citing the federal policy favoring arbitration. At the very least, the search for possible bias will increase the costs of and delays in the process.

Regulating arbitrators coincides with and furthers the adversarialization of the arbitral process. If impartiality and disclosures apply to all arbitrators, more actions to disqualify will be lodged— perhaps for the exclusively litigious end of frustrating the recourse to arbitration. This type of advocacy ruined judicial litigation. Arbitration thrived because of the adversarial failings of the legal system. If arbitration begins to emulate the maladies of court proceedings, it, too, could suffer a decline and eventually falter.

In the area of enforcement, the Eleventh Circuit has suggested that the right of recourse against awards be subject to the imposition of sanctions if the court concludes that the challenge is frivolous or perfunctory. The court's perspicacity is uncontestable, "The laudatory goals of the FAA will be achieved only to the extent that courts ensure arbitration is an alternative to litigation, not an additional layer in a protracted contest." *See B.L. Harbert Int'l, L.L.C. v. Hercules Steel Co.,* 441 F.3d 905 (11th Cir. 2006). The statement of position warrants serious attention. Procedural sophistication and complexity are antithetical to the effectiveness and functionality of arbitration. They are lawyer urgings that add little to the fairness and legitimacy of the arbitral process. They could have a crippling impact. Formalization should only be resorted to in the event of flagrant abuse.

While there are misgivings, debates, and controversies, arbitration—despite imperfections—is in a golden era. The Court sustains every aspect of the operation of the arbitral process in both the domestic and transborder sphere. Doctrine is adapted to achieve the objectives of policy; everything is sacrificed to bring about an accessible form of private adjudicatory justice. The judicial support not only is consistent, but also unequivocal. As a consequence, arbitration has expanded its range to new dispute areas and its scope of application beyond contract itself. With the extension of the contract to nonsignatory parties and the deference paid to adhesionary agreements, arbitral clauses implied at law may soon become a new feature of the U.S. court doctrine on arbitration.

The new reach of arbitration creates a need for information at both the public and professional level. The present volume provides a comprehensive description and appraisal of the arbitral process under United States law. It defines essential terms and doctrines. In addition, it thoroughly explains the statutory law in the area (the Federal Arbitration Act and the Uniform Arbitration Act of 2000). Thereafter, it addresses the major decisional law themes: Federalization, freedom of contract, and arbitrability. It investigates the traditional and the less established applications of the arbitral mechanism. It also assesses the law that applies to the enforcement of arbitral awards—a critical phase of the arbitral process.

In addition, the book contains an account of international commercial arbitration. International commercial arbitration is instrumental to the conduct of international commerce and the harmonization of transborder law and legal procedure. The discussion highlights the central significance of the 1958 New York Arbitration Convention. It evaluates the rulings of the United States Supreme Court in the area for their contribution to applicable doctrine and the systemic autonomy of the process. The book enables the reader to confront standard arbitration problems as well as issues that have yet to surface but which appear inevitable and likely to constitute formidable challenges to the arbitral process' operation and continued viability.

CHAPTER ONE

BASIC TERMS, CHARACTERISTICS, AND ISSUES

A Definition

Arbitration is a private and informal trial procedure for the adjudication of disputes. It is an extrajudicial process. It functions as an alternative to conventional litigation. It yields binding determinations through less expensive, more efficient, expert, and fair proceedings. Although it can engender settlements, arbitration is not intended to operate as a means for achieving dispute resolution directly through party agreement. Arbitration is neither negotiation nor mediation. The parties confer upon the arbitrators full legal authority to adjudicate their disputes, *i.e.,* to render a final disposition on the matters submitted that can be enforced through coercive legal means. Party agreement sets the process in motion, but it does not dictate (necessarily) the procedure nor (certainly) the outcome. Once the parties entrust the arbitral tribunal with the authority to rule, they—subject to a possible settlement—relinquish control of the proceedings, the dispute, and its resolution to the arbitrators and—to a lesser extent—the administering arbitral institution.

The recourse to arbitration is consensual. The parties agree by contract to submit existing or prospective disputes to arbitration. The agreement to arbitrate is the centerpiece of the process—both in terms of legal doctrine and from a practical vantage point. The parties have the freedom—the legal right—to engage in arbitration and to make specific provisions for the implementation and operation of their arbitration. By entering into an arbitration contract, the parties voluntarily abandon their right to judicial relief and, in effect, create a private system of adjudication that presumably is better adapted to their transactional needs.

Arbitration Agreements

A contract for arbitration can take one of two forms: The submission or the arbitral clause. The submission is an arbitration agreement in which the parties agree that an existing dispute will be submitted to arbitration. The arbitral clause is a contract under which the parties agree to submit future disputes to arbitration. In either form, an arbitration agreement must be in writing and should satisfy the requirements for contract validity.

The arbitral clause is the most common type of arbitration agreement. It generally contains simple, straightforward, standard language providing for the resolution of disputes through arbitration: "Any dispute arising under this contract shall be submitted to arbitration under the rules of [a chosen arbitral institution]." Ordinarily, the arbitral clause is a provision within a larger contract; it, however, can be a separate agreement. In such instances, the main contract should provide for the incorporation of the arbitration agreement and the latter, likewise, should contain an unambiguous declaration that it applies to the main contract. As a matter of law, the arbitral clause—whether it is a stand-alone agreement or a provision within the larger contract—is always distinct from the principal contract. The separability doctrine provides that the arbitral clause has its own legal identity.

Once a dispute arises, the parties to an arbitral clause usually enter into a submission agreement. The submission functions as the threshold step to arbitration. It establishes the matters of disagreement. In so doing, it defines the arbitrators' jurisdictional authority. The submission eventually leads to the initiation of the arbitral proceeding through the appointment of arbitrators.

A valid written agreement to arbitrate deprives the courts of jurisdiction to entertain any matter covered by the agreement. Judicial authority to adjudicate remains stymied even when an arbitral award is vacated or the arbitral process is functioning badly. The reference to arbitration establishes exclusive jurisdiction in the arbitral tribunal. Court assistance, however, is available during the arbitral proceedings. It may become necessary, for example, to compel arbitration or enforce subpoenas.

Separability and *Kompetenz-Kompetenz*

The separability doctrine works in tandem with *kompetenz-kompetenz*. *Kompetenz-kompetenz*, or jurisdiction to rule on jurisdictional challenges, provides that the arbitral tribunal has the authority to rule on matters involving the validity or the scope of the agreement to arbitrate. The arbitral tribunal, therefore, can rule on allegations that there is a flaw in the main contract that affects the validity of the arbitral clause. It can also assess claims of adhesion or unconcionability against the arbitral clause. Further, the tribunal can decide claims that the dispute in question is not covered by the arbitral clause.

Under U.S. law, the arbitrators' right to rule on jurisdiction is not conferred by statute. It, like separability, arises from case law. Moreover, it is available at the parties' discretion; it is a function of contract. *See First Options of Chicago, Inc. v. Kaplan*, 514 U.S. 938 (1995).

The separability and *kompetenz-kompetenz* doctrines reinforce the autonomy of the arbitral process. They give arbitrators judge-like authority and are likely to dissuade parties from engaging in perfunctory challenges to arbitrator jurisdiction. Court supervision of the arbitrator's determination of such issues is likely to be lax. It is usually delayed until the final award is rendered. For all intents and purposes, the arbitral tribunal itself decides questions pertaining to the validity and scope of its adjudicatory authority.

Arbitrability

Arbitrability establishes which disputes can be lawfully submitted to arbitration. A finding of inarbitrability can act as a defense to the enforcement of an arbitration agreement or arbitral award. Arbitrability limits the parties' right to engage in arbitration and the arbitrators' authority to rule. Inarbitrability can arise as a result of the subject matter of the dispute or because of contractual flaws in the arbitration agreement.

Under subject-matter inarbitrability, a dispute cannot be submitted to arbitration—as a matter of law—because it involves matters directly linked to the public interest. Matters of criminal culpability generally are deemed inarbitrable because of their subject matter. Therefore, unless plea-bargaining is considered a form of arbitration, allegations of bribery or criminal violations of RICO or of the tax regulations would be inarbitrable because the offending private commercial conduct implicates the public interest. To some extent, subject-matter inarbitrability overlaps with the public policy exception to arbitration. In both circumstances, public interest considerations prevent the recourse to arbitration.

The most difficult problems pertaining to subject-matter arbitrability arise when disputes involve government regulation of commercial activity through, for example, antitrust or securities laws. The difficulty is acute both domestically and in the context of international business transactions. Such statutory claims involve the authority of the government to implement regulatory policy, the individual parties' freedom of contract, whether the transactions are "one-off" (single time) deals or have a larger social significance, and whether arbitrators have sufficient integrity, as well as the necessary jurisdiction, independence, and distance, to rule on matters of regulatory law.

The United States Supreme Court has rejected the traditional view that regulatory or statutory matters are inarbitrable. *See Mitsubishi Motors Corp. v. Soler Chrysler–Plymouth, Inc.,* 473 U.S. 614, 632 (1985) ("The mere appearance of an antitrust dispute does not alone warrant invalidation of the selected forum on the undemonstrated assumption that the arbitration clause is tainted."). The federal judicial position is that such claims, regardless of whether they arise in international or domestic contracts, can be submitted to arbitration. *See Gilmer v. Interstate/Johnson Lane Corp.,* 500 U.S. 20 (1991).

Inarbitrability also functions on the basis of contract. In these circumstances, the matter does not involve the application of public law or invocation of the public interest. The challenges converge on the contract of arbitration—its existence, making, or scope. The contention of inarbitrability can be premised upon the lack of an agreement to arbitrate, a contract deficiency in an existing agreement, or the limited scope of application of an otherwise existing and valid agreement. There also can be a failure to follow the terms of the agreement in organizing the arbitration. Contract is the gateway to arbitration. *See First Options of Chica-*

go, Inc. v. Kaplan, 514 U.S. 938 (1995). Without an actual, enforceable, and applicable agreement, there is no legal obligation to arbitrate.

Case Law Rules on Arbitrability

A few doctrinal rules should be highlighted in connection with the inarbitrability defense. First, courts generally interpret a broadly-worded arbitration agreement as referring to all transactional disputes that arise between the parties. Therefore, a broad reference to arbitration (''any dispute arising under this contract'') encompasses—as a matter of law—contract problems relating to performance, delivery, consideration, conformity to specifications, excuse and other defenses, as well as statutory claims pertaining to the public regulation of commercial conduct (bankruptcy, antitrust, securities, and tax). A broad reference to arbitration also encompasses civil rights claims. *14 Penn Plaza v. Pyett*, 129 S.Ct. 1456 (2009), however, indicates that specific mention must be made of discrimination claims. In some circumstances, it may include jurisdictional questions—if the parties include an addendum to that effect in the arbitration agreement. It is, therefore, necessary to expressly exclude matters that the parties do not wish to submit to arbitration.

Second, state contract law generally governs the construction of an arbitration agreement. Therefore, questions pertaining to the formation of the contract and its validity—adhesion, unconscionability, and restrictions imposed to protect consumer rights—are resolved pursuant to the relevant state law. Because the U.S. law on arbitration has been federalized, any state contract law provision that disables arbitration agreements in particular is subject to challenge under federal preemption. If it is to survive a preemption challenge, the statutory disability must at least apply to contracts in general and not single out arbitration agreements. Rulings that arbitration agreements are adhesionary and unconscionable have been especially common in employment and consumer cases in the state and federal courts in California. *See, e.g., Chalk v. T–Mobile USA Inc.*, 560 F.3d 1087 (9th Cir. 2009). As a general matter, however, courts uphold arbitration agreements as valid contracts no matter what their deficiencies in formation.

Third, the United States Supreme Court has articulated a highly tolerant view of what subject areas can be submitted to arbitration on the basis of two doctrinal precepts. The latter doctrine was elaborated primarily in the security arbitration cases (*McMahon* and *Rodriguez*). First, arbitration is as effective as a court proceeding in adjudicating disputes. Therefore, rights are not extinguished or diminished by the submission of claims to arbitration. Because arbitration will give full effect to rights created by statute or otherwise, statutory disputes can lawfully be submitted to arbitration. Second, relatedly, each arbitration stands on its own and does not have any significance beyond the private agreement and relationship that gave rise to it. Inarbitrability as a protector of the public interest, therefore, is of little relevance in the setting of most arbitrations.

Finally, the unstated view in many of the United States Supreme Court's rulings is that arbitration is in the parties' and society's best interest as a matter of law. Some access to justice is better than no access at all. This position undermines the role of the contract inarbitrability defense. As long as a reference to arbitration has been made, the parties must always have intended to agree to arbitrate disputes no matter what the flaws in the contract might be. The presumption that arbitration is in the best interest of all the affected parties works to remedy all contract deficiencies that might have voided the agreement.

The Advantages of Arbitration

Arbitral adjudication responds well to the character of commercial transactions and the disputes to which they give rise. First, arbitration is a private dispute resolution process. Arbitral proceedings are not open to the public and awards generally have not been published. Business associates, competitors, and clients generally have no knowledge of the dispute, the proceedings, or the outcome. The recourse to arbitration, therefore, allows commercial parties to maintain a competitive position despite transactional problems. Second, the parties to the arbitration have the right to select the arbitrators. The designated arbitrators ordinarily have considerable expertise in the relevant field. Their commercial experience allows them to reach determinations that reflect standard practices. By choosing to arbitrate, therefore, business parties avoid inexpert judges, legalistic solutions, and unwanted publicity.

Third, arbitral adjudication can be more flexible and less adversarial and protracted than its judicial counterpart. It can result in an economy of time and money. The commercial experience of the arbitral tribunal lessens the significance of legal precedent, eliminates the need for complex rules of evidence, and minimizes discovery, the use of experts, and other informational trial procedures. These features reduce the prospect of tactical litigious warfare. As a general matter, the arbitral tribunal is bound to provide the arbitrating parties with a fair and reasonable opportunity to be heard, to admit and weigh the pertinent evidence, and to decide the matters submitted in a rational and timely fashion. Procedural informality, placing trust in the arbitrators' professional capabilities, and allowing commercial equity to trump jural considerations have been the hallmarks of commercial arbitration.

In international commerce, the neutrality of arbitration as to nationality and legal tradition is a fourth factor that contributes to its "business appeal." In fact, the reference to arbitration is indispensable in multinational commercial ventures. It eliminates the conflicts associated with the assertion of national court jurisdiction, the choice of applicable law, and the enforcement of foreign judgments. Arbitration also tempers the disparities between different legal systems. In the context of transborder business, arbitration functions as a *de facto* transborder legal system, providing an adjudicatory process free of national bias, parochial laws and practices, and able to dispense sensible commercial justice.

Finally, it should be underscored that arbitration's more flexible approach to adjudication is less destructive of business relationships and allows the parties to continue to do business once the dispute has been resolved. In arbitration, commercial parties can make their case and let a neutral expert decide the outcome. In effect, arbitration functions as a type of "in-house" adjudicatory process through which disputes are decided pursuant to the usages of the commercial community.

The Process

Arbitration is not a panacea. In some instances, arbitration can provide a better, or the best, means for addressing disputes, but it is nothing more or less than an alternative remedy—one of several mechanisms for achieving fairness and finality in the determination of conflict. Like the judicial trial or party negotiations, arbitration has advantages and disadvantages. The decision to arbitrate represents a calculation of procedural gains and losses in an effort to achieve maximum advantage. In each case, the question of whether to pursue traditional litigation, arbitration, or structured negotiation requires a clear understanding of the circumstances of the dispute and of the available remedies.

The choice of remedies is never an easy one. Choosing between a public judicial trial and private arbitral proceedings demands the exercise of judgment, balancing complex factors and shifting considerations, and speculating about the future. Moreover, the choice involves trading the protection of rights available in the constitutionally-sound but cumbersome public process of judicial litigation for the functionality and finality of private arbitral proceedings in which the arbitrator is the sovereign decider.

Assuming an agreement to arbitrate exists and that it is an enforceable contract, the proceedings usually take place in accordance with the rules of an administering arbitral institution, like the American Arbitration Association (AAA), the National Arbitration Forum (The Forum), JAMS, or the International Chamber of Commerce (ICC). The institutional rules provide the framework for the operation of the various stages of the arbitral process: (1) the constitution of the arbitral tribunal; (2) the establishment of the submission to arbitration or the tribunal's terms of reference; (3) the selection of procedural rules for the proceedings; (4) the conduct of the proceedings; (5) the closure of the proceedings; (6) the tribunal's deliberations; and (7) the rendering of an award. The selection of administrative rules is a way for the parties to customize their arbitration.

Following receipt of a "demand for arbitration," the administering arbitral institution notifies the other party of the demand and requests that the parties nominate arbitrators pursuant to their agreement. The administering institution can supply the parties, if necessary, with arbitrator lists. As a general matter, the parties select an uneven number of arbitrators to avoid a deadlock—one arbitrator is usually agreed upon for smaller matters and a three-member panel presides over larger, more complex cases. When a three-member panel is chosen, each party names its arbitrator and the two party-appointed arbitrators name a third arbitrator, known as the neutral, who acts as the chair of the panel.

Despite their allegiance to a party, party-appointed arbitrators are now expected to act in a disinterested professional manner. Some courts disagree and hold that partisan expectations still accompany party appointment. Recent institutional practice, however, provides that all arbitrators—including party-appointed arbitrators—should assess the submitted matter with complete impartiality. Contemporary appointment rules further insist upon thorough disclosures and transparency by arbitrators.

Before the proceedings can begin, the designated arbitrators must accept their appointment and the statement of claims that has been submitted. The arbitrators are obligated to disclose any conflicts of interest or other matter that might impair their ability to rule in an impartial manner. The failure to disclose necessary and available information can result in the vacatur of the award on the basis of evident partiality. The arbitrators can refuse to serve on the panel or disqualify themselves. The parties can lodge an action to disqualify an arbitrator before the administering arbitral institution or a court of law. With the acquiescence of the parties and under the direction of the administering arbitral institution, the arbitral tribunal chooses a place for the arbitration and sets a time for the initial hearing. At this stage of the process, parties submit a deposit for arbitrator and administrative fees with the administering arbitral institution.

An arbitration can be conducted on a purely documentary basis. In an "arbitration on the documents," the parties supply the administering arbitral institution with a statement of their position and allegations, as well as their supporting evidence. The arbitral tribunal or the sole arbitrator then rules on the basis of the submitted materials. Arbitrations can also consist of a documentary record with an abbreviated hearing or of a set of elaborate hearings that include pretrial procedures and live testimonial evidence. Actual proceedings can be as varied as the type of parties involved and the circumstances of the dispute. The character of the proceeding is generally determined by the arbitration agreement or by the parties' ability to agree once a dispute arises. If no contractual disposition exists and the parties are unable to agree, the arbitral tribunal—under the supervision of the administering arbitral institution—would decide on the protocol for the arbitration.

The proceedings begin once preliminary procedural matters have been resolved. The parties' traditional expectation is to have reasonably fair and flexible proceedings. The arbitrators usually have sufficient procedural authority to thwart trial tactics that unnecessarily lengthen the proceedings. Generally, the parties want to be able to make their case. They then want the arbitral tribunal to decide the matter.

Arbitral systems ordinarily do not include a right to pretrial discovery. Parties are generally required to exchange documents and witness lists prior to the commencement of the proceedings. The arbitral tribunal has the authority to decide whether proffered evidence is relevant and to evaluate the significance of the evidence that it admits. While the arbitrating parties have the right to be heard, neither side can abuse its rights by manufacturing specious arguments, issues, and requests for evidence—thereby tactically prolonging the proceeding for litigious advantage.

When the parties have presented their evidence and witnesses and summarized their respective positions, the arbitral tribunal closes the proceedings and adjourns to deliberate. The tribunal's deliberations are private, conducted only between the arbitrators. A decision can be, and usually is, reached by simple majority vote. Especially in domestic practice, arbitral tribunals render awards without issuing an opinion containing the reasons for, or an explanation of, the determination. The award usually follows a standard format: a statement of the facts, a description of the issues, the parties' respective positions, and a disposition of the matters submitted. The practice of not providing an opinion with domestic awards is intended to discourage judicial review.

The Significance of Arbitration

Arbitration raises serious questions about the function of adjudication, the purpose of law and the legal system, and the objective of law practice. Lawyers—once skeptical of arbitration and inclined to disparage it as a makeshift trial process—are now an integral part of arbitration practice. Lawyers function as arbitrators, draft arbitration agreements, and represent parties in arbitral proceedings and related litigation. Lawyers' acceptance of and participation in arbitration have modified the process of arbitral adjudication and transformed the role and work of the legal profession. Moreover, the greater role of arbitration in U.S. law has modified the concept of due process.

Increased lawyer presence in arbitration has made arbitral proceedings more formal and adversarial. The staples of trial practice—pretrial discovery, depositions, interrogatories, the use of expert witnesses and of cross-examination, and contests about the admissibility of evidence—have been transplanted into some arbitrations. While "judicializing" arbitration incorporates more due process protections into the proceedings, it also undermines arbitration's efficiency and expedition. Nonetheless, the ability of arbitral procedure to remain functional even when it has been adversarialized attests to its adaptability and resilience.

The recourse to arbitration may represent the only way to maintain a fundamental rule of law in American society. The arbitral process may amount to a privatized system of civil litigation. Overburdened courts—saddled with criminal proceedings and illegal drug prosecutions—are unable to supply civil litigants with any meaningful access to justice. Arbitration does provide access, legal representation, hearings, equal and fair treatment of the parties, and a final and enforceable decision.

A Survey of the Case Law

Three sets of arbitration trilogies represent the pillars of U.S. arbitration law. The first, the *Steelworkers* trilogy, announced in 1960 that arbitration had a special role to play in the resolution of labor and management disputes in the unionized workplace. *See United Steelworkers of Am. v. American Mfg. Co.*, 363 U.S. 564 (1960); *United Steelworkers of Am. v. Warrior & Gulf Navigation Co.*, 363 U.S. 574 (1960); *United Steelworkers of Am. v. Enterprise Wheel & Car Corp.*, 363 U.S. 593 (1960). Labor arbitration cases came to embody the basic legal principles that would govern a self-contained, parallel system of civil litigation. Much of what the courts decided in regard to labor arbitration eventually would be incorporated—despite the difference in governing statute—into the FAA and would govern the other forms of arbitration. Matters of labor arbitration are governed by the Labor Management Relations Act of 1947 (LMRA), not the FAA—in particular, § 301 LMRA.

The second, the "Federalism" trilogy, came a number of years later. It made clear that the rule of law in arbitration proceeded from the FAA. The FAA, especially Sections Two and Ten which validate arbitration agreements and awards, governed all cases that had an arguable connection to interstate commerce and thereby allowed for the assertion of federal authority and application of federal law. The command of the FAA reached federal courts sitting in state law cases, state legislation that might directly or incidentally affect arbitration, and state courts ruling in ordinary contract cases. *See Allied–Bruce Terminix Cos., Inc. v. Dobson*, 513 U.S. 265 (1995).

It was indispensable, in the Court's assessment, to have a single directive in matters of arbitration. A single standard would create an effective judicial doctrine. A multiplicity of views, the freedom to disagree, and the unfettered exercise of choice would undermine the necessary unity of approach and result. Properly read, FAA § 2 embodies a federal right to arbitrate that eclipses the political authority of states. Acquiescing to state government authority or other possible positions would have meant, in effect, a nationwide denial of due process. Tolerating exceptions would have robbed arbitration of its universal reach and application. *See, e.g.,*

Buckeye Check Cashing, Inc. v. Cardegna, 546 U.S. 440 (2006).

Finally, the third trilogy consisted of a group of cases on international litigation. *See The Bremen v. Zapata Off–Shore Co.*, 407 U.S. 1 (1972); *Scherk v. Alberto–Culver Co.*, 417 U.S. 506, *reh'g denied*, 419 U.S. 885 (1974); *Mitsubishi Motors Corp. v. Soler Chrysler–Plymouth, Inc.*, 473 U.S. 614 (1985). The reference to arbitration was even more necessary in the international context. Without a viable system of international arbitration, transborder commerce could not take place. International merchants and transactions would be overwhelmed by risk if there were no system of accountability. It was, therefore, an imperative that national courts affirm the dispute resolution provisions in the parties' agreement. The enforcement of arbitral agreements and awards was the source of stability for international commerce.

These decisions played a decisive role in crafting the judicial doctrine on arbitration. For example, the ruling in *Mitsubishi*, part of the international litigation trilogy, gave rise to the holdings in *McMahon* and *Rodriguez*. *Shearson/Am. Express, Inc. v. McMahon*, 482 U.S. 220 (1987); *Rodriguez de Quijas v. Shearson/Am. Express, Inc.*, 490 U.S. 477 (1989). These two cases eventually led to the creation of the securities arbitration industry. *Gilmer v. Interstate/Johnson Lane Corp.*, 500 U.S. 20 (1991), integrated the principles of the *Steelworkers* Trilogy into the nonunionized workplace, thereby posing a substantial challenge to the rule of *Alexander v. Gardner-Denver*, 415 U.S. 36 (1974), as well as generating the field of employment arbitration. In fact, in *14 Penn Plaza v. Pyett*, 129 S.Ct. 1456 (2009), the Court integrated the *Gilmer* arbitrability rule into CBA arbitration and reduced the status of *Gardner-Denver* to a "narrow holding" that could essentially be ignored.

CHAPTER TWO

FREEDOM OF CONTRACT

The primary rule that governs the law, practice, and regulation of arbitration is the principle of freedom of contract. In *Volt Information Sciences, Inc. v. Board of Trustees of Leland Stanford Junior University*, 489 U.S. 468 (1989), the United States Supreme Court gave expression to this fundamental principle when it held that:

> the FAA does not require parties to arbitrate when they have not agreed to do so . . . nor does it prevent parties who do agree to arbitrate from excluding certain claims from the scope of their arbitration agreement. . . . It simply requires courts to enforce privately negotiated agreements to arbitrate, like other contracts, in accordance with their terms. . . . Arbitration under the Act is a matter of consent, not coercion, and parties are generally free to structure their arbitration agreements as they see fit. . . .

Freedom of contract allows arbitrating parties to write their own rules of arbitration—in effect, it permits them to establish the law of arbitration for their transaction. The parties can customize the arbitral process to fit their needs, eliminate legal rules or trial techniques that might prove inconvenient or unsuitable, and maintain procedural elements they believe necessary to achieving fairness, finality, and functionality.

Courts generally uphold the parties' efforts to customize the arbitral proceedings. For example, the parties can provide that compliance with formal evidentiary rules is necessary for a fair arbitral trial, or that arbitrators are bound to apply the rules of law, or that the arbitral adjudication of matters relating to trade secrets must be conducted *in camera*. Moreover, the hearing must incorporate the right to pretrial discovery, to call witnesses and question them directly, and to engage in adversarial cross-examination.

This "deregulatory" approach to arbitration enhances the position of the stronger party to the transaction. It also requires that the parties identify their adjudicatory needs ahead of time and understand how arbitration responds to them. Finally, it places a "front-end load" on the parties' dealings, demanding that they spend time negotiating an agreement that is responsive to these matters.

Volt

The opinion in *Volt Information Sciences* introduced the contract freedom dimension to the Court's doctrine on arbitration. In *Volt*, the Court stated that the parties could provide that their agreement to arbitrate was governed by a state law which negated the contractual reference to arbitration. The FAA, therefore, could command that arbitration agreements be enforced, but the reach of that legislative directive was defined—implemented and contained—by the basic principles of contract law. The parties to the agreement could make whatever lawful stipulations they deemed suitable and the courts were obligated to enforce the agreement as written. In effect, party choice in each case dictated the law of arbitration. And, the exercise of choice could thwart the very reference to arbitration.

The absolute view of freedom of contract and its incorporation into FAA § 2 confounded for a time the federalization policy. Moreover, the reference to contract freedom appears to have been a haphazard doctrinal invention, useful in avoiding immediate interpretative problems, but potentially unpredictable and unwieldy. The Court applied contract law reasoning in two subsequent cases. The first, *Mastrobuono v. Shearson Lehman Hutton, Inc.*, 514 U.S. 52 (1995), generated a strong but lone dissent. To some degree, the decision in *Mastrobuono* contradicted the reasoning and ruling in *Volt*, yet endorsed its view of the significance of party autonomy in the law of arbitration. The second case, *First Options of Chicago, Inc. v. Kaplan*, 514 U.S. 938 (1995), a unanimous decision, is a landmark case. There, the Court defines more specifically its position on contract freedom and explores in greater detail its consequences upon the legal regulation of arbitration.

Mastrobuono

Mastrobuono is a key part of the Court's federalization policy. Despite *Mastrobuono*'s factual and analytical similarity to *Volt*, the Court ruled against the application of state law. In doing so, the Court placed a qualification upon the power given to contract principles in *Volt*. After *Mastrobuono*, the contractual reference to state law would be fully respected only when the choice-of-law promoted the recourse to arbitration or when the parties expressly recognized that the state law contained a restriction on the right to arbitrate and expressly acknowledged that the restriction applied to their arbitration.

The plaintiffs in *Mastrobuono* opened a securities account with Shearson Lehman Hutton and signed a standard client's agreement. Paragraph thirteen of that agreement contained an arbitral clause under which the parties agreed to resolve disputes through NASD arbitration. It also provided for the application of New York law to the agreement. After closing the account, the plaintiffs filed suit alleging that Shearson personnel mishandled their funds. The brokerage company, however, prevailed on its motion to stay the court proceeding and to compel arbitration.

Thereafter, an arbitral tribunal awarded the plaintiffs $160,000 in compensatory damages and $400,000 in punitive damages. Shearson appealed, arguing that—pursuant to the contract—New York law governed the arbitral proceeding and that the rule in *Garrity v. Lyle Stuart, Inc.*, 40 N.Y.2d 354 (1976), a landmark state case, prohibited the arbitrators from awarding punitive damages. The United States Supreme Court granted *certiorari* to consider whether "a contractual choice-of-law provision may preclude an arbitral award of punitive damages that otherwise would be proper." The Court held in the negative, reversing the federal district court and Seventh Circuit Court of Appeals, which had held that the arbitral tribunal had no authority to award punitive damages given the provisions of the controlling New York state law.

Through Justice Stevens, the majority opinion initially established that the reference to arbitration was a matter of contractual choice. The purpose of the judicial implementation of the FAA was to enforce arbitration agreements as written. The Court cited language from *Volt* to sustain its modest view of the judicial role under the federal legislation:

> But it does not follow that the FAA prevents the enforcement of agreements to arbitrate under different rules than those set forth in the Act itself. Indeed, such a result would be quite inimical to the FAA's primary purpose of ensuring that private agreements to arbitrate are enforced according to their terms. *Arbitration under the act is a matter of consent, not coercion,* and parties are generally free to structure their arbitration agreements as they see fit. Just as they may limit by contract the issues which they will arbitrate...so too may they specify by contract the rules under which that arbitration will be conducted. (Emphasis added.)

The majority opinion in *Mastrobuono* then asserted that the contract freedom doctrine in *Volt* supported its determination. Straining its reasoning even further, the Court stated that an independent "conflict-of-laws analysis" might point to the application of New York state law, but would preclude the application of the New York bar on the award of punitive damages by arbitrators because the parties had not expressly decided to exclude such damages in their agreement, thereby making the state law provision subject to preemption under the federalization policy. Moreover, even if the parties intended New York state law to govern their contractual obligations, including their reference to arbitration, the choice of New York state law would "include only New York's substantive rights and obligations, and not the state's allocation of power between alternative tribunals." Further, "[w]e think the best way to harmonize the choice-of-law provision with the arbitration provision is to read 'the laws of the State of New York' to encompass substantive principles that New York courts would apply, but not to include special rules limiting the authority of arbitrators. Thus, the choice-of-law provision covers the rights and duties of the parties, while the arbitration clause covers arbitration. . . ." The distinction was twisted enough to discourage analytical scrutiny; in the end, the reasoning only served to justify a foregone conclusion.

Further, the Court argued that the reference in the agreement to NASD arbitration rules provided some justification for allowing the arbitrators to award punitive damages. Suffice it to state that the NASD Code of Arbitration Procedure, although it referred to the question of punitive damages in arbitration, did not establish a clear institutional rule on that matter. As the Court itself stated in another attempt to disavow its own reasoning, "[w]hile not a clear authorization of punitive damages, this provision appears broad enough at least to contemplate such a remedy." Finally, equity demanded that the cost and burden of the contractual ambiguity be shouldered by the party opposing the award of punitive damages when that party drafted the contract and created the ambiguity between the choice-of-law and arbitration provisions. "The reason for this rule is to protect the party who did not choose the language from an unintended or unfair result." And, "the choice-of-law clause introduces an ambiguity into an arbitration agreement that would otherwise allow punitive damages awards."

Kaplan

In *Kaplan*, the Court held that courts, rather than arbitral tribunals, have jurisdiction to resolve questions of arbitrability (presumably, contractual inarbitrability, *i.e.*, whether a contract of arbitration exists and covers a specific dispute or set of disputes), unless the agreement to arbitrate provides that the arbitral tribunal has the authority to decide the matter. To buttress its determination, the Court espoused a view of arbitration and of arbitration law expressly based on contract freedom principles, under which the contract of arbitration could function essentially as a completely self-contained body of arbitration law. The contract freedom view of arbitration reduced matters of arbitration and the public interest in adjudication to a question of contractual consent between the parties in individual cases. It was problematic not only in terms of the facts of *Kaplan*, but also as a pronouncement on arbitration doctrine.

The Kaplans were private investors and owners of an investment company (MKI). They, individually, and MKI, as a separate business entity, incurred substantial losses during the October 1987 stock market crash and thereafter in other stock transactions. First Options, a brokerage firm that clears stock trades on the Philadelphia Stock Exchange, was their creditor. First Options, MKI, and the Kaplans entered into four "work out" agreements to repay the debts, only one of which (between First Options and MKI) contained an arbitration agreement. When efforts to collect the debts failed, First Options filed a demand for arbitration against MKI and the Kaplans. The Kaplans refused to submit to arbitration and challenged the agreement to arbitrate. The arbitral tribunal nonetheless asserted jurisdiction and rendered an award against both MKI and the Kaplans. The question submitted to the Court was whether the arbitral tribunal had jurisdiction to adjudicate the disputes between First Options and the Kaplans.

The Court was unanimous in its resolution of the question. Its reasoning can be divided into three basic and interrelated parts. First, the Court's memory of its statement that arbitration was a "mere form of trial" seems to have faded. It acknowledged the "practical importance" of the arbitrability question and recognized that arbitration involved the surrender of the right to the judicial resolution of disputes. Second, it declared that the courts (rather than arbitral tribunals) have primary authority to resolve the arbitrability question, grounding its holding in, and portraying its determination as, a standard of review question. Finally, in a substantially, if not completely, contradictory corollary, the Court proclaimed the contract of arbitration as the true source of final authority on the arbitrability question.

At the outset of the opinion, the Court described the arbitrability question as a narrow concern, but conceded that it "has a certain practical significance." In particular, who decides whether there is a legal basis for compelling the parties to arbitrate can make "a critical difference" to the party resisting arbitration. By agreeing to arbitrate, a party abandons the right to obtain a judicial resolution of contractual disputes, even though some limited judicial supervision of arbitral awards is available. The Court now appeared to believe that the waiver of rights gave the arbitrability question importance because it signified that the parties, in effect, have chosen a form of justice other than judicial justice.

As a consequence, the Court concluded that the "emphatic federal policy" favoring arbitration did not govern the arbitrability question. In fact, on the threshold matter of arbitrability, the appropriate standard of review consisted of a fully independent form of judicial review that replaced the normally "hospitable" federal court "inquiry" into issues of arbitration law. While all other arbitration questions were governed by the favorable federal policy, the Court believed that substantial unfairness would result if an unwilling, and—more importantly—an unobligated, party were forced to arbitrate. The Court created a presumption that the arbitrability question was to be decided by the courts. To rebut the presumption, the party seeking to submit the arbitrability question to arbitration must establish to a preponderance that the parties' agreement authorized the arbitrator to rule on the question of arbitrability. "Courts should not assume that the parties agreed to arbitrate arbitrability unless there is 'clear and unmistakable' evidence that they did so."

The two substantive components of the *Kaplan* holding, however, could not coexist. On the one hand, the Court viewed arbitrability as a critical rights determination and mandated judicial disposition of the issue; on the other hand, it ruled that the question, no matter how significant, could be reassigned to arbitral disposition through the vehicle of private contract. At this point, none of the Court's complex reasoning on the standard of review question mattered because arbitration clauses (especially adhesionary ones) would now routinely include a delegation of arbitrability questions to the arbitral tribunal. In consumer, employment, and other contexts, courts would simply be excluded from the jurisdictional phase of arbitration by party agreement. The authority of contract clearly trumped the judicial authority to supervise or decide matters of arbitration law.

The question of arbitrability is central to the legal regulation of arbitration. It involves in some instances determining whether a valid arbitration agreement exists and, if so, whether it covers the dispute in question. As the Court itself observes, the agreement's validity and scope of application establish the boundary between judicial and arbitral jurisdiction, between public and private adjudication, and represent the parties' willingness to waive their legal right to judicial relief. Given the importance of the choice, it would seem that the law should determine when it has been made.

In *Kaplan*, the Court had the opportunity to integrate the *kompetenz-kompetenz* doctrine (jurisdiction to rule on jurisdictional challenges) into the U.S. law of arbitration. It does so indirectly by holding that arbitrators can rule upon the validity and scope of arbitration agreements if the arbitration agreement authorizes them to rule on these matters. The *Kaplan* holding amounts to an adoption of the *kompetenz-kompetenz* doctrine on an *ad hoc*, contractual basis. It is, however, curious that the *Kaplan* Court neither refers to the *kompetenz-kompetenz* doctrine itself nor acknowledges the relevance of FAA § 3, which provides for court determination of contractual inarbitrability questions.

Howsam and *Bazzle*

Two recent cases (*Howsam* and *Bazzle*) confirm the rule of contract doctrine in U.S. arbitration law, while also affirming the decisional and procedural sovereignty of the arbitrator. The parties' express provisions govern, but their absence or a lack of clarity empowers the arbitrator to decide on the agreement's meaning. The rulings also limit the ability of courts to intervene in arbitrations, confining them to absolutely threshold jurisdictional matters.

In *Howsam v. Dean Witter Reynolds, Inc.*, 537 U.S. 79 (2002), the United States Supreme Court held that a dispute over an NASD six-year eligibility requirement was a "question of arbitrability" that should be decided by an arbitrator and not the courts. Karen Howsam, an investor who bought an interest in four limited partnerships upon the advice of Dean Witter, filed a demand for arbitration for misrepresentation. The Client Service Agreement allowed Howsam to choose the arbitration forum. She selected NASD (National Association of Securities Dealers) arbitration.

Upon learning of Howsam's attempt to compel arbitration, Dean Witter filed suit in federal district seeking a judicial declaration that the dispute was ineligible for arbitration. The NASD Arbitration Rules excluded disputes that were more than six years old from arbitration. The district court dismissed the action, ruling that the arbitrator should interpret and apply the NASD rule. Dean Witter appealed and the Tenth Circuit reversed. According to the Circuit Court, application of the NASD rule presented a question of "arbitrability." These questions of threshold jurisdiction should be decided by a court, not an arbitrator. The United States Supreme Court granted *certiorari* to resolve a conflict among appellate courts in the application and interpretation of this NASD rule.

Referring to prior cases, however, the *Howsam* Court initially stated that the "question of arbitrability"—whether the parties agreed to arbitration the dispute—is "an issue for judicial determination unless the parties clearly and unmistakably provide otherwise." Accordingly, the Court analyzed the NASD time-limit provision to determine if it fell within the scope of its ruling. In the Court's view, the "question of arbitrability" often had a narrow meaning in actual litigation. It applied only in limited circumstances "where contracting parties would likely have expected a court to decide the gateway matter, where they are not likely to have thought that they had agreed that an arbitrator would do so, and, consequently, where reference of the gateway dispute to the court avoids the risk of forcing parties to arbitrate a matter that they may well not have agreed to arbitrate." Therefore, the Court stated, "procedural questions which grow out of the dispute and bear on its final disposition are presumptively not for the judge, but for an arbitrator to decide."

Accordingly, arbitrators should decide "allegation[s] of waiver, delay, or a like defense to arbitrability" as they are not questions of whether parties have agreed to submit a dispute to arbitration. In so concluding, the Court referred to the language of the Revised Uniform Arbitration Act of 2000 (RUAA) providing that an "arbitrator shall decide whether a condition precedent to arbitrability has been fulfilled." According to the commentary that accompanies the RUAA "in the absence of an agreement to the contrary, issues of procedural arbitrability, *i.e.*, whether prerequisites such as time limits…have been met, are for the arbitrator to decide."

Reasoning that the NASD time-limit rule "closely resembles the gateway questions that this court has found not to be questions of arbitrability," the Court ruled that the applicability of the NASD time-limit rule was presumptively for the arbitrator to decide. Moreover, NASD arbitrators are "comparatively more expert about the meaning of their own rule" and consequently better able to apply it. Aligning the authority to decide with actual expertise would result in a "fair and expeditious resolution of the underlying controversy—a goal of arbitration systems and judicial systems alike."

In 2003, the United States Supreme Court rendered its landmark decision in *Green Tree Fin. Corp. v. Bazzle,* 539 U.S. 444 (2003). *Bazzle* involved loan agreements between Green Tree and homeowners. The arbitral clause in the loan agreements provided for the arbitration of all disputes "by one arbitrator selected by us with consent of you." Individual cases eventually were certified as a class and compelled to arbitration. The arbitral clause, however, made no mention of classwide arbitration. The South Carolina state Supreme Court held that, under state contract law, the silence of the agreement permitted claims to be submitted to class action arbitration. The question of whether the agreement allowed for classwide arbitration divided the United States Supreme Court. Four Justices constituted a plurality; one Justice wrote a concurring opinion, and four Justices formed the dissent. The split did not appear to reflect ideological opposition among the Justices. Rather, it indicated intellectual differences on an important issue of arbitration law.

Justice Breyer authored the plurality opinion. In addressing the issue, the Court returned to an elusive concept of arbitrability that it originally propounded in *First Options of Chicago, Inc. v. Kaplan*. In *Kaplan*, the Court stated that courts decide the basic issues of arbitrability (whether there is a valid contract of arbitration that covers the question in litigation), unless the parties authorize the arbitrators to rule on these matters. The recent decision in *Howsam* confirmed this division of labor between the courts and arbitrators. Unless the parties provide otherwise, the courts decide the threshold arbitrability questions, while the arbitrators rule upon issues that pertain to the implementation of the arbitration (*e.g.*, the application of a time-limit bar to the submitted claim). *Bazzle* adds that the interpretation of the content of the arbitration agreement falls within the sovereign decisional authority of the arbitrator. Simply stated, "Under the terms of the parties' contracts, the question—whether the agreement forbids class arbitration—is for the arbitrator to decide." The impact of the plurality opinion upon the law of arbitration is generally favorable. It extends the reach of the arbitrator's discretion, limits the role of the courts in regard to the arbitral process, and enhances the systemic autonomy of arbitration.

The Court was divided on the distinction between substantive and procedural arbitrability. The late Chief Justice William Rehnquist authored the principal dissenting opinion. Contending that *Kaplan* and *Howsam* were distinguishable, he asserted that the courts must decide what the parties have agreed to in their arbitration agreement. The content of the agreement can involve much more than merely implementing the agreed-upon recourse to arbitration. "It can go to the method and manner of the agreed-upon arbitration. What has been agreed can also transcend the procedural details of the arbitration." For the late Chief Justice, then, the question in *Bazzle* fell within *Kaplan*'s reach, not *Howsam*'s: "I think that the parties' agreement as to how the arbitrator should be selected is much more akin to the agreement as to what shall be arbitrated, a question for the courts under *First Options*, than it is to 'allegations of waiver, delay, or like defenses to arbitrability,' which are questions for the arbitrator under *Howsam*." According to the dissent, the parties did not agree to classwide arbitration and the South Carolina state Supreme Court "imposed a regime that was contrary to the express agreement of the parties . . . ." The state court's failure to respect the parties' contract warranted the reversal of its decision.

Justice Thomas dissented on the basis that the FAA should not govern "a state court's interpretation of a private arbitration agreement." In his dissent, Rehnquist acknowledged that state contract law regulated arbitration agreements, but emphasized that state laws that contravened federal law on arbitration were subject to preemption. Finally, Justice Stevens—who concurred and would have upheld the South Carolina state Supreme Court rather than remand the case—concluded that: "There is nothing in the Federal Arbitration Act that precludes . . . [the] determinations by the Supreme Court of South Carolina." According to Justice Stevens, that court simply held "as a matter of state law that class-action arbitrations [were] permissible if not prohibited by the applicable arbitration agreement, and that the agreement between [the] parties [was] silent on the issue."

When the Court granted *certiorari* in *Bazzle*, the expectation was that it would address classwide arbitration and begin to formulate a basic standard of fairness in consumer arbitration—including the function of unconscionability and the possibly limited validity of arbitration agreements in this setting.

These matters, however, did not preoccupy the *Bazzle* Court. Instead, the Court framed the issue from a jurisdictional perspective—who determines the content of the arbitration agreement? In effect, by converting the question of litigation to a jurisdictional matter, the Court impliedly ruled that the fairness and legitimacy questions in consumer arbitration were to be resolved by the parties' agreement and by the arbitrators. This conclusion reinforces the view, also stated in *Kaplan*, that the practice of arbitration should not be allowed to generate a great volume of litigation. The Court's ruling thereby buttressed the independence and autonomy of the arbitral process.

Opt-In Provisions

The exercise of contract freedom in arbitration gave rise—at least, temporarily—to so-called opt-in provisions. By including an opt-in clause in their arbitration agreement, the parties could provide for the judicial review of the merits of awards rendered pursuant to their agreement. By contract, the parties—in effect—provided for a level of court scrutiny that was not available under the express language of the federal statute. In fact, the provision for *de novo* judicial review violated the objective and historical gravamen of the governing law.

This usage of contract freedom divided the federal circuits. The Fifth and Third Circuits uphold the practice without equivocation. *See Gateway Techno., Inc. v. MCI*, 64 F.3d 993 (5th Cir. 1995); *Roadway Package System, Inc. v. Kayser*, 257 F.3d 287 (3d

Cir.), *cert. denied*, 534 U.S. 1020 (2001). Several Circuits—critical and skeptical of the practice—begrudgingly enforced such agreements if the requirement for merits review was clear, unambiguous, and unmistakable. *See, e.g., Schoch v. InfoUSA, Inc.*, 341 F.3d 785 (8th Cir. 2003); *Bowen v. Amoco Pipeline Co.*, 254 F.3d 925 (10th Cir. 2001). A number of circuit courts reject the practice outright as an illicit use of contract prerogatives. *See Chicago Typographical Union v. Chicago Sun–Times*, 935 F.2d 1501 (7th Cir. 1991); *Hoeft v. MVL Group, Inc.*, 343 F.3d 57 (2d Cir. 2003). Some of these courts suggested that any reconsideration of the merits of awards be restricted to an internal arbitral procedure—essentially, a second arbitral tribunal that acted as an appellate body.

In a landmark case, the Ninth Circuit oscillated between a negative and positive position on the issue. In *LaPine Technology Corp. v. Kyocera Corp.*, 130 F.3d 884 (9th Cir. 1997), now known as *LaPine I*, the Ninth Circuit held that federal courts were required to honor arbitration agreements as written and to apply a heightened standard of judicial review when the parties so provided in their agreement. If parties indisputably contracted for a more rigorous review of awards on the basis of errors of fact or law, federal courts were not limited to the review grounds specified in the FAA.

Kyocera, LaPine, and Prudential–Bache engaged in an enterprise to manufacture and market computer disk drives. LaPine designed the drive and licensed it to Kyocera, the manufacturer. Prudential–Bache purchased the drives from Kyocera and sold them to LaPine, who then marketed them to customers. In 1986, negotiations began to restructure the deal due to financial problems that LaPine was experiencing. The deal was memorialized in a Definitive Agreement (DA) on November 13, 1986, which contained an arbitration clause. On November 14, 1986, a revised DA was distributed and included an Amended Trading Agreement (ATA) that required Kyocera to sell the drives to LaPine directly. Kyocera objected to this provision and refused to comply with the ATA. LaPine then claimed breach of contract and instituted an action in the district court.

Kyocera's motion to compel arbitration was granted. The arbitration clause provided that "[t]he court shall vacate, modify or correct any award: (i) based upon any of the grounds referred to in the Federal Arbitration Act, (ii) where the arbitrators' findings of fact are not supported by substantial evidence, or (iii) where the arbitrators' conclusions of law are erroneous." The dispute was submitted to a three-member arbitral panel, and the "Terms of Reference" contained a provision for judicial review similar to the one in the arbitration clause. The arbitral tribunal rendered a final decision and Kyocera filed a motion to vacate, alleging that: (1) the findings of fact were not supported by substantial evidence, (2) the award contained errors of law, and (3) these were grounds for vacatur and modification under the FAA. The district court denied the motion to vacate and stated that it would not review the arbitration award under the heightened standard for judicial scrutiny provided for by the parties in the arbitration clause or in the Terms of Reference. Instead, the district court employed the more deferential standard contained in the FAA.

On appeal, the Ninth Circuit held that the district court erred in refusing to apply the heightened standard for judicial review agreed to by the parties in the arbitration clause. The court stated that, to fully honor the agreement, it had to be enforced according to its terms. The court cited *Volt*, stating that:

> In recognition of Congress' principal purpose of ensuring that private arbitration agreements are enforced according to their terms, we have held that the FAA preempts state laws which "require a judicial forum for the resolution of claims which the contracting parties agreed to resolve by arbitration." But it does not follow that the FAA prevents the enforcement of agreements to arbitrate under different rules than those set forth in the Act itself. Indeed, such a result would be quite inimical to the FAA's primary purpose of ensuring that private agreements to arbitrate are enforced according to their terms. Arbitration under the Act is a matter of consent, not coercion, and parties are generally free to structure their arbitration agreements as they see fit. Just as they may limit by contract the issues which they

will arbitrate, so too may they specify by contract the rules under which that arbitration will be conducted.

The Ninth Circuit thereby agreed with the Fifth Circuit that "federal courts have the authority, and, indeed, the obligation, to conduct heightened judicial review of an arbitration award in accordance with the parties' agreement." The Ninth Circuit held that the "contract expressly and unambiguously provide[d] for review of 'errors of law'; to interpret this phrase short of de novo review would render the language meaningless and would frustrate the mutual intent of the parties." In so holding, the Ninth Circuit rejected the Seventh Circuit's reasoning that parties could not contract to create federal jurisdiction and its recommendation that "[i]f parties want, they can contract for an appellate arbitration panel to review the arbitrator's award."

The Ninth Circuit also rejected the argument that Article 24 of the Rules of the International Chamber of Commerce, which provides for final and binding arbitral awards, trumped the heightened judicial review standard established by the parties. The court concluded that, to the extent that the Terms of Reference and Article 24 conflicted, the provisions in the Terms of Reference controlled. Thus, where the parties contracted and agreed to arbitration, they did so based on the belief that the federal district court would review the arbitral decision for errors of law and fact.

In a brief concurrence, Judge Kozinski stated that, while the parties may contract to the time, place, and manner of arbitration, he did not "believe parties may impose on the federal courts burdens and functions that Congress has withheld" nor dictate to the federal courts how to conduct their business. Judge Kozinski, however, concluded that the terms of the agreement should be followed by the courts in this case because the standard of review that was provided for in the arbitration clause "[was] no different from that performed by the district courts in appeals from administrative agencies and bankruptcy courts, or on habeas corpus."

Judge Mayer dissented, stating that no authority was cited by Kyocera "which empower[ed] litigants to dictate how an Article III court must review an arbitration agreement" and that "[a]bsent this, they [the parties] may not" dictate how review should be conducted. Citing *Chicago Typographical Union*, Judge Mayer noted that heightened review should be achieved through an appellate arbitration panel.

In a more recent ruling, the Ninth Circuit—sitting *en banc*—reversed its holding by asserting in *Kyocera Corp. v. Prudential–Bache Trade Services, Inc.*, 341 F.3d 987 (9th Cir. 2003), that contracting parties could not instruct courts on how they should supervise arbitral awards. The rule of contract law, according to the court, ended with the arbitral tribunal's rendering of the award. Thereafter, the provisions of the enacted law governed. The judicial review of awards took place pursuant to FAA § 10.

In its *en banc* decision, the appellate court held that the statutorily mandated standard of review may not be expanded by contract and that the scope of judicial review of arbitral awards is limited to that which is set out in the FAA. The court noted that FAA § 9 states that a court must confirm an award "unless the award is vacated, modified or corrected as prescribed in sections 10 and 11 of this title." More specifically, the court acknowledged that "confirmation is required even in the face of erroneous findings of fact or misinterpretations of law." FAA §§ 10 and 11 "allow a federal court to correct a technical error, to strike all or a portion of an award pertaining to an issue not at all subject to arbitration, and to vacate an award that evidences affirmative misconduct in the arbitral process or the final result or that is completely irrational or exhibits a manifest disregard for the law." The court concluded that these grounds allow the federal courts to exercise only an "extremely limited review authority." The court pointed out that, pursuant to the United States Supreme Court's decision in *Volt*, parties have complete freedom in designing the arbitration process in the way that best suits their needs. That freedom ends, however, once a case reaches the federal courthouse. At that point, the private arbitration process is concluded and the federal court steps in and "must act pursuant to [the FAA] standards and no other."

After a discussion of the case law in the other federal circuit courts, the court followed the Sixth, Seventh, Eighth, and Tenth Circuits and held that "private parties have no power to determine the rules by which federal courts proceeds, especially when Congress has explicitly prescribed those standards." The court reasoned that, while private parties are free to design the arbitration process and even to design a standard of review for an appellate arbitration panel, they cannot dictate the standard of review in a federal court once the arbitration award is final.

The court severed the offending provisions from the remainder of the agreement and held that Kyocera had not presented any valid ground for vacating, modifying, or correcting the arbitral award under the FAA §§ 10 and 11. The arbitrators, Kyocera had argued, "exceeded their power" when they made a decision based on unsubstantiated facts or legal conclusions that were errors of law. The court dismissed the argument as an attempt to have the court engage in a review of legal and factual errors. Section 10(a)(4), the court stated, "provides for vacatur only when arbitrators purport to exercise powers the parties did not intend for them to possess or otherwise display a manifest disregard for the law." Arbitrators may make errors of law or fact as long as they act in good faith. The court also dismissed Kyocera's argument that the award should be vacated under § 10(a)(1) for "fraud and undue means."

On March 25, 2008, the United States Supreme Court rendered its long-awaited opinion in *Hall Street Associates, LLC v. Mattel, Inc.,* 128 S.Ct. 1396 (2008). A majority of six justices determined that FAA §§ 9–11 were "exclusive." The governing statute provided for "expedited judicial review to confirm, vacate, or modify arbitration awards," and could not be "supplemented by contract." It is quite extraordinary that, given the issue for which *certiorari* was granted, the majority opinion never expressly refers to opt-in provisions. Rather, it frames its holding in terms of the exclusivity of the FAA grounds for confirmation and vacatur. By ignoring the contractual vehicle for statutory modification, the court makes the statute the principal, nearly exclusive element of consideration. Moreover, the Court never explicitly addresses the contract freedom idea—previously, a staple of the judicial doctrine on arbitration. Only the dissents, especially Justice Stevens', expound upon the idea that contracting parties have the right to set the terms of, and protocol for, their arbitrations. The majority's singular focus upon the statutory language implies that contract freedom is estranged from the final stage of the arbitral process. It applies primarily, if not exclusively, to the initial engagement in the process and the proceedings themselves. Once the tribunal renders the award, the process eludes contract and reenters the domain of law.

The discussion of manifest disregard is perplexing. It is well-settled that manifest disregard originated in *Wilko v. Swan*, 346 U.S. 427 (1953), and functions as one of three common law grounds for the judicial supervision of arbitral awards. All three common law grounds are intended to prevent labor arbitrators from dispensing a personal and idiosyncratic brand of industrial justice in their awards. The case law indicates uniformity in the construction of manifest disregard. Most courts agree that manifest disregard addresses unusual and exceptional circumstances; it does not apply to mere legal error or dubious interpretations of the contract. The classical formulation is that it pertains to a situation in which the arbitrators describe the applicable law and then completely ignore it in reaching their determination.

Be that as it may, Justice Souter's representations as to manifest disregard are both groundbreaking and fantastic. Supporting his speculation with only indirectly relevant authority, Justice Souter maintains that manifest disregard may have been intended to be a "shorthand" reference to all of the grounds expressly contained in FAA § 10 or the FAA § 10 grounds targeting arbitrator misconduct or excess of authority. The majority opinion seems to say that manifest disregard is a phrase, a linguistic construct that refers to all or some of the existing content of the statute. The assertion is implausible and unconvincing. If it persists, manifest disregard, which continues to wobble in the case law between the analytically inconceivable and standard error, may gain in enigma and thereby become an even more significant and obtuse notion in the law of vacatur.

The Court examines FAA § 10 and 11 and concludes that they establish an unambiguous substantive standard for the judicial supervision of arbitral awards that rejects individual modifications by contract. The basis for the judicial vacatur of awards is founded upon "egregious departures" and "extreme arbitral conduct," the statute lists specific instances of abhorrent arbitrator conduct that could invalidate the arbitral award. Because of the specificity of enumeration and given that the FAA provisions do not contain a "textual hook for expansion" of their content, the "contracting parties ... cannot [be] authorize[d] to supplement review for specific instances of outrageous conduct with review for just any legal error." The Court adds pointedly that " '[f]raud' and a mistake of law are not cut from the same cloth."

The statute dictates the applicable rule. When the statutory provisions contain "no hint of flexibility," they are not default legal rules articulated to apply only in the absence of party provision. The majority declares that "fighting the text" is not a sensible means of establishing governing legal rules. The gravamen of the statute in Sections 9 to 11 cannot be mistaken: They substantiate "a national policy favoring arbitration with just the limited review needed to maintain arbitration's essential virtue of resolving disputes straightaway." Permitting parties to introduce *de novo* review into the process by agreement would "bring arbitration theory to grief in post-arbitration process." "[F]ull-bore legal and evidentiary appeals" will erode arbitration's finality, flexibility, and frugality. Judicialization will transform the remedy into the pathology it endeavors to cure.

In *dicta*, the majority tries to temper the effect of its exclusivity holding by contending that review of arbitral awards is available outside the framework of the FAA. In other words, although the statutory grounds are "exclusive" (otherwise stated, not modifiable by contract), the parties could obtain "more searching review" under other regimes for judicial supervision. The assertion is peculiar, if not incomprehensible. By way of illustration, the Court explains that parties "may contemplate enforcement under state statutory or common law ... where judicial review of different scope is arguable." It is difficult to divine what "arguable" means in this formulation. More importantly, the contention does not account for the federal preemption doctrine. If a form of review is unacceptable under the federal law, it should likewise be unavailable under state statutory regimes. Assuming that a state law of arbitration would permit parties to alter the statutory basis for judicial supervision of awards by contract, a provision for *de novo* merits review and for examining the arbitrator's evidentiary determinations would deprive the arbitral process of its autonomy and injure the institution of private adjudication. Undercutting the national policy on arbitration by enforcing the particularities of state law is precisely the result that the preemption doctrine was intended to prevent.

In terms of doctrine, the dissenting opinions focus upon the express language of the statute and the contract freedom idea. In a separate dissent, echoing his interpretative approach in *First Options of Chicago, Inc. v. Kaplan*, 514 U.S. 938 (1995), Justice Breyer concludes that the FAA "does not *preclude* enforcement of such an agreement." Justice Stevens' dissenting opinion articulates the essential opposition to the majority opinion. He maintains that the FAA's statutory regime can readily co-exist with contract freedom and special provisions for judicial supervision agreed to by the parties. The common law, historically, has given contract freedom substantial bearing in the regulation of arbitration and the statute readily tolerates "agreements fairly negotiated by the parties." "An unnecessary refusal to enforce a perfectly reasonable category of arbitration agreements defeats the primary purpose of the statute." The actual text of the statute "does not compel ... a reading that is flatly inconsistent with the overriding interest in effectuating the clearly expressed intent of the contracting parties."

From the vantage point of U.S. domestic law, *Hall Street Associates* is a useful, perhaps necessary addition to the Court's doctrine on arbitration.

Making the statutory text the preeminent, even exclusive source of law provides greater clarity and focus. Allowing parties to treat the statutory framework as a default mechanism not only depreciates the institutional standing of legislation, but also subjects the law of arbitration to the chaotic rule of the jungle. The interests of economically superior parties would always triumph and the law would become unstable, subject to modification at the will and whim of the stronger parties. A workable epistemology of law requires a degree of constancy that cannot be provided by perpetually shifting rule predicates. Contract freedom can be energetic and dominant, but it must be exercised within the boundaries of basic legal civilization. Courts and legislatures cannot simply be displaced by circumstantial aberrations. The anarchy of contract, unless it is tamed by a customary discipline, cannot provide a sufficient basis for the rule of law.

In its wake, *Hall Street Associates* has generated substantial judicial debate about the continued viability of manifest disregard of the law as a basis for challenging the enforceability of arbitral awards. The Court itself contributed to the discussion by reversing and remanding the Ninth Circuit decision in *Improv West Associates v. Comedy Club*, 129 S.Ct. 45 (2008), to reconsider its partial vacatur of an award for manifest disregard of the law in light of *Hall Street Associates*. The Ninth Circuit upheld its prior determination, holding that manifest disregard remained a viable basis for the nullification of awards. *See Comedy Club, Inc. v. Improv West Associates*, 2009 WL 205046. Ruling courts, thus far, are divided on the question. Some have determined that *Hall Street Associates* sounded the death knell of manifest disregard, while others have concluded that it remains part of the law of vacatur.

CHAPTER THREE

THE FEDERAL ARBITRATION ACT

Introduction

The United States Arbitration Act, 9 U.S.C. §§ 1–16, more commonly known as the Federal Arbitration Act or the FAA, is a landmark piece of legislation that ended the era of judicial hostility to arbitration in the United States. It validates agreements to arbitrate and provides limited grounds for the judicial review of awards. Its objective is to legitimize arbitration and to give it the systemic autonomy it needs to function effectively as an adjudicatory mechanism.

The FAA consists of three chapters. The first sixteen provisions constitute chapter one of the statute and are the domestic U.S. law of arbitration. The two other chapters incorporate the international instruments on arbitration, both of which have been ratified by the United States, namely, the New York Arbitration Convention and the Inter–American Arbitration Convention. All of these statutes share a similarity of substance and rationale; they all distinctly favor the recourse to arbitration.

Congress conceived the FAA as a means by which commercial parties could gain access to a private adjudicatory remedy through contract. It authorized the federal courts to give effect to arbitration agreements. The FAA was seen as a procedural enactment that created a statutory mechanism for the enforcement of arbitral agreements and awards. "The principal support for the Act came from trade associations dealing in groceries and other perishables and from commercial and mercantile groups in the major trading centers.... Practically all who testified in support of the bill ... explained that the bill was designed to cover contracts between people in different states who shipped, bought, or sold commodities...."

Court construction—done principally by the United States Supreme Court—has modified considerably the original language and content of the statute. The reach of the FAA, for example, now extends far beyond the adjudication of specialized commercial claims. Judicial opinions have given the right to arbitrate not only a substantive character, but a constitutional stature as well. The right to arbitrate is now effectively a part of the Bill of Rights. Moreover, the courts viewed the federalism questions that arose in connection with the FAA as an opportunity to transform the legislation into a substantive law enactment. What began as a procedure for special interests became the cornerstone remedy of civil litigation.

FAA § 1

Section One defines the FAA's scope of application, *i.e.*, it identifies the circumstances in which the federal arbitration law governs the adjudication of questions that arise under arbitration provisions. The issue is of critical concern because the FAA's scope of application defines the reach of its nearly irrebuttable presumption in favor of arbitration. At first blush, it appears that the FAA is intended to apply exclusively in actions before federal courts involving the application of federal law. The legislative text nowhere mandates that state courts apply its provisions, especially in matters governed by state law.

Rulings by the United States Supreme Court enhanced substantially the FAA's scope of application. As the opinion in *Southland Corp. v. Keating,* 465 U.S. 1 (1984), and the later decision in *Allied-Bruce Terminix Cos., Inc. v. Dobson*, 513 U.S. 265 (1995), demonstrate, the current rule is that the FAA is binding in diversity cases in which state law applies and upon state courts ruling in state law cases that can be linked in some fashion to interstate commerce. It also preempts state laws that contradict its content. The FAA—in reality—is the national American law of arbitration.

Under the language of Section One, the FAA applies to maritime and commercial matters that are part of interstate commerce or which involve foreign commerce. In 2003, the U.S. Supreme Court, reversing a decision of the Alabama state Supreme Court, held that a debt-restructuring agreement was "a contract evidencing a transaction involving commerce" within the meaning of the

FAA and, thus, the arbitration provision included in that agreement was enforceable. *See Citizens Bank v. Alafabco, Inc.*, 539 U.S. 52 (2003).

The Court noted that the FAA covers a "written provision in any ... contract evidencing a transaction involving commerce." It construed the term "involving commerce" in the FAA as the functional equivalent of the more common term "affecting commerce"—an interpretation that typically signals the broadest permissible exercise of Congress' Commerce Clause power. The FAA provides for the enforcement of arbitration agreements within the full reach of the Commerce Clause. It encompasses a wider range of transactions—not just those actually "in commerce" or "within the flow of interstate commerce."

Ultimately, the Court overruled the Alabama state Supreme Court because it had erroneously adhered to an "improperly cramped view of Congress' Commerce Clause power" that rested on a misreading of the Court's decision in *United States v. Lopez,* 514 U.S. 549 (1995). The Court clarified that the decision in *Lopez* was not intended to "restrict the reach of the FAA," nor announce a new rule governing Congress' power over economic activity that included the debt-restructuring agreements in *Alafabco*. While the Court conceded that "the power to regulate commerce, though broad indeed, has limits," Congress' commerce power can be exercised in individual cases without showing any specific effect upon interstate commerce if, in aggregate, the economic activity in question represented a general practice subject to federal control.

Section One states that the FAA does not apply to the resolution of disputes that arise from employment contracts. Presumably, the Congress that enacted the FAA wanted to protect the special right of recourse that was available to workers in the specialty areas of foreign or interstate commerce. The apprehension was that the use of arbitral dispute resolution would undermine these rights. The Court eventually narrowed considerably the scope of the "employment contract exclusion." *See Circuit City Stores, Inc. v. Adams*, 532 U.S. 105 (2001). The ruling in *Gilmer v. Interstate/Johnson Lane Corp.*, 500 U.S. 20 (1991), directly challenged the utility and relevance of the provision. There, notwithstanding the language of Section One, the Court upheld an arbitral clause that was said to govern disputes arising out of a stockbroker's employment contract.

The *Gilmer* opinion was seen by a majority of the lower federal courts as a legitimation of the recourse to arbitration in the nonunionized workplace. As the *Circuit City* Court stated, the majority of these courts—as a result—gave the employment contract exclusion a "narrow reading:"

[T]he exclusionary clause of § 1 of the Arbitration Act should be narrowly construed to apply to employment contracts of seamen, railroad workers, and any other class of workers actually engaged in the movement of goods in interstate commerce in the same way that seamen and railroad workers are. We believe this interpretation comports with the actual language of the statute and the apparent intent of the Congress which enacted it. The meaning of the phrase 'workers engaged in foreign or interstate commerce' is illustrated by the context in which it is used, particularly the two specific examples given, seamen and railroad employees, those being two classes of employees engaged in the movement of goods in commerce.

In *Circuit City Stores, Inc. v. Adams*, the United States Supreme Court held that the employment contract exclusion in Section One of the FAA only applied to the employment contracts of interstate transportation workers. Employers, therefore, could require all other employees to submit employment related disputes to arbitration. The Court reversed the Ninth Circuit holding that the language in FAA § 1 exempted all employment contracts from the FAA's scope of application.

The federal courts are steadfast in their application of the employment contract exclusion under FAA § 1 and cite the United States Supreme Court precedent in *Circuit City v. Adams* to support their restrictive view of the provision. Their objective is to comply with the Court's policy perspective that the FAA should have broad application to assure the vitality of arbitration in civil dispute resolution. Two recent cases illustrate the point. In *Hill v. Rent–A–Center, Inc.*, 398 F.3d 1286 (11th Cir. 2005), the Eleventh Circuit held that an employee who incidentally delivered goods across state lines was subject to the FAA. He was not a "transportation worker" and could be compelled to arbitrate employment-related disputes. Similarly, in *Lenz v. Yellow Transportation, Inc.*, 431 F.3d 348 (8th Cir. 2005), the Eighth Circuit excluded the contract of a customer service representative for a transportation company from the narrow "transportation worker exception" in FAA § 1. The court reasoned that the employee's duties were only tangentially related to the transportation of goods; he did not directly work with goods that were in interstate commerce and he did not directly supervise transportation workers. His "central task was to answer the questions of and provide information to Yellow customers, not to supervise packages moving in interstate commerce."

The reach of arbitration in the employment area can be extended by state law despite the transportation employee exclusion. In *Palcko v. Airborne Express Inc.,* 372 F.3d 588 (3d Cir. 2004), the Third Circuit held that, although an employee was covered by the exemption in FAA § 1, the FAA did not preempt a state law that allowed the employment arbitration agreement to be enforced. Like *Mastrobuono*, the holding confirms that the validity of legal doctrines in the arbitration area reside in their ability to sustain the recourse to the arbitral process. Even the would-be supremacy of the FAA yields to the latter objective.

FAA § 2

Section Two is the centerpiece of the FAA. It legitimizes arbitration agreements as contracts and impliedly creates a federal right to engage in arbitration. Section Two constitutes the core provision of the legislation. It recognizes that both the arbitral clause and the submission agreement are lawful contracts. Neither agreement violates any public policy prohibition relating to contracts. Arbitral agreements are "valid, irrevocable, and enforceable"—a statement that clearly repudiates the past judicial practice of upholding arbitration agreements only once the arbitral tribunal had rendered an award. Arbitration agreements are subject to challenge only on contract grounds, primarily for reasons of defective formation.

The case law contains a number of opinions that hold that the FAA does not require an arbitration agreement to be signed in order to be effective. There are circumstantial exceptions to the basic rule which is—once again—an expression of the "strong federal policy on arbitration." *See Edwards v. Blockbuster, Inc.*, 400 F.Supp.2d 1305 (E.D. Okl. 2005); *Tinder v. Pinkerton Sec.*, 305 F.3d 728 (7th Cir. 2002); *In re Taravella*, 734 So.2d 149 (La.App. 1999). According to the First Circuit, a properly-worded email can constitute a valid and enforceable employment arbitration agreement. *See Campbell v. General Dynamics Govt. Sys. Corp.*, 407 F.3d 546 (1st Cir. 2005). In fact, "the E–Sign Act [15 U.S.C. § 7001(a)] prohibits any interpretation of the FAA's 'written provision' requirement that would preclude giving legal effect to an agreement solely on the basis that it was in the electronic form." The critical factor in assessing validity is whether the e-mail notification constituted sufficient notice to employees that continued employment would make the arbitral clause binding. Moreover, the e-mail needed to state clearly that the employment relationship was being changed and continued employment amounted to acceptance of the agreement for mandatory arbitration. Employees were further required to reply by acknowledging receipt and their acceptance of the new dispute resolution policy.

An "opportunity to read" the agreement and a signature generally manifest express, legally-binding consent to the arbitration agreement. Signing the agreement or an acknowledgement of receipt, without actually reading the documents, is enough. *See Pennington v. Frisch's Restaurants, Inc.,* 147 Fed.Appx. 463 (6th Cir. 2005). The Fifth Circuit held that illiteracy alone was not a sufficient basis for invalidating an arbitration agreement. It also stated, however, that the other party's awareness of the illiteracy might constitute fraud—rendering the arbitral clause unenforceable. Therefore, a signature was not enough if there had been no meeting of the minds. *See American Heritage Life Ins. Co. v. Lang,* 321 F.3d 533 (5th Cir. 2003).

Finally, courts are exceedingly unlikely to allow problems of contract formation, like adhesion or failure of consideration, to thwart enforcement of arbitration agreements. The federal policy supporting arbitration generally prohibits the invalidation of these agreements. The policy, therefore, has modified the express language of the statute. Following the lead of the United States Supreme Court, federal courts have upheld adhesionary and unilateral provisions for arbitration as valid contracts. *See Rodriguez de Quijas v. Shearson/Am. Express, Inc.*, 490 U.S. 477 (1989).

The liberal application of contract validity requirements to arbitration agreements has been challenged most consistently and effectively in California. For example, in *Armendariz v. Foundation Health Psychcare Services, Inc.*, 6 P.3d 669 (2000), the California state Supreme Court established that certain minimum requirements were necessary to create a legally enforceable arbitration agreement in the employment context. It created a five-point test by which to assess the validity of an arbitration agreement and the measure of due process and fairness in the structuring of an arbitration. Accordingly, employment contracts needed a "modicum of bilaterality" to be enforceable. Moreover, the arbitration procedure had to provide the plaintiff with the opportunity to vindicate fully its statutory rights by providing for neutral arbitrators, minimal discovery, a written award, comprehensive remedies, and reasonable costs.

In *Boghos v. Lloyd's of London*, 30 Cal.Rptr.3d 787 (Cal. 2005), the California state Supreme Court refused to extend its ruling in *Armendariz* to common law claims—for example, insurance disputes that involve tort, contract or business claims. Previously, the court had extended the *Armendariz* doctrine to nonwaivable, nonstatutory employment claims that were based on fundamental public policy. *See Little v. Auto Stiegler, Inc.*, 63 P.3d 979 (Cal. 2003), *cert. denied*, 540 U.S. 818 (2003).

A line of cases developed that focused upon the "outer" jurisdictional consequences of an arbitration agreement. In particular, whether an arbitration agreement between private parties could displace the authority and jurisdiction of government agencies to investigate and pursue remedies on behalf of aggrieved claimants.

In a significant doctrinal ruling, the United States Supreme Court held that an agreement between an employer and an employee to arbitrate workplace disputes did not bar the EEOC from obtaining either injunctive or victim-specific relief. *See EEOC v. Waffle House, Inc.*, 534 U.S. 279 (2002). The EEOC had brought suit in state court seeking injunctive relief and back pay, reinstatement, and damages on behalf of an employee who had been discharged after he had a seizure at work. The EEOC asserted a claim under Title I of the Americans with Disabilities Act (ADA) on behalf of the employee, who was not a party to the suit. The Court held in a 6–3 ruling that the EEOC was not barred from seeking either injunctive or victim-specific relief for the employee.

In the lower court opinion, the Fourth Circuit had distinguished injunctive relief from victim-specific relief. According to that opinion, the EEOC was statutorily entitled to file claims for injunctive relief, but the FAA prohibited the filing of a claim for victim-specific relief when the victim signed a mandatory arbitration clause as a condition of employment. The United States Supreme Court granted *certiorari* to resolve the circuit split on the question.

The Court began by stating that the EEOC had the same authority under the ADA that it had under the Civil Rights Act, namely, to bring injunctive actions to force employers to halt unlawful employment practices. The Court also stated that the FAA "does not mention enforcement by public agencies" and "does not purport to place any restriction on a nonparty's choice of judicial forum." The ADA "clearly makes the EEOC the master of its own case and confers on the agency the authority to evaluate the strength of the public interest at stake." According to the Court, it was the EEOC's "province" both to select a forum and to decide how public resources should be used to obtain victim-specific relief.

The Court reaffirmed the EEOC's independent power to investigate and to bring its own enforcement actions under Title VII and the ADA. Because of its independent power, the EEOC was not bound by an arbitration agreement signed by an employee, nor did the agreement limit the EEOC's discretion as to what remedies it would seek on behalf of the employee. The Court also criticized the lower court's distinction between injunctive and victim-specific relief, characterizing it as simultaneously over- and under-inclusive. It concluded that the EEOC had the statutory right to pursue both injunctive and victim-specific remedies in court on behalf of the employee despite the agreement to arbitrate.

In all likelihood, the opinion will have only a minor impact on practice. It will not disturb existing arbitration doctrine. As the Court itself notes, "the EEOC only files suit in a small fraction of the charges that employees file." In "year 2000, the EEOC received 79,896 charges of employment discrimination... [and] only filed 291 lawsuits and intervened in 111 others." The Court further recognized that "the EEOC files less than two percent of all antidiscrimination claims in federal court." Thus, "permitting the EEOC access to victim-specific relief in cases where the employee has agreed to binding arbitration, but has not yet brought a claim in arbitration, will have a *negligible* effect on the federal policy favoring arbitration." And, it remains "an open question whether a settlement or arbitration judgment would affect the validity of the EEOC's claim or the character of relief the EEOC may seek."

In his dissent, Justice Thomas (a former head of the EEOC) argued that, if an employee agreed to arbitration, the EEOC was bound by that agreement because the EEOC could not do "on behalf of an employee that which an employee has agreed not to do for himself," namely, to seek monetary relief before a court. Justice Thomas further contended that, while "the EEOC has the statutory right to *bring* suit, it has no statutory entitlement to *obtain* a particular remedy." Thus, "whether a particular remedy is 'appropriate' in any given case is a question for a court and not for the EEOC." Because the employee had waived his right to obtain relief in a judicial forum by signing an arbitration agreement, the EEOC was precluded from seeking victim-specific relief in a judicial forum.

Lower courts have adhered to the holding in *EEOC v. Waffle House*, that the EEOC has the statutory authority to investigate employment discrimination claims even if the employer and employee signed an arbitration agreement. *See EEOC v. Ralphs Grocery, Co.*, 300 F.Supp.2d 637 (N.D. Ill. 2004). Although the EEOC is not bound by an employee's agreement to arbitrate, an employee, however, cannot intervene in an EEOC lawsuit against the employer; to do so would constitute an avoidance of his obligation to arbitrate disputes. In this sense, FAA § 1 functions as a statement of subject-matter inarbitrability.

FAA § 3

Section Three of the FAA outlines the legal effects of an arbitration agreement that is "valid, irrevocable, and enforceable" under Section Two. A valid agreement to arbitrate divests the courts of jurisdiction to entertain the dispute. A federal court cannot assert jurisdiction over a dispute that is properly the subject of an arbitration agreement. When the court is notified of the existence of an arbitration agreement, it can engage in only two types of inquiry: (1) whether the agreement to arbitrate is a valid contract (a Section Two question); and (2) whether the dispute in question is covered by ("referable to") arbitration (a Section Three question) (each inquiry addresses an aspect of the doctrine of contractual inarbitrability). Once this scrutiny has been exercised, the court is obligated by statute to stay the court proceeding "until such arbitration has been had in accordance with the terms of the agreement . . . ."

Courts have the authority to decide challenges to the contractual validity of the arbitration agreement or to its scope of application under the language of FAA §§ 2 and 3. The governing statute does not contain a *kompetenz-kompetenz* provision. The *lacuna* invites the use of dilatory tactics and can cause a two year or longer delay in getting to arbitration. This omission underscores the need to revise and update the FAA.

Despite such gaps, the FAA remains a highly functional regulatory scheme on arbitration. Its provisions are generally quite favorable to arbitration and the case law is a source of constant updates and adaptation. In fact, the absence of *kompetenz-kompetenz* has been remedied, to some extent, by the case law. In its ruling in *First Options of*

Chicago, Inc. v. Kaplan, 514 U.S. 938 (1995), the United States Supreme Court affirmed the power of the courts to rule on jurisdictional challenges (presumably, under Sections Two and Three of the FAA), but also held that the parties could agree to submit such jurisdictional disputes to the arbitrators. Such contractual grants of authority to arbitrators are likely to become a standard feature of both boilerplate and negotiated arbitration agreements.

Other aspects of the language of Section Three warrant comment. The reference at the outset of the provision to actions "brought in any of the courts of the United States" confirms that the FAA is addressed exclusively to the federal courts. There is no hint in the text of a Congressional intent to establish rules for state courts or to elaborate rules of federal law that supersede state provisions. Also, the last clause of the section states that a party moving to stay a judicial trial on the ground of the existence of a valid arbitration agreement that encompasses the dispute submitted to the court must "not [be] in default in proceeding with such arbitration." To conserve its right to arbitrate disputes, a party must act diligently and invoke the process in a timely manner. If neither party has recourse to the agreed-upon arbitral mechanism, the agreement to arbitrate is rescinded by conduct—at least for purposes of the dispute in question. In effect, the parties are estopped from blocking judicial jurisdiction in the matter.

Finally, both Sections Two and Three fail to provide for a defense to the enforcement of arbitration agreements and awards on the basis of the subject matter of the dispute. In fact, the FAA contains no mention whatsoever of the subject-matter inarbitrability defense—not even in Section Ten, which governs the enforcement of awards. The absence of the defense perhaps underscores the procedural character of the FAA provisions. There was no need to refer to substantive considerations in the text of the FAA because other statutes would supply the substantive limits on the right to arbitrate. Moreover, the FAA is intended to apply to interstate maritime and commercial transactions. There was, therefore, no need to limit the reach of legislation that already circumscribed its own scope of application. It applied to standard commercial disputes. In this sense, FAA § 1 functions as a statement of subject-matter inarbitrability.

The Act also ignores public policy in its regulation of arbitral agreements and awards. The courts added a common law ground to that effect in their rulings under the statute, but the legislation itself contains no mention of public policy. As with subject-matter inarbitrability, Congress may have concluded that other statutes would define the role of public policy in arbitration on a subject-matter-by-subject-matter basis. The FAA thereby remains a procedural statute. Whatever factors explain their absence in the FAA, the subject-matter inarbitrability defense and the public policy exception have a limited presence in the U.S. law of arbitration.

Recent case law has endorsed an unequivocal approach to granting stays under FAA § 3 that is fully in compliance with the strong federal policy in favor of arbitration. The principal, and to some extent preemptory, element of a petition for a stay is the existence of a valid agreement to arbitrate disputes. According to one federal district court, there is "little reason to require that an arbitration be commenced by a defendant against itself before a stay [of a court proceeding] can be ordered." Provided there is an enforceable contract of arbitration, a judicial action can be stayed even though no arbitral proceeding has been initiated. As "long as a written agreement to arbitrate exists[,] there is no specific requirement that arbitration actually be pending before a stay of litigation can be granted." The opinion represents a liberal interpretation of FAA § 3's requirement that "the party applying for the stay is not in default in proceeding with such arbitration." *See Sims v. Montell Chrysler, Inc.*, 317 F.Supp.2d 838, 841 (N.D. Ill. 2004).

FAA § 4

Section Four authorizes the federal courts to compel party compliance with the agreement to arbitrate. It also implies that the federal courts have a duty to assist the arbitral process when the exercise of coercive legal authority is necessary to the operation of the process. Along with Section Two, the content of the provision expressly reverses the prior judicial hostility to arbitration. It commands that courts take an active role in sustaining the contractual recourse to arbitration. In order to benefit from the court's authority, one of the parties to the arbitration agreement must invoke the court's jurisdiction by establishing that a written agreement to arbitrate exists and that the other party has failed to abide by the agreement. The court with proper jurisdiction to hear such a motion is the court that would have had jurisdiction over the matter had the parties not agreed to arbitration.

The remainder of the provision contains intricate and therefore confusing language. The applicable regime appears to be that, before the requested court can issue an order compelling a party to arbitrate, it must ascertain that an arbitration agreement does, in fact, exist. Once the existence of the agreement is established, the requested court must determine whether the recalcitrant party's refusal to comply is unwarranted in the circumstances. The party allegedly in breach of the agreement has the right to request a jury trial on both issues.

The designated procedure is cumbersome and unusual. It testifies to the FAA drafters' preoccupation with legal procedural regularity. They agreed that arbitration should be made available to merchants, but were determined that such recourse should not compromise due process rights. Emphasizing constitutional protections and guarantees in an action to compel arbitration may be both excessive and counterproductive. Having contract matters that arise at the threshold of the arbitral process determined by a jury as a matter of right invites the type of delay that can readily frustrate the recourse to arbitration. Resolving such matters by court decision is more efficient and does not compromise the process rights of the parties—especially in cases involving commercial matters.

Section Five adds further content to the duty of the courts to assist and cooperate with arbitral proceedings. At the request of one of the parties, a court can nominate an arbitrator when the parties cannot agree upon the designation or one party refuses to comply with its contractual obligation to appoint an arbitrator. The provision gives proper recognition to the principle of freedom of contract: The parties, through their agreement, control the procedure for nominating arbitrators. It is only in circumstances in which the dynamics of contract freedom fail, *i.e.*, when the agreement is silent and no agreement can be reached subsequently or when there is a refusal to comply with the agreed-upon procedure, that the court can intervene (upon the request of a party) and remedy the stalemate. While the agreement to arbitrate eliminates judicial jurisdiction to rule on the dispute, judicial authority surrounds the operation of the arbitral process. When the agreed-upon rule of law fails, the courts can enforce the contractual obligations. Arbitrators appointed by the court have the same status and authority as party-appointed arbitrators.

FAA § 7

Section Seven gives arbitrators broad evidence-gathering powers. Their authority extends to nonarbitrating parties. Arbitrators can order such parties to appear and testify or to comply with requests for documents or other evidentiary elements. The language of Section Seven is unequivocal: "[t]he arbitrators ... may summon ... *any* person...." (Emphasis added.) Therefore, when the FAA governs the arbitral proceeding, the arbitral tribunal has the same subpoena powers as a court of law. If the third party refuses to comply, the tribunal can petition the proper court to order compliance under penalty of contempt. In issuing its order, the arbitral tribunal must satisfy ordinary notification requirements and a majority of the arbitrators must sign the order.

By including subpoenas in the procedural protocol of the arbitral trial, the drafters of the FAA intended to give arbitrators the tools necessary to engage in effective record-building. Arbitrators, it was assumed, could not decide without a thorough access to, and understanding of, the facts of the litigation. The recent case law is divided on how extensive the arbitrator's subpoena powers are under FAA § 7. In *Hay Group, Inc. v. E.B.S. Acquisition Corp.*, 360 F.3d 404 (3d Cir. 2004), the Third Circuit held that FAA § 7 conferred limited subpoena powers and did not give arbitrators the authority to compel nonparties to comply with pre-hearing discovery requests. The Second Circuit, however, ruled that FAA § 7 should be interpreted broadly to allow arbitrators to subpoena any evidence that is material to the case. In the court's view, arbitrators have the authority to compel testimony and documents from non-party witnesses at both preliminary and final hearings. The courts should uphold, and not seek to restrain, the arbitrator's power to issue subpoenas under the FAA. *See Stolt–Nielsen S.A. v. Celanese AG,* 430 F.3d 567 (2d Cir. 2005).

FAA § 9

Section Nine establishes that a party, within one year of the rendering of the arbitral award, may apply for a judicial order confirming the award. There is a circuit split as to whether the one-year time limit is mandatory or simply conditional. *See Photopaint Tech., L.L.C. v. Smartlens Corp.,* 335 F.3d 152 (2d Cir. 2003) (one-year period is mandatory not permissive and, therefore, applies in all circumstances). Moreover, there are problems regarding the meaning of the term rendition. Does it take place when the arbitrators finish drafting the award or when the administering arbitral institution delivers the award to the parties? The provision recites the standard requirements for exercising court jurisdiction and for conducting the enforcement procedure. It also takes the principle of contractual freedom into account: The parties may choose the court that will issue the order confirming the award prospectively in their agreement. Confirmation begins the process of coercive judicial enforcement of the award against a noncomplying party.

FAA § 10

Section Ten articulates the grounds upon which a federal district court with proper jurisdiction can refuse to confirm or set aside an arbitral award. The action, known as "vacatur," renders the award unenforceable. The basis for denying legal effect to an arbitral award is quite limited. In the main, only significant procedural deficiencies in the arbitral process can thwart the enforcement of an award. The limited number of grounds and their restrictive scope reflect the FAA's liberal disposition toward arbitration. The courts have fully endorsed the limitation of their supervisory authority. Any one of the four grounds in Section Ten could become a significant obstacle to the enforcement of awards. Courts could have given wide meaning and application to the words "undue means," "evident partiality," "misconduct," or "imperfect execution of powers" and engaged in a rigorous scrutiny of awards. In point of fact, the federal courts ordinarily conduct a modest, even perfunctory, review of awards. A nearly irrebuttable presumption exists in the federal case law that arbitral awards, once rendered, are legally enforceable. The vacatur of an award remains an unusual result.

As to the statutory grounds themselves: They are four in number; they avoid any reference to a substantive basis for review (thereby, impliedly eliminating the possibility of a merits review of awards); they expressly relegate judicial scrutiny to violations of basic procedural fairness; and they indicate, by their number and content, a statutory policy favoring the enforcement of awards. Courts will nullify awards only when the arbitral trial was manifestly unfair and significant arbitrator abuse characterized the proceedings. Arbitral trials, however, must abide by basic due process requirements: The right to receive notice, to be heard, and to have the tribunal consider the parties' arguments.

Grounds (a) and (b): The existence of wholesale illegitimacy in the arbitral proceedings, such as bribery, threats of violence, or other forms of intimidation, will invalidate an award. Corrupting the process through "undue means" will entail an equally corrupt determination. Proceedings infected by such "vices" have no integrity and lack the foundation for rendering enforceable results.

Grounds (c) and (d): The arbitrators must also avoid technical violations of their adjudicatory responsibilities. Their conduct of the proceedings cannot "prejudice" the right of either party to a fair hearing. They cannot rule on matters not submitted. And, they must provide the parties with a ruling that resolves their dispute. The courts liberally construe these grounds. For example, they give arbitrators wide latitude in conducting the arbitral proceedings. Arbitrators are not required to follow the rigor of judicial procedure, but rather must only avoid violations of the minimal safeguards of fairness. The general professionalism and experience of arbitrators make vacatur on this basis unlikely.

Ground (e): In those rare instances in which an award is vacated, the court can order the arbitrators to rehear the matter and render another award, provided the arbitration agreement has not lapsed and the court believes a rehearing serves the best interest of the parties and the ends of justice. Resubmission of the matter to the original arbitrators obviates the need for an entirely new proceeding. The resubmission possibility signifies that corrective judicial supervision is exceptional and limited to fundamental matters and that its effect can be contained to a reconsideration of the matter by the arbitrators. It indicates that the courts' function is to preserve—whenever and however possible—the parties' reference to arbitration. The content of Section Ten safeguards the systemic autonomy of the arbitral process by strictly limiting judicial supervision and by having the courts preserve the results of the process.

The decisional law has added several common law grounds for effectuating the judicial supervision of arbitral awards. They include: "manifest disregard of the law"; capricious, arbitrary, or irrational arbitral determinations; and violations of public policy. Most of these grounds overlap with each other and have been applied restrictively by the courts. They originated in the special setting of labor arbitration and were meant to police labor arbitrators' fidelity to and application of the collective bargaining agreement. Over time, they were given a more generalized application by courts in the arbitration area. Their existence in the governing decisional law contradicts the express language and purpose of Section Ten and the judicial policy favoring arbitration. Allowing courts to second-guess arbitrators is hardly supportive of the autonomy of arbitration. In the final analysis, the incorporation of these grounds did not make vacatur more likely. They simply made confirmation more complicated and costly.

FAA § 11

Section Eleven makes possible the correction and modification of arbitral awards that contain formal, objectively-ascertainable errors. It reinforces the statutory objective to uphold the contractual reference to arbitration, to establish a cooperative relationship between the judicial and arbitral processes, and to eliminate the dilatory undermining of the arbitral process.

Upon the request of one of the parties, U.S. federal courts have the power to modify or correct awards for inadvertent technical errors that might preclude enforcement. The errors in question must be "evident" and unrelated to the merits of the determination. Moreover, Ground (b) of Section Eleven recognizes implicitly a commonplace severance procedure. In circumstances in which arbitrators exceed their authority and rule on matters not submitted to arbitration, the court may enforce that part of the award that is valid by severing it from those portions that represent an illicit exercise of adjudicatory authority. Severance is possible only when the various parts of the award are not interrelated or interdependent.

Section Eleven is likely to develop a greater role in the challenge of awards as the arbitration process expands its range of application and lawyers adversarialize the process and the parties. The decisional law has provided that Section Eleven can be used to seek clarification of an award when the award is arguably ambiguous. Such an action may also represent a means of expressing disagreement with the determination and of seeking a modification of the ruling.

In 2000, the United States Supreme Court held that the FAA's venue provisions, §§ 9–11, were permissive in character. *See Cortez Byrd Chips, Inc. v. Bill Harbert Constr. Co.*, 529 U.S. 193 (2000). The ruling allowed motions to confirm, vacate, or modify an arbitration award to be brought either in the district where the award had been rendered or in any proper district under the general venue statute. The general venue statute provides for venue in a diversity action in "a judicial district in which a substantial part of the events or omissions giving rise to the claim occurred, or a substantial part of property that is the subject of the action is situated." 28 U.S.C. § 1391(a)(2). The Court explained that "the three venue sections of the FAA [were] best analyzed together, owing to their contemporaneous enactment and the similarity to their pertinent language."

The Court warned that "[e]nlightenment [would] not come merely from parsing the language [of the statute]." Instead, the Court looked to the statute's legislative history:

When the FAA was enacted in 1925, it appeared against the backdrop of a considerably more restrictive general venue statute than the one current today. At the time, the practical effect of 28 U.S.C. § 112(a) was that a civil suit could usually be brought only in the district in which the defendant resided. The statute's restrictive application was all the more pronounced due to the courts' general inhospitality to forum selection clauses. Hence, even if an arbitration agreement expressly permitted [an] action to be brought in the district in which arbitration had been conducted, the agreement would probably prove to be in vain. The enactment of the special venue provisions in the FAA thus had an obviously liberalizing effect, undiminished by any suggestion, textual or otherwise, that congress meant simultaneously to foreclose a suit where the defendant resided. Such a consequence would have been as inexplicable in 1925 as it would be passing strange 75 years later.

The Court stated that interpreting the FAA venue provisions to require motions to confirm, vacate, or modify the award only in the district where the arbitration took place "would be more clearly at odds with both the FAA's 'statutory policy of rapid and unobstructed enforcement of arbitration agreements,' or with the desired flexibility of parties in choosing a site for arbitration." The Court pointed out that, "[a]lthough the location of the arbitration may well be the residence of one of the parties, or have some other connection to a contract at issue, in many cases the site will have no relation whatsoever to the parties or the dispute." The Court further explained that "parties may be willing to arbitrate in any inconvenient forum, say, for the convenience of the arbitrators, or to get a panel with special knowledge or experience, or as part of some compromise, but they might well be less willing to pick such a location if any future court proceedings had to be held there." The Court was concerned that the flexibility to make these types of practical choices would be "inhibited by a venue rule mandating the same inconvenient venue if someone later sought to vacate or modify the award."

The Court also noted that a restrictive interpretation of the venue provisions would put them in "needless tension" with FAA § 3, which "provides that any court in which an action 'referable to arbitration under an agreement in writing' is pending 'shall on application of one of the parties stay the trial of the action until such arbitration has been had in accordance with the terms of the agreement.' " The Court explained that the existing precedent gives the "court with the power to stay the action under § 3...the further power to confirm any ensuing arbitration award." Under a restrictive interpretation of the venue provisions, if an arbitration were held outside the district of that litigation, a subsequent proceeding to confirm, modify, or vacate the award could not be brought in the district of the original litigation, a result that the Court found unacceptable.

Finally, the Court held that a restrictive "interpretation would create anomalous results in the aftermath of arbitrations held abroad." FAA §§ 204, 207, and 302 "together provide for liberal choice of venue for actions to confirm awards subject to the 1958 Convention on the Recognition and Enforcement of Foreign Arbitral Awards and the 1975 Inter–American Convention on International Commercial Arbitration. But, reading §§ 9–11 to restrict venue to the site of the arbitration would preclude any action under the FAA in courts of the United States to confirm, modify, or vacate awards rendered in foreign arbitrations not covered by either convention." The Court noted that, "[a]lthough such actions would not necessarily be barred for lack of jurisdiction, they would be defeated by restrictions on venue, and anomalies like that are to be avoided when they can be." The Court admitted that "[t]here have been, and perhaps there still are, occasional gaps in the venue laws, [but] Congress does not in general intend to create venue gaps, which take away with one hand what Congress had given by way of jurisdictional grant with the other. Thus, in construing venue statutes it is reasonable to prefer the construction that avoids leaving such gaps."

The Court concluded by explaining that the "[a]ttention to practical consequences…points away from the restrictive reading of §§ 9–11 and confirms the view that the liberalizing effect of the provisions in the day of their enactment was meant to endure through treating them as permitting, not limiting, venue choice today." Therefore, the Court held that the permissive view of FAA venue provisions prevailed.

FAA § 15

Section Fifteen is misplaced because it deals with the impact of foreign State sovereignty on arbitration by regulating the impact of the Act of State doctrine upon the enforcement of arbitral agreements and awards. Its contents do not belong in the domestic law section of the U.S. statute on arbitration.

Act of State applies primarily, if not exclusively, in the transborder context, more than likely when a U.S. national or corporate entity alleges that it is aggrieved by the conduct of a foreign State within that State's territorial borders. Act of State functions as an objection to the exercise of U.S. judicial jurisdiction in much the same manner as the sovereign immunity defense. Under the latter, a foreign State cannot be sued before U.S. courts because of its status as a State: It is immune from suit because of its sovereignty. Under the former, a foreign State cannot be sued before a U.S. court because its actions took place within its own territory and were undertaken to further the interests of the nation. They were done for a public purpose.

Further, the matter is nonjusticiable because it implicates U.S. foreign policy interests and thereby the constitutional separation of powers doctrine under which the Executive Branch has exclusive authority over U.S. diplomatic policy. Unlike sovereign immunity, Act of State is unique to U.S. law; it emerged and is embedded in U.S. constitutional separation of powers. It involves State conduct that is roughly equivalent to the exercise of eminent domain powers in the domestic setting.

FAA § 16

Despite the relative complexity of its language, Section Sixteen makes a simple point. It confirms and gives legislative approval to the court-created "policy favoring arbitration." The right of interlocutory appeal exists against any court order that is antagonistic to arbitration, *e.g.*, an order refusing to stay a judicial proceeding in favor of arbitration or refusing to compel arbitration. There is, however, no right of interlocutory appeal against an order that supports the recourse to arbitration. A federal court order, for example, that confirms the parties' right to proceed with arbitration is only subject to ordinary appeal.

The dichotomy of regimes is meant to advance the interests of arbitration and to affirm the FAA policy to legitimate arbitration. The gravamen of Section Sixteen also creates a bond of cooperation between the judicial and arbitral processes. One commentator has assessed Section Sixteen in these terms:

It is a pro-arbitration statute designed to prevent the appellate aspect of the litigation process from impeding the expeditious disposition of an arbitration. Its inherent acknowledgment is that arbitration is a form of dispute resolution designed to save the parties time, money, and effort by substituting for the litigation process the advantages of speed, simplicity, and economy associated with arbitration. Its theme is that judicial involvement in the process should be kept to the barest minimum to avoid undermining those goals.

D. Siegel, *Practice Commentary*, 9 U.S.C.A. [Arbitration] at 306 (West Supp. 1996).

A critical legal problem under Section Sixteen is determining when judicial action in regard to arbitration is a final disposition and subject to appeal. In December 2000, the United States Supreme Court rendered its ruling in *Green Tree Financial Corp.-Alabama v. Randolph*, 531 U.S. 79 (2000). There, the Court held that, when a district court compels the parties to arbitrate their differences and dismisses all claims brought before it, that determination constitutes a "final decision" under FAA § 16(a)(3) and is subject to appeal:

The District Court's order directed that the dispute be resolved by arbitration and dismissed respondent's claims with prejudice, leaving the court nothing to do but execute the judgment. That order plainly disposed of the entire case on the merits and left no part of it pending before the court. The FAA does permit parties to arbitration agreements to bring a separate proceeding in a district court to enter judgment on an arbitration award once it is made (or to vacate or modify it), but the existence of that remedy does not vitiate the finality of the District Court's resolution of the claims in the instant proceeding.... The District Court's order was therefore 'a final decision with respect to an arbitration' within the meaning of § 16(a)(3), and an appeal may be taken.

The *Rooker-Feldman* doctrine is relevant to FAA § 16. It is intended to prevent "a party losing in state court from seeking what in substance would be appellate review of the state judgment [in the lower federal courts] based on the losing party's claim that the state judgment itself violate[d] the loser's federal rights." It originated in *Rooker v. Fidelity Trust Co.*, 263 U.S. 413 (1923), and *District of Columbia Court of Appeals v. Feldman*, 460 U.S. 462 (1983). It is meant to discourage forum-shopping and the relitigation of cases based on a strained federal rights argument. It works *in tandem* with FAA § 16 in that it generally precludes reconsideration of an order to compel arbitration. The preclusion of appeal under *Rooker-Feldman* obviously is not temporary or merely delayed. Moreover, it applies to the jurisdictional divide between state and federal courts, rather than to the exercise of appellate jurisdiction among federal courts on arbitration matters. *Rooker-Feldman* is a bar when a party challenges the application of law in a state court litigation, but not when the challenge is directed to the constitutionality of the state law that was applied in the proceeding before the state court.

Pieper v. American Arbitration Association, 336 F.3d 458 (6th Cir.), *cert. denied*, 540 U.S. 1182

(2004), demonstrates the standard application of the doctrine. After being compelled to arbitrate by an Ohio state court, Pieper filed suit before a federal district court alleging that "the dispute was not properly subject to arbitration and seeking injunctive relief that would bar [the] AAA from beginning the arbitration hearings." The federal court concluded that it lacked subject matter jurisdiction to engage in the appellate review of state court proceedings. On appeal, the ruling was upheld because "under the *Rooker-Feldman* doctrine[,]" the lower federal court "was without jurisdiction to grant relief" because *Rooker-Feldman* "generally prohibits federal courts from reviewing state-court judgments."

Despite the clarity of its application in the foregoing case, *Rooker-Feldman* raises a number of unresolved issues that indicate it may not work in concert with FAA § 16 in all circumstances. When a state court denies a motion to compel arbitration, federal law would command interlocutory recourse to an appellate court. Does *Rooker-Feldman* foreclose recourse to the lower federal courts in this instance? Does that mean that recourse to federal appellate courts also is precluded? These circumstances also raise the possible arguments that either the state court applied a state law contrary to the FAA—which, therefore, should be preempted— or the state court misconstrued the applicable law such that it denied the affected party its federal right to arbitrate under FAA § 2. The latter argument assumes that FAA § 2 does in fact create such a right and some sort of accompanying federal question jurisdiction. The case law acknowledges the "anomalies," but has not proposed any resolution of the issue.

These unprovided-for complications at least raise the question of whether *Rooker-Feldman* is intended only to have a pro-arbitration effect, allowing state court determinations favorable to arbitration to escape lower federal court scrutiny. The doctrine was articulated in a federalism-jurisdictional context and not in circumstances of support for or compliance with the federal policy on arbitration. It is difficult to imagine how state court proceedings that prevent the recourse to arbitration under state law would not result in an action before federal courts. The issue, however, has yet to receive a thorough examination in the decisional law.

CHAPTER FOUR

ARBITRATION AND FEDERALISM

Introduction

The FAA was enacted during the era of *Swift v. Tyson*, 41 U.S. (16 Pet.) 1 (1842). The decision in *Swift v. Tyson* provided that federal courts hearing state law cases on a diversity basis were bound by state court opinions only when the cases involved the construction of state constitutions or statutes. When such provisions were not implicated, the federal courts were free to devise their own rules of decision independently of state court rulings. *Erie Railroad Co. v. Tompkins*, 304 U.S. 64 (1938), overruled *Swift v. Tyson*, providing that "there is no general federal common law," and that "Congress has no power to declare substantive rules of common law applicable in a state, whether they be local in their nature or general, whether they be commercial law or a part of the law of torts." Under *Erie,* in cases of diversity jurisdiction, the federal courts applied state law except in circumstances in which the controversy was governed by the U.S. Constitution or an Act of Congress.

From the perspective of *Erie*, the question became whether the FAA was merely a set of procedural regulations or legislation that created sub-stantive rights and was, therefore, binding upon the federal courts in all cases. Moreover, if federal question jurisdiction did not exist, could federal courts ruling on the basis of diversity apply the FAA—even if the litigation involved predominantly state interests and state law is otherwise controlling? The question was especially significant if the state law on arbitration conflicted with the FAA.

Under *Erie*, the court could have envisaged the displacement of applicable state law on arbitration as an impermissible preemptive application of general federal common law. The application of state arbitration laws by federal courts sitting in diversity could have fragmented any national consensus on arbitration and undermined the FAA's clear mandate to make arbitration an autonomous and viable alternative adjudicatory process. Another view of the federalism dimension of the FAA in diversity cases, however, could be advanced. Because *Erie* mandated the application of state law in all diversity cases but those in which the U.S. Constitution or federal legislation was controlling, courts could hold that the FAA was applicable as a federal enactment, ruling—in effect—that the FAA represented more than the enactment of merely procedural regulations and that it actually created substantive federal rights.

Early Cases

In *Bernhardt v. Polygraphic Co. of America*, 350 U.S. 198 (1956), the United States Supreme Court took an *"Erie*-sensitive" position, holding that the FAA was a federal procedural enactment that could not dislodge the application of state law in federal diversity cases. Allowing claims to be submitted to arbitration through the federal courts in diversity cases might lead to adjudicatory outcomes not otherwise available under state law. The undermining of state law would violate the directive in *Erie*.

In *Robert Lawrence Co. v. Devonshire Fabrics, Inc.*, 271 F.2d 402 (2d Cir. 1959), the Second Circuit advanced a different view of the FAA's status, declaring that it represented the enactment of federal substantive law on arbitration agreements under the constitutional powers of the U.S. Congress. The federal law was applicable in both state and federal courts and also controlled in diversity cases:

> We, therefore, hold that the Arbitration Act in making agreements to arbitrate 'valid, irrevocable, and enforceable' created national substantive law clearly constitutional under the maritime and commerce powers of the Congress and that the rights thus created are to be adjudicated by the federal courts whenever such courts have subject matter jurisdiction, including diversity cases, just as the federal courts adjudicate controversies affecting other substantive rights when subject matter jurisdiction over the litigation exists. We hold that the body of law thus created is substantive not procedural in character and that it encompasses questions of interpretation and construction as well as questions of validity, revo-

cability and enforceability of arbitration agreements affecting interstate commerce or maritime affairs, since these two types of legal questions are inextricably intertwined.

Prima Paint

Prima Paint Corp. v. Flood & Conklin Manufacturing Co., 388 U.S. 395 (1967), is the landmark case on this question. The *Prima Paint* Court underscored the FAA's primary objective and expressed its resolve to give it full effect. The FAA's basic purpose was to foster the enforcement of arbitration agreements, "[i]n so concluding, we not only honor the plain meaning of the statute but also the unmistakably clear congressional purpose that the arbitration procedure, when selected by the parties to a contract, be speedy and not subject to delay and obstruction in the courts." State law challenges to the validity of arbitration agreements constituted a dilatory infringement—an attempt to defeat the effect of the arbitration agreement and to frustrate the objective of the federal legislation.

The Court further stated that the question in *Prima Paint* "was not whether Congress may fashion federal substantive rules to govern questions arising in simple diversity cases,...[but] whether Congress may prescribe how federal courts are to conduct themselves with respect to subject matter over which Congress plainly has power to legislate." In other words, *Prima Paint* did not involve the issue of federalism and states' rights, but rather whether Congress could provide substantive directives to the federal courts in areas in which Congress had specific legislative powers.

The Court answered the federalism question while appearing to disregard it; Congress could create federal law where it had legislative authority to act. Therefore, in diversity cases in which questions arose regarding the validity of the recourse to arbitration, the federal courts were under an obligation to apply the controlling federal legislation. The application of federal law appeared to be restricted by the requirement that the contracts containing arbitration clauses affect interstate commerce.

The primary question in *Prima Paint* was whether a party's allegation of contractual fraud—specifically, fraud in the inducement of the agreement— might void both the main contract and the arbitral clause. If the claim had any credibility, jurisdiction over the parties' dispute should be redirected to the courts because the arbitral tribunal had no legal basis upon which to exercise its adjudicatory authority. The foundation of its authority, the arbitral clause, was suspect and, therefore, inoperative (at least, temporarily as a result of the allegation). If the court determined that the claim of fraud in the inducement was unfounded, the reference to arbitration presumably would be reinvigorated and the arbitral tribunal would have jurisdiction to decide the other contract disputes.

The *Prima Paint* Court's answer to the dilemma between the validity of contract and the policy favoring arbitral independence was the separability doctrine. Allegations of contractual deficiency must be directed specifically at the clause itself; the deficiency of the main agreement did not necessarily impinge upon the arbitration agreement. The separability doctrine heightened the adverse party's burden of proof, made dilatory objections less likely, and could avoid the reference to the courts by maintaining the arbitral tribunal's jurisdiction.

The otherwise applicable state law of New York, however, did not recognize the separability doctrine. The court, not the arbitral tribunal, would rule upon the claim of fraud in the inducement. The federal courts had no power to amend the state law of New York and, under *Erie*, were required to apply the governing state law as enacted. *Erie* appeared to demand that the federal courts reach a determination of the matter that contravened the federal policy on arbitration. The Court skirted the issue by declaring that the FAA was a congressional command, binding upon the federal courts, that directed them on how to rule on matters of arbitration. The federal courts sitting in diversity cases were required to apply the FAA (which included the separability doctrine)—the FAA thereby dislodged the application of otherwise controlling state law in diversity jurisdiction cases. The *Erie* doctrine, therefore, was of limited application in arbitration cases involving diversity of citizenship.

The vitality of the separability doctrine and *Prima Paint* in the U.S. law of arbitration was recently reaffirmed by the United States Supreme Court.

The Court in *Buckeye Check Cashing, Inc. v. Cardegna*, 546 U.S. 440 (2006), made clear that the separability doctrine was a vital part of U.S. arbitration law and dictated practice in both state and federal courts: "We reaffirm today that, regardless of whether the challenge is brought in federal or state court, a challenge to the validity of the contract as a whole, and not specifically to the arbitration clause, must go to the arbitrator." The Court made evident the settled law on the question:

> ...[A]s a matter of substantive federal arbitration law, an arbitration provision is severable from the remainder of the contract.... [U]nless the challenge is to the arbitration clause itself, the issue of the contract's validity is considered by the arbitrator in the first instance.... [T]his arbitration law applies in state as well as federal courts.

The Court concluded that Florida public policy and contract law, and even its concept of criminal culpability, did not overwhelm separability or federal preemption: "We simply reject[] the proposition that the enforceability of the arbitration agreement turn[s] on the state legislature's judgment concerning the forum for enforcement of the state-law cause of action." Additionally, the Court declared that separability arose from FAA § 2, as well as §§ 3 and 4, thereby making it fully enforceable in state courts.

At the outset of its opinion, the Court made a distinction between different types of challenges that could be lodged against arbitration agreements. It recognized two types of challenges: (1) *Southland*-like challenges, and (2) challenges to the "contract as a whole." In a footnote, the Court identified a third type of challenge, *i.e.*, whether a contract (presumably, of arbitration) was entered into by the parties. These brief statements constitute a rudimentary outline of the jurisdictional doctrine of *kompetenz-kompetenz* and principles of arbitration law that are recognized as basic law in other, likeminded jurisdictions, like France and England.

It appears that the Court was establishing a distinction between subject-matter and contractual inarbitrability and elaborating the basis for a challenge on either ground. *Southland* challenges involve the application of statutes that provide for the exclusive resolution of dispute through courts. When the parties agreed to arbitrate such disputes, courts must decide whether the arbitration agreement is effective in light of the statutory subject matter barrier to arbitration. The consideration of that question inexorably leads to another which is even more decisive: Whether the "blocking" statute's jurisdictional exclusivity (if it is state legislation) is preempted by federal law under FAA § 2.

The Court's two additional statements in this matter relate to inarbitrability based on contract, rather than subject matter. They represent the traditional basis upon which to bring jurisdictional challenges to the arbitral tribunal in most legal systems. Arbitrator authority to rule can be challenged on the basis that the parties never entered into an arbitration agreement—a ground that the Court recognizes in the footnote; that a contract to arbitrate exists, but is deficient in formation and unenforceable; that the agreement to arbitrate is good as a contract, but it does not apply or extend to the controversy at hand; and, finally, that the arbitral clause is fully enforceable and applicable, but it has not been correctly applied according to its terms to the litigation in question. In other words, the instituted arbitration deviates from the agreed-upon provisions in the contract that relate, presumably, to material matters.

The Federalism Trilogy

The full implications of the ruling in *Prima Paint* on federalism and the FAA became clearer over time. The Court's rulings in *Moses H. Cone Memorial Hospital v. Mercury Construction Corp.*, 460 U.S. 1 (1983), *Southland Corp. v. Keating*, 465 U.S. 1 (1984), and *Dean Witter Reynolds, Inc. v. Byrd,* 470 U.S. 213 (1985), demonstrated that the Court gave the Congressional objective underlying the FAA fundamental importance. The Court would uphold that objective regardless of state law provisions.

Moses H. Cone involved a contract dispute between a North Carolina hospital and an Alabama building contractor. The contract for the construction of additions to the hospital's main building provided that disputes would be resolved by the architect within a specified period of time. If a dispute went unresolved, it would be submitted to binding arbitration. When a dispute arose over costs and could not be resolved, the hospital filed an action before a North Carolina state court, seeking in part a declaratory judgment that there was no right to arbitrate "under the contract due to waiver, latches, estoppel, and failure to make a timely demand for arbitration." The building contractor then filed an action before the federal district court to compel arbitration under FAA § 4. The district court stayed the action pending resolution of the hospital's suit in state court. On appeal, the Fourth Circuit reversed the stay and issued instructions to compel arbitration. The United States Supreme Court upheld the appellate opinion:

The basic issue presented in Mercury's federal suit was the arbitrability of the dispute between Mercury and the Hospital. Federal law in the terms of the Arbitration Act governs that issue in either state or federal court. Section 2 is the primary substantive provision of the Act, declaring that a written agreement to arbitrate "in any maritime transaction or a contract evidencing a transaction involving commerce...shall be valid, irrevocable, and enforceable, save upon such grounds as exist at law or in equity for the revocation of any contract."

Section 2 is a congressional declaration of a liberal federal policy favoring arbitration agreements, notwithstanding any state substantive or procedural policies to the contrary. The effect of the section is to create a body of federal substantive law of arbitrability, applicable to any arbitration agreement within the coverage of the Act. In *Prima Paint Corp. v. Flood & Conklin Mfg. Corp.*, . . . [w]e held that the language and policies of the Act required the conclusion that the [contractual] fraud issue was arbitrable. Although our holding in *Prima Paint* extended only to the specific issue presented, the courts of appeals have since consistently concluded that questions of arbitrability must be addressed with a healthy regard for the federal policy favoring arbitration. We agree. The Arbitration Act establishes that, as a matter of federal law, any doubts concerning the scope of arbitrable issues should be resolved in favor of arbitration, whether the problem at hand is the construction of the contract language itself or an allegation of waiver, delay, or a like defense to arbitrability.

In the recesses of its opinion, the Court asserted that: "The Arbitration Act is something of an anomaly in the field of federal-court jurisdiction. It creates a body of federal substantive law establishing and regulating the duty to honor an agreement to arbitrate, yet it does not create any independent federal-question jurisdiction.". *Id.* at 26 n.32. The Court's characterization of the FAA as an "anomaly" for jurisdictional purposes, and its conclusion that the FAA did not create "federal-question jurisdiction" for purposes of litigation involving arbitration were to gain importance as the law evolved. Indeed, the most recent cases pose the question, albeit critically in dissent, of whether the Court's construction of the FAA has not, in effect, resulted in the creation of federal-question jurisdiction for purposes of arbitration. Such a result challenges fundamental principles of federalism, the legislative history of the statute, and the express language of Section One. Further, given the would-be anomalous lack of federal-question jurisdiction, the Court declared that "there must be diversity of citizenship or some other independent basis for federal jurisdiction" before a federal court could issue an order to compel arbitration under Section Four of the Act in a diversity case governed by state law. *Id.* The answer begged the question; under *Erie*, diversity of citizenship was a sufficient basis for asserting federal court jurisdiction, but not for applying federal law. Diversity alone should not compel or authorize a federal court to apply the FAA, unless the statute and the right to arbitrate have a constitutional dimension.

The Court recently decided *Vaden v. Discover Bank*, 129 S.Ct. 1262 (2009). The issue in *Vaden* involved the long-standing "anomaly" that the FAA fails to create federal question jurisdiction. Rather than focusing upon FAA § 2 as is often the case in such litigation, the focal point in *Vaden* was FAA § 4. Section Four governs the procedure for compelling arbitration and provides, in relevant part, that: "A party aggrieved by the alleged failure, neglect, or refusal of another to arbitrate under a written agreement for arbitration may petition any United States district court which, save for such agreements, would have jurisdiction under Title 28, in civil action or in admiralty of the subject matter of a suit arising out of the controversy between the parties, for an order directing that such arbitration proceed in the manner provided for in such agreement."

In 1990, Ms. Vaden, an individual consumer, secured a credit card from Discover Bank. Her account was administered by a Discover affiliate, Discover Financial Services ("DFS"). Upon sending her a plantinum card in 1999, Discover modified the card member agreement to the effect that either party could elect to arbitrate disputes. Thereafter, in 2003, DFS sued Vaden in state court because she failed to pay the outstanding balance on her card. In response, Vaden filed class action counterclaims on the basis of state law. Among other things, she alleged that the fees and interest were excessive and violated statutory limits. Whereupon DFS filed an action in federal court to compel arbitration pursuant to the modified cardmember agreement. It contended that federal subject matter jurisdiction existed because Discover Bank was subject to the Federal Deposit Insurance Act ("FDIA"). The FDIA preempted the state law counterclaims.

The district court agreed and ordered arbitration. The Fourth Circuit upheld the lower court, ruling that "when a party comes to federal court seeking to compel arbitration, the presence of a federal question in the underlying dispute is sufficient to support subject matter jurisdiction." Discover Bank

v. Vaden, 396 F.3d 366, 367 (2005). Federal courts could assert jurisdiction over any dispute "arising under" federal law pursuant to 28 U.S.C. § 1331. The court remanded to have the district court determine the true party in interest and whether a federal question existed. The district court ruled that Discover Bank was the real party in interest and that Vaden's state law claims were preempted by the FDIA. In effect, the existence of federal statutory claims somewhere in the controversy gave the court subject matter jurisdiction under FAA § 4 to compel arbitration. Vaden appealed and the Fourth Circuit upheld the district court determination.

The Court granted *certiorari* to resolve a circuit split on whether an underlying dispute involving federal law could create federal jurisdiction to compel arbitration. The Second, Fifth, Sixth, and Seventh Circuits view jurisdiction under Section Four narrowly and look only to the contractual dispute to which the motion to compel refers (in *Vaden*, debt collection). The First, Fourth, and Eleventh Circuits take a more expansive view of subject matter jurisdiction under FAA § 4. These courts will "look through" the petition to compel arbitration to the underlying dispute to find subject matter jurisdiction (in *Vaden*, the FDIA claims).

In its opinion, the Court sided with the First, Fourth, and Eleventh Circuits. The Court resolved the circuit split by adopting the more liberal and expansive test for federal jurisdiction, but nonetheless concluded that the application of that test in this case did not yield federal question jurisdiction. The Court emphasized that the order to compel arbitration, the purpose of seeking federal jurisdiction, could be achieved on a different, but equally effective, statutory basis. Although the case was properly before state courts, FAA § 2 demanded that the latter order the litigation to arbitration:

In sum, § 4 of the FAA instructs district courts asked to compel arbitration to inquire whether the court would have jurisdiction, "save for [the arbitration] agreement," over "a suit arising out of the controversy between the parties." We read that prescription in light of the well-pleaded complaint rule and the corollary rule that federal jurisdiction cannot be invoked on the basis of a defense or counterclaim. Parties may not circumvent those rules by asking a federal court to order arbitration of the portion of a controversy that implicates federal law when the court would not have federal-question jurisdiction over the controversy as a whole. It does not suffice to show that a federal question lurks somewhere inside the parties' controversy, or that a defense or counterclaim would arise under federal law. Because the controversy between Discover and Vaden, properly perceived, is not one qualifying for federal-court adjudication, § 4 of the FAA does not empower a federal court to order arbitration of that controversy, in whole or in part.

Discover, we note, is not left without recourse. Under the FAA, state courts as well as federal

courts are obliged to honor and enforce agreements to arbitrate.... Discover may therefore
petition a Maryland court for aid in enforcing the
arbitration clause of its contracts with Maryland
cardholders.

[. . .]

It is difficult to assess the significance of *Vaden* to
the U.S. law of arbitration. It is even more difficult
to see how the FAA gives rise, in almost any circumstance, to federal question jurisdiction except
through the fiat of judicial pronouncement and recourse to the federal preemption doctrine. The latter is itself a judicial graft. Most of the provisions of
the Act are directed to federal courts and are purely
procedural in character. The Court continues to
transform the governing statute to have it reflect
the image of its favorable-to-arbitration policy.

The *Moses H. Cone* Court further asserted that:
"[A]lthough enforcement of the Act is left in large
part to the state courts, it nevertheless represents
federal policy to be vindicated by the federal courts
where otherwise appropriate." The content of the
statement violated fundamental federalism principles. It also contradicted the view articulated in
Prima Paint that the FAA stood as a congressional
directive to the federal courts on matters of arbitration. The language of FAA Section One does not—in
any manner—sustain the view that state courts are
primarily responsible for the enforcement of the
FAA. The rule that the FAA was binding upon state
courts had now crept into the Court's decisional law

and would be reinforced and broadened in later opinions.

The Court also provided an explanation for the integration of state courts into the arbitration regime established by the FAA. First, by way of the general mores of the common law, most state courts, in the Court's view, have agreed voluntarily to be bound by the stay provision in Section Three of the Act. State court practice eliminated any need to clarify the allegedly ambiguous jurisdictional reference in Section Three to actions brought "in any of the courts of the United States." Whether the state court precedent was either so voluminous or so clear on the question was certainly debatable, but the Court's discovery of ambiguity in the language of Section Three was strained at best and contradicted its reading of the provision in *Prima Paint*, not to mention the legislative history of the statute.

Second, and this reasoning gets to the nub of the federalism question and more readily explains the motivation of the holding, the Court observed that a disparity in the enforcement of arbitration agreements among the federal and state courts would undermine the congressional intent underlying the FAA. The practicality rationale was persuasive in some respects, but it was hardly a solution to the federalism and state rights problems that were generated by the Court's holding. In resorting to this rationale, the Court referred to "Congress's intent to mandate enforcement of all covered arbitration agreements." If "covered ... agreements" included all those clauses that were the subject of litigation before the federal and state courts, the FAA applied to any and all agreements to arbitrate. And, the law of arbitration had been federalized.

Southland Corp. v. Keating, 465 U.S. 1 (1984), decided a year later, had an even more pronounced impact upon federalism. The issue in *Keating* centered upon the constitutionality of a section of the California Franchise Investment Law, Cal. Corp. Code § 31512 (West 1997), which had been interpreted to require exclusive judicial adjudication of claims brought under the statute. Keating's claim, brought on behalf of Seven–Eleven franchisees against Southland Corporation, the Seven–Eleven franchisor, alleged, among other things, that Southland had breached its fiduciary duty and violated the disclosure requirements of the California Franchise Investment Law. After a trial court determination holding the nonwaiver provisions of the Franchise Investment Law valid, a California court of appeals held that, if the Franchise Investment Law rendered arbitration agreements unenforceable, it conflicted with the provisions of the FAA and was, therefore, invalid under the Supremacy Clause of the United States Constitution. The California state Supreme Court interpreted the investment law provision to require exclusive judicial adjudication of claims brought under the statute; it held that claims asserted under the investment law were inarbitrable; and it further concluded that the California statute did not contravene the federal legislation on arbitration. *Keating v. Superior Court*, 183 Cal.Rptr. 360 (1982).

The United States Supreme Court determined that the federal legislation created a duty not only upon the federal courts, but also upon the state courts to apply the federal policy on arbitration embodied in the FAA. "In enacting section 2 of the Federal Act, Congress declared a national policy favoring arbitration and withdrew the power of the states to require a judicial forum for the resolution of claims which the contracting parties agreed to resolve by arbitration." Agreeing with the essential reasoning of the California appellate court opinion, the Court further held that, "in creating a substantive rule applicable in state as well as federal courts, Congress intended to foreclose state legislative attempts to undercut the enforceability of arbitration agreements. We hold that § 31512 of the California Franchise Investment Law violates the Supremacy Clause."

Dean Witter Reynolds, Inc. v. Byrd, 470 U.S. 213 (1985), was the final segment of the federalism trilogy. *Byrd* involved a dispute between a customer and the Dean Witter Reynolds securities brokerage firm. Byrd filed a complaint against Dean Witter Reynolds in a U.S. district court, claiming jurisdiction based on the existence of a federal question as well as diversity of citizenship, alleging violations of the U.S. Securities Act of 1934 and of various state law provisions relating to securities regulation. The broker-dealer contract, however, contained an arbitration agreement. Based upon that agreement, Dean Witter filed a motion to sever the pendant state claims and compel arbitration, staying the arbitration during the resolution of the federal court action. At both the federal trial and appellate levels, the motion to sever the pendant state claims and compel arbitration was denied because of the "intertwining" doctrine, barring the arbitration of state law claims that are factually inseparable from claims under the federal securities act. According to the appellate court reasoning, the intertwining doctrine maintained the federal courts' "exclusive jurisdiction over the federal securities claim" by preventing the earlier arbitral determination of the state claim from binding the federal proceeding through collateral estoppel. Also, "by declining to compel arbitration, the courts avoid bifurcated proceedings and perhaps redundant efforts to litigate the same factual question twice."

Despite the persuasiveness of this reasoning, the United States Supreme Court reversed the decision, holding that the pendant state claims should be compelled to arbitration. In a unanimous opinion, the Court stated that "the Act leaves no place for the discretion by a district court, but instead mandates that district courts *shall* direct the parties to proceed to arbitration on issues as to which an arbitration agreement has been signed." The Court emphasized the underlying controlling congressional intent of the federal legislation on arbitration, namely, "that the purpose behind the act's passage was to ensure judicial enforcement of privately made agreements to arbitrate...[and] [w]e therefore reject the suggestion that the overriding goal of the [FAA] was to provoke the expeditious resolution of claims."

The federalism trilogy, *Moses H. Cone*, *Keating*, and *Byrd*, left little doubt about its ultimate consequence; it effectively federalized the domestic U.S. law of arbitration. The Court discovered in the FAA a "strong federal policy supporting arbitration" and a congressional command to the courts to enforce it. It referred to three constitutional concepts to expand the reach of the FAA and to achieve a uniform national legal position on arbitration: a broad view of interstate commerce under the Commerce Clause, the dominance of federal law under the Supremacy Clause, and the constitutional power of the Congress to direct the conduct of the federal courts. As a result, the FAA was binding upon federal courts in diversity cases and upon state courts ruling on matters that had some link to interstate commerce. The FAA also overrode the legislative authority of states to regulate arbitration given the supremacy of federal law. In effect, all statutes and litigation in the United States that implicate arbitration must conform to the provisions and underlying policy of the FAA.

From *Prima Paint* to the federalism trilogy, the Court supported the autonomy of the arbitral process at the price of substantially undermining, if not eradicating, state authority in the area. The Court's decisional law emphasized the FAA's mandate and the need to eliminate judicial hostility to arbitration. There was a judicial duty to recognize and give effect to arbitration agreements. The Court's pronouncements also added content to the FAA and heightened its systemic standing. The Court was determined to achieve a cohesive and coherent national law and policy on arbitration.

Volt

Volt Information Sciences, Inc. v. Board of Trustees of Leland Stanford Junior University, 489 U.S. 468 (1989), involved a contractual agreement between Stanford University and Volt Information Sciences, Inc., one of several contractors working on a large construction project on the Stanford campus. Its contract to install a system of electrical conduits contained standard provisions on dispute resolution and choice-of-law that provided for arbitration and the application of local law. After a dispute arose, Volt demanded arbitration and Stanford initiated a legal action against Volt for breach of contract and fraud and also sought indemnification from two other contractors not bound by an arbitration agreement. The California courts denied Volt's motion to compel arbitration. According to state procedural law, California courts had the discretion to stay arbitral proceedings pending the resolution of related litigation against third parties not bound by the arbitration agreement. The purpose of the provision was to avoid conflicting rulings on the same matter by different tribunals. *See* Cal. Civ. Proc. Cod. Ann. 1281.2(c) (West 1982).

The question before the United States Supreme Court was two-fold: Had the parties in *Volt* intended to have California law govern not only the contract, but also the arbitration agreement and any ensuing arbitration? If so, was the applicable law valid under the Supremacy Clause of the Federal Constitution given that the application of state law resulted in a stay of the arbitration proceeding? In turn, these issues engendered a more wide-ranging, albeit circuitous, question: Could party intent be used to defeat the agreed-upon recourse to arbitration? In other words, although the parties agreed to resolve their contractual disputes through arbitration, could they also have expressly provided for the application of a state law that might, upon the exercise of judicial discretion, undermine that intent?

California state courts held that the choice-of-law clause (mandating the application of local law) also governed the arbitration agreement. Because California law applied and its procedural law allowed courts to stay arbitral proceedings in circumstances of "intertwining" arbitral and legal proceedings, Volt's request to compel arbitration could lawfully be denied. This determination permitted state law to predominate over the FAA. In practical terms, it simply provided Stanford, the noncomplying party, with a loophole by which to avoid arbitration.

In prior rulings, primarily in the federalism trilogy, the Court had held unequivocally that state legislation could not be used to prevent the recourse to arbitration. Even the promotion of adjudicatory efficiency was not a significant enough concern to override the FAA's policy mandate. These prior rulings should have led the Court to espouse the approach ultimately adopted by the dissent. Arguing for a reversal, the dissent in *Volt* emphasized the state law's detrimental impact upon and inconsistency with the provisions of the FAA and its objectives. State law, after all, was being used to thwart agreed-upon recourse to arbitration.

With a 6–2 majority, the Court nonetheless held that the parties' contractual intent was clear (or, at least, the state court's interpretation of it could not be challenged) and that the intent to have state law govern could effectively defeat the parties' agreement to arbitrate. The Court's previous preoccupation with elaborating legal rules uniformly favorable to arbitration was conspicuously absent. Instead, it embraced the view that the FAA meant to have arbitration agreements enforced as written. Parties who expressly agreed to arbitrate disputes could also agree, by implication from a choice-of-law provision, to repudiate that agreement—whenever a court decided to exercise its discretion to stay arbitral proceedings under state procedural law.

The new doctrinal development in *Volt* centered upon the role of contract freedom in arbitration law: Under the FAA, arbitration agreements were enforceable according to their specific contract language. The emphasis of the decisional law moved from protecting the contractual right to arbitrate (the reversal of judicial hostility to arbitration) to the enforcement of stipulated obligations in the contract of arbitration (party autonomy). "[W]e have recognized that the FAA does not require parties to arbitrate when they have not agreed to do so." Even the dissent agreed with the new doctrinal emphasis:

> [T]he FAA does not pre-empt state arbitration rules, even as applied to contracts involving interstate commerce, when the parties have agreed to arbitrate by those rules to the exclusion of federal arbitration law. I would not reach that question, however, because I conclude that the parties have made no such agreement.

Recent Decisions

Allied-Bruce Terminix Cos., Inc. v. Dobson, 513 U.S. 265 (1995), fully aligned itself with the federalism trilogy and thereby reaffirmed the judicial policy on federalization. In *Terminix*, an Alabama homeowner entered into a termite protection agreement with a local Terminix franchisee. The agreement contained a dispute resolution provision, which stated that *"any controversy or claim"* arising under the contract *"shall be settled exclusively by arbitration."* When the owner sold the home to another Alabama resident, the parties discovered that the house was swarming with termites, leading the new owner to file suit in state court against the seller and Terminix. The termite protection contract had been transferred to the new owner at the time of the sale. Terminix and its franchisee, however, objected to the assertion of jurisdiction by the state court on the basis of the arbitral clause in the contract and FAA § 2. On appeal, the Alabama state Supreme Court upheld the trial court's refusal to stay the court action pending arbitration, stating that the federal law on arbitration was inapplicable to the transaction because the transaction's connection to interstate commerce was too tenuous. The United States Supreme Court disagreed and reversed the determination.

Throughout the majority opinion, Justice Breyer restated the basic propositions associated with the "hospitable" federal court "inquiry" into matters of arbitration. The primary purpose for the enactment of the FAA in 1925 was to purge the judiciary of its bias against arbitration. The FAA's protection of arbitration from judicial prejudice applied wherever federal law could reach; in particular, the federal courts must apply the provisions of the FAA even when they exercise diversity jurisdiction over state litigation; state courts also must apply the FAA whenever a basis for applying federal law can be found, even in cases the merits of which are otherwise governed by state law. In effect, the Court stood firm on the federalization policy articulated in the federalism trilogy, in particular, *Southland Corp. v. Keating* ("we find it inappropriate to reconsider what is by now well-established law"). The Court held fast to the notion that "the Federal Arbitration Act pre-empts state law" and that "state courts [let alone federal courts] cannot apply state statutes that invalidate arbitration agreements." The Court declared unequivocally: "[T]he Act does displace state law to the contrary."

Doctor's Associates, Inc. v. Casarotto, 517 U.S. 681 (1996), is a recent ruling by the Court on the question of the supremacy of the FAA over state laws on arbitration. The 8–1 decision added nothing new to the Court's doctrine on arbitration, but rather confirmed the strength of the federalization development. With *Casarotto*, the Court's stance on this question of arbitration law became completely unambiguous. Finally, in *Buckeye Check Cashing, Inc. v. Cardegna*, 546 U.S. 440 (2006), the Court rejected the impact of Florida law on the enforceability of arbitration agreements. In *Preston v. Ferrer*, 128 S.Ct. 978 (2008), it upheld the primacy of the FAA over California legislation. State regulatory "side bars" cannot limit or minimize the strong federal policy on arbitration. Federalization and federal preemption have become unequivocal.

CHAPTER FIVE

THE ARBITRABILITY OF
STATUTORY CLAIMS

Introduction

Like contractual inarbitrability, the question of subject-matter inarbitrability is of central importance to the law of arbitration. It defines the lawful adjudicatory role of arbitration. Should arbitration function primarily, if not exclusively, as a mechanism for resolving private contractual disputes (relating to performance, delivery, or payment)? Should its jurisdictional reach be expanded to include claims that arise in the context of contractual relationships and involve legal rights created by statute? Extending arbitration to the resolution of regulatory law claims blurs the jurisdictional distinction between judicial and arbitral adjudication, between the role of the law and the function of contract. It attributes to arbitration some degree of public law-making authority. It affects the relevant statutory framework and the underlying public interest by confining some part of its interpretation and implementation to a private adjudicatory process.

For example, a commercial transaction that results in a failure of timely payment or delivery can also implicate laws that are meant to curb economic monopolies. When the transaction contains an arbitral clause, should the law permit the arbitrators to rule both on the breach of contract claim and a counterclaim sounding in antitrust? The defendant, for instance, might argue that the would-be breach of an illegal contract is no breach at all or that the regulatory claim commands that the entire litigation be brought to court. Would a statutory command for exclusive judicial jurisdiction over the regulatory claim require a severance of the litigation into a judicial and arbitral component? A stay of arbitration pending the court action or the opposite? If the claims are so inter-related that severance is not possible, should judicial or arbitral jurisdiction predominate?

The answers to these questions in the domestic U.S. law of arbitration have been influenced by considerations of arbitral autonomy, the federal policy supporting arbitration, and the Court's arbitrability rulings in matters of international commercial arbitration. On the one hand, it can be argued, as a matter of basic doctrine, that some subject-matter limits must be imposed upon and are necessary to the process of arbitral adjudication. The marketplace may be a private arena, but it is also a stage upon which public interests appear and play a role. Bankruptcies involve both the interests of creditors and the public's interest in the orderly dissolution and possible reorganization of liability-ridden enterprises. The sale of securities is a private transaction done in the context of a financial market, the integrity of which is of critical importance to society at large. Commercial competition may enhance the profitability of private enterprises, but it also affects the position of consumers and the general operation of the American economic system. The public dimension of the issues raised by commercial conduct can sometimes warrant exclusive judicial jurisdiction over the issues that are created.

On the other hand, the possibility of staying or bifurcating arbitral proceedings because of regulatory law claims can invite dilatory tactics and lessen substantially the adjudicatory effectiveness of arbitration. Parties can always manufacture a claim that enables them to shift the litigation to a court (at least, temporarily), thereby causing delay and greater expense and perhaps frustrating the recourse to arbitration itself. In the absence of a clear and easily applicable rule for claims that are "intertwined," a body of complex and difficult rules would need to be elaborated to establish proper jurisdictional lines, placing greater stress upon the process. As Justice Breyer makes clear in *First Options of Chicago, Inc. v. Kaplan*, none of these consequences is desirable in the context of arbitration. Such rule predicates would eliminate the simplicity and clarity of the reference to arbitration, and they could transform the law of arbitration into a litigious, unworkable, and self-defeating body of legal principles. This approach would ultimately contravene the letter and spirit of the FAA, especially Section Two, and result in a deterioration of the system of alternative remedial recourse. If the basic precepts of federalism cannot limit the federal policy on arbitration, it is unlikely that any other legal value or principle could thwart it.

Also, the Court's inarbitrability rulings in international arbitration cases have had a direct and profound impact upon the elaboration of a domestic rule of subject-matter inarbitrability. In two landmark cases, *Scherk v. Alberto–Culver Co.*, 417 U.S. 506 (1974), and *Mitsubishi Motors Corp. v. Soler Chrysler–Plymouth, Inc.*, 473 U.S. 614 (1985), the Court held that international arbitrators could rule upon statutory claims that arose in the performance of an international contract. At the time they were rendered, *Scherk* and *Mitsubishi* were expressly limited to matters involving transborder commercial arbitration. The reasoning that characterized these cases, however, began to creep into domestic arbitration cases. Eventually, the Court simply began to ignore the international specificity of the holdings and integrated them into the domestic decisional law. As a result, precedent prohibiting the domestic recourse to arbitration for the adjudication of certain statutory claims was reversed, engendering a new interpretation of the domestic provisions of the FAA: Nothing in the Act prohibited the submission of statutory disputes to arbitration. *See, e.g., Shearson/Am. Express, Inc. v. McMahon*, 482 U.S. 220 (1987); *Rodriguez de Quijas v. Shearson/Am. Express, Inc.*, 490 U.S. 477 (1989). Finally, as a result of its holdings in *Scherk* and *Mitsubishi*, the Court came to believe—or at least to state—that arbitration was a "mere form of trial," its use had no impact upon the implicated substantive rights. *See Rodriguez de Quijas,* 490 U.S. at 480 (*quoting Wilko v. Swan,* 346 U.S. 427, 433 [1953]). Therefore, the holdings in the international cases became the doctrinal foundation for the Court's elaboration of a domestic law rule that statutory claims could be submitted to arbitration.

ERISA and Bankruptcy

There are few, if any, federal statutes or rights that result in a determination of inarbitrability. The courts are too supportive of arbitration to find that statutory texts prohibit recourse to arbitration. In *Pritzker v. Merrill Lynch, Pierce, Fenner & Smith, Inc.,* 7 F.3d 1110 (3d Cir. 1993), for example, the Third Circuit reversed a prior ruling and held that "claims of statutory violations of the Employee Retirement Income Security Act of 1974...(ERISA) [were] subject to arbitration pursuant to section 2 of the Federal Arbitration Act...." The strong federal policy favoring arbitration also rendered many bankruptcy matters arbitrable. The general rule is that the trustee in bankruptcy "is bound by the terms of an arbitration clause to the same extent as the debtor would be...." To defeat the recourse to arbitration, the trustee bears a heavy burden "of demonstrating that the Bankruptcy Code provisions, policy or legislative history [ ] conflict with [the] enforcement of an arbitration clause...." The public policy underlying the Bankruptcy Code no longer outweighs "the policies of the Arbitration Act":

The fact that the matter before the court is a core proceeding does not mean that arbitration is inappropriate.... The description of a matter as a core proceeding simply means that the bankruptcy court has the jurisdiction to make a full adjudication. However, merely because the court has the authority to render a decision does not mean it should do so. The discussion in *Hays* regarding core and non-core proceedings is not read by this court as suggesting that core proceedings may not be subject to arbitration. Rather, it appears that the *Hays* court sought to distinguish between actions derived from the debtor, and therefore subject to the arbitration agreement, and bankruptcy actions in essence created by the Bankruptcy Code for the benefit ultimately of creditors of the estate, and therefore not encompassed by the arbitration agreement.

[...]

In the present matter, in terms of efficiency, arbitration is perhaps better suited to resolve the disputes of all the parties. The former partners are presently in arbitration with Hilton International. The addition of the Debtor to the proceeding will enable all claims to be resolved in one forum. In any event, the factors of cost and expediency do not weigh mightily against arbitration. The fact that arbitration may not be as efficient or as expeditious has been held not to justify refusal to enforce arbitration clauses in itself, even in bankruptcy....

As a general rule, the policy behind Chapter 11 Reorganization recognizes the expedient and economic resolution of business affairs. However, inquiry regarding conflict between the statutes should not be [so] broad as to swallow the policies of the Arbitration Act, especially when confirmation is not delayed by arbitration.... Following the reasoning of *Hays* in this case, the court cannot perceive any greater impact on the Bankruptcy Code in compelling arbitration than denying it....

[...]

The case law further demonstrates that the recourse to arbitration in the bankruptcy context can be defeated by express party agreement. For example, the parties can provide in their confirmed Chapter 11 plan that the bankruptcy court will have exclusive jurisdiction to adjudicate pending adversarial proceedings. Moreover, arbitration can be excluded in circumstances in which it affects core proceedings and its influence on such proceedings has an adverse effect upon the underlying purposes of the Bankruptcy Code.

Several federal circuits have recently expanded the reach of arbitration in bankruptcy matters. They have lessened the significance of the previously central distinction between "core and non-core" matters and emphasized that the recourse to arbitration would be disallowed only if it jeopardized the objectives of the Bankruptcy Code. According to the U.S. Second Circuit, for example, bankruptcy courts do not have the discretion to override an arbitration agreement unless they find that the bankruptcy proceedings are based on provisions of the Bankruptcy Code that "inherently conflict" with the Arbitration Act or that the arbitration of the claim would "necessarily jeopardize" the objectives of the Bankruptcy Code. In *MBNA Am. Bank, N.A. v. Hill*, 436 F.3d 104 (2d Cir. 2006), the lower court had held that the consumer's claim that MBNA violated the automatic stay provision of the Bankruptcy Code was a "core" bankruptcy proceeding and the bankruptcy court was the most appropriate forum for resolving the dispute. The appellate court disagreed, holding that the bankruptcy court must enforce the arbitration agreement between debtor and creditor. It ordered the class action to arbitration.

The Third Circuit has ruled in a similar vein. In *In re Mintze*, 434 F.3d 222 (3d Cir. 2006), it held that a bankruptcy court does not have the authority to deny enforcement to an otherwise valid arbitration agreement. In so holding, the court referred to the precedent set by *Hays and Co. v. Merrill Lynch*, 885 F.2d 1149 (1989). It stated that the "core/non-core" distinction has been vital to determining whether a bankruptcy court has jurisdiction to adjudicate fully the proceeding, but the latter can refuse to enforce the arbitration agreement only if there is an inherent conflict between the objectives of the Arbitration Act and the Bankruptcy Code. The need for an inherent conflict applies to both core and non-core matters.

The ruling of an Ohio appellate court appears to contradict the decisional law of the federal courts on this question. In *Benjamin v. Pipoly*, 800 N.E.2d 50 (Ohio. App. 2003), the court held that state public policy prohibits the recourse to arbitration in bankruptcy matters. According to the court, a contract that turns bankruptcy liquidation proceedings over to private arbitration infringes upon the authority of public officials in contravention of state public policy. In enacting the law of bankruptcy, the state legislature did not intend to yield power to private arbitrators instead of state officials especially because arbitration was "shielded from public scrutiny" and the "judicial review of [awards] would be sharply limited." The court, therefore, concluded that a private arbitration agreement that "impinges upon a broad statutory scheme that invests sweeping powers in a state official" violates public policy. This result and reasoning may be subject to federal preemption because they single out arbitration agreements for discriminatory treatment and limit the range and validity of arbitration agreements in violation of FAA § 2.

Antitrust

In *Hunt v. Up North Plastics, Inc.*, 980 F.Supp. 1046 (D. Minn. 1997), the court ruled that a domestic antitrust claim was arbitrable. The sales transaction between the parties included an arbitral clause that provided that "any disagreement arising out of the sale or use of the products ... shall be submitted to binding arbitration held under the rules then in effect of the American Arbitration Association." Hunt alleged that Up North, Ag–Bag, and Poly America, Inc. conspired to fix prices and allocate customers of silage products in violation of the federal antitrust laws. Up North and Poly America filed a motion to compel arbitration. The court granted the motion. In doing so, it rejected— *inter alia*—Hunt's argument that domestic antitrust actions were inarbitrable. Although the Eighth Circuit had not yet expressly overruled *Helfenbein v. International Industries, Inc.,* 438 F.2d 1068 (8th Cir. 1971) (declaring that domestic antitrust violations were not subject to arbitration), the court explained that a number of recent decisions nevertheless called that holding into question.

First, the court made reference to the United States Supreme Court's decisions in *Mitsubishi Motors Corp. v. Soler Chrysler-Plymouth, Inc.*, 473 U.S. 614 (1985), which held that an antitrust dispute arising pursuant to an international commercial contract was arbitrable, and *Shearson/American Express, Inc. v. McMahon,* 482 U.S. 220 (1987), which held that federal securities claims were arbitrable. In the court's view, these decisions "call into question the rationale of earlier cases exempting antitrust and other statutory claims from arbitration." Second, the court acknowledged that a number of other circuits—including the Ninth and Eleventh Circuit—had found domestic antitrust disputes arbitrable. And, lastly, the court pointed out that the decision in *Swensen's Ice Cream Co. v. Corsair Corp.*, 942 F.2d 1307 (8th Cir. 1991), expressly stated that, since the United States Supreme Court handed down its rulings in *Mitsubishi* and *Shearson/American Express,* the ruling in *Helfenbein* "may no longer be a correct statement of the law." Consequently, the court held that the antitrust claim was arbitrable.

In *Seacoast Motors of Salisbury, Inc. v. Daimler-Chrysler Motors*, 271 F.3d 6 (1st Cir. 2001), *cert. denied*, 535 U.S. 1054 (2002), the First Circuit considered the question of whether antitrust claims could be submitted to arbitration. In ruling that they could, the court emphasized the position that the United States Supreme Court had taken in *Mitsubishi Motors Corp.* and the lower court progeny to which it gave rise. The court acknowledged that these cases discredited both the result and reasoning in the earlier ruling in *American Safety Equipment Corp. v. J.P. Maguire & Co.,* 391 F.2d 821 (2d Cir. 1968). The public interest in the enforcement of regulatory provisions no longer demanded the inarbitrability of statutory claims. In the court's words, *American Safety* needed to be put "to rest"—"time ha[d] passed by [its] doctrines . . . .":

> There is no question here of an advance waiver of antitrust claims: arbitration clauses do not eliminate substantive rights but submit them for resolution in an arbitral, rather than a judicial forum. . . . [W]hile some antitrust cases do involve large issues in which the public has an interest, others are essentially business quarrels peculiar

to the parties. For those in the former category, government agencies remain free to pursue the defendant regardless of private actions, whether before courts or [before] arbitrators. . . .

FLSA

The reach of arbitration also touches federal labor statutes. In *Coughlin v. Shimizu America Corp.*, 991 F.Supp. 1226 (D. Or. 1998), the U.S. district court in Oregon held that an employee was not deprived of rights under the Fair Labor Standards Act (FLSA) by being compelled to arbitrate an overtime pay dispute. Coughlin had been hired by Shimizu America Corporation on December 2, 1987, and was transferred in 1993 to its Tigard, Oregon office. On April 12, 1993, Coughlin signed an employment agreement with Shimizu. The agreement contained a standard arbitration clause. In 1994, Shimizu issued new employee handbooks, employment agreements, and arbitration forms. Coughlin, however, did not sign any of these documents. On June 20, 1997, Coughlin brought suit against Shimizu for overtime wages, alleging that Shimizu's conduct violated both federal and state laws. Coughlin claimed that he was entitled to judicial relief because he had not signed the arbitration agreement in 1994. Alternatively, he argued that the arbitration agreement was invalid because it denied him important statutory rights afforded by the FLSA. Shimizu sought to compel arbitration under the April 12, 1993 employment agreement, claiming that Coughlin was not a new, but rather a transferred employee.

The court held that Coughlin failed to establish that there was no arbitration agreement. It ruled that the April 12, 1993 employment agreement governed the relationship. It compelled the arbitration of the overtime wages dispute because it determined that the arbitration agreement did "not deprive Coughlin of any substantive rights." Coughlin had argued that, under the FLSA, prevailing employers were not generally awarded attorney's fees. The arbitration clause in the April 12, 1993 employment agreement, however, stated that the prevailing party in the arbitration would be awarded attorney's fees. Coughlin contended that "he [was] deprived of a substantive right if he [could] be subjected to the payment of attorney's fees" under the arbitration agreement but not under the statute. The court rejected this argument, stating that Coughlin "ha[d] all the remedies available under the FLSA if he prevail[ed] in arbitration that he would have if he prevail[ed] in . . . court."

Title VII

Claims arising under statutes that prohibit discriminatory conduct can also be submitted to arbitration. The U.S. Court of Appeals for the Fifth Circuit has held that a securities dealer who agreed to arbitrate "any dispute, claim or controversy that might arise between himself and his firm" was compelled to arbitrate Title VII discrimination claims against his employer. *See Mouton v. Metro-*

politan Life Ins. Co., 147 F.3d 453, 456 (5th Cir. 1998). The court rejected the plaintiff's contention that the claim was exempt from compulsory arbitration because of an insurance business exemption, and it dismissed the plaintiff's argument that he could not be compelled to arbitrate because he did not knowingly and voluntarily waive his access to a judicial forum.

The court ruled that: "Questions of arbitrability must be addressed with a healthy regard for the federal policy favoring arbitration" and that "any doubts concerning the scope of arbitrable issues should be resolved in favor of arbitration." In *dicta*, the court asserted that, even if the arbitration provisions at issue were ambiguous, "to acknowledge the ambiguity is to resolve the issue, because all ambiguities must be resolved in favor of arbitrability." Moreover, an arbitration clause need not speak directly to employment-related disputes for it to mandate the arbitration of Title VII claims. Because the plaintiff agreed to arbitrate "any dispute, claim or controversy that may arise between himself and Metropolitan," the language was sufficiently broad to encompass Title VII claims.

The United States Supreme Court decision in *14 Penn Plaza v. Pyett*, 129 S.Ct. 1456 (2009), confirms the arbitrability of discrimination claims. For the Court, their arbitrability arises as a matter of express party agreement, as long as the enacting legislation does not unequivocally provide for exclusive judicial resolution.

Whistleblower Claims

According to the U.S. Court of Appeals for the Second Circuit, a claim of retaliatory discharge brought pursuant to 12 U.S.C. § 1831j can be submitted to arbitration pursuant to a broad arbitration clause in the plaintiff's employment agreement. In enacting § 183lj, the Congress, according to the court, did not intend to preclude the arbitration of retaliatory discharge claims. *See Oldroyd v. Elmira Sav. Bank, FSB,* 134 F.3d 72 (2d Cir. 1998).

Plaintiff Richard Oldroyd was employed as vice-president and director of Management Information Systems at Elmira Savings Bank (ESB) when he contacted the Office of Thrift Supervision to report illegal activities at ESB. Oldroyd's employment with ESB was subsequently terminated, and Oldroyd brought an action in the U.S. District Court for the Western District of New York, alleging retaliatory discharge under 12 U.S.C. § 183lj, the whistleblower protection provision of the Financial Institutions Reform, Recovery, and Enforcement Act of 1989 (FIRREA). Denying ESB's motion to stay the claim pending arbitration, the district court found that, although the § 1831j action was generally arbitrable because Congress had not expressed a contrary intent, it was not within the scope of the arbitration clause contained in Oldroyd's employment contract. The district court, therefore, ordered the claim to proceed and ESB appealed.

In vacating the district court's order, the Second Circuit found that the arbitration clause in Oldroyd's employment contract was a "prototypical broad arbitration provision." The clause stated: "Any dispute, controversy or claim arising under or in connection with this Agreement shall be settled exclusively by arbitration." In the court's view, the employment agreement's contractual language was broad enough to encompass the retaliatory discharge claim. The claim amounted to a cause of action for unlawful termination and "more than half of Oldroyd's employment contract relates to the subject of termination from employment."

The arbitrability of a § 1831j claim was not contrary to the intent of Congress. In agreeing with the district court on this point, the Second Circuit rejected Oldroyd's argument that, because portions of the FIRREA contemplate litigation of § 1831j claims, Congress meant to preclude arbitration in this statutory setting. In so doing, the court noted that "[s]everal other federal statutes, under which claims have been held to be arbitrable by this Circuit and the Supreme Court, contain similar provisions in their enforcement sections."

Truth-in-Lending

Because of its class action feature, the Truth–In–Lending Act (TILA) initially presented some courts with an opportunity to express their reluctance about the arbitrability of statutory rights. According to these courts, if classwide proceedings were not available in arbitration, a TILA party was deprived of an essential remedy available under the statute because of the reference to arbitration. The

U.S. Court of Appeals for the Third Circuit, however, held that claims arising under the Truth–In–Lending Act (TILA) and the Electronic Fund Transfer Act (EFTA) could be submitted to arbitration. The arbitrability of claims applied even though class action relief might not be available in arbitration. In the court's assessment, the affected statutes were not enacted to guarantee access to class action procedures. *See Johnson v. West Suburban Bank*, 225 F.3d 366 (3d Cir. 2000), *cert. denied*, 531 U.S. 1145 (2001).

According to the court, "nothing in the legislative history or the statutory text of the TILA clearly expresses congressional intent to preclude the ability of parties to engage in arbitration." The court determined that parties who sign valid arbitration agreements and "lack the procedural right to proceed as part of a class...retain the full range of rights created by the TILA." Additionally, the court held that "when the right made available by a statute is capable of vindication in the arbitral forum, the public policy goals of that statute do not justify refusing to arbitrate.... While arbitrating claims that might have been pursued as part of class actions potentially reduces the number of plaintiffs seeking to enforce the TILA against creditors, arbitration does not eliminate plaintiff incentives to assert rights under the Act."

In assessing legislative intent in the various implicated statutes, the court stated that it was obligated to "give equal consideration to Congress' policy goals in enacting the FAA.... The statute was intended to overcome judicial hostility to agreements to arbitrate." Arbitration had some well-established and attractive advantages: "it is usually cheaper and faster than litigation; it can have simpler procedural and evidentiary rules; it normally minimizes hostility and is less disruptive of ongoing and future business dealings among the parties; and it is often more flexible in regard to scheduling." Therefore, the congressional intent to promote arbitration carried with it equal, if not more, weight than the policy concerns argued by Johnson for the protection of class actions under the TILA.

The court of appeals reversed the district court ruling and held that an "irreconcilable conflict" did not exist between arbitration and the goals of the TILA or the EFTA. Claims arising under the TILA or the EFTA were "subject to arbitration notwithstanding the desire of a plaintiff who previously consented to arbitration to bring his or her claims as part of a class."

Magnuson-Moss Warranty Claims

The Fifth Circuit has held that Magnuson–Moss Warranty Act (MMWA) claims were subject to compulsory arbitration. The Fifth Circuit found that the arbitration of the MMWA claims was not inconsistent with the statutory purposes of the MMWA. Furthermore, the court concluded that compelling the arbitration of MMWA claims was consistent with the federal policy of favoring arbitration under the FAA. *See Walton v. Rose Mobile Homes L.L.C.*, 298 F.3d 470 (5th Cir. 2002).

In identifying the purposes of the MMWA, the Fifth Circuit noted that the legislation was enacted to "improve the adequacy of information available to consumers, prevent deception, and improve competition in the marketing of consumer products." Contrasting these purposes with the FAA, the court found "no inherent conflict between arbitration and these purposes." According to the court, FAA applicability to MMWA claims was a fair remedy as "consumers can still vindicate their rights under warranties in an arbitral forum" and warranties can "provide adequate and truthful information to consumers, while still requiring binding arbitration."

In *Davis v. Southern Energy Homes, Inc.*, 305 F.3d 1268 (11th Cir. 2002), *cert. denied*, 538 U.S. 945 (2003), the Eleventh Circuit ruled that the MMWA did not prohibit the use of binding arbitration. The appellate court held that claims based on a written warranty under the Act could be submitted to binding arbitration. It compared the purposes underlying the MMWA and the FAA to determine if a conflict existed. Because the United States Supreme Court had consistently upheld the binding arbitration of claims arising under consumer protection laws, the court concluded that the FAA's objectives did not conflict with the legislative purpose underlying the MMWA. Lastly, the court noted that Congress intended to reduce the parties' unequal bargaining power through the MMWA. Unequal bargaining power by itself, however, could not prevent the enforcement of a valid arbitration agreement regarding statutory claims.

McCarran–Ferguson Act

There have been a few exceptions to the rule of the wide-ranging arbitrability of statutory matters. The McCarran–Ferguson Act (MFA), 15 U.S.C. § 1012, for example, establishes the generally preemptive effect of state law in the regulation of the business of insurance and the interpretation of insurance contracts. The statute provides: "No Act of Congress shall be construed to invalidate, impair, or supersede any law enacted by any state for the purpose of regulating the business of insurance...unless such Act specifically relates to the business of insurance." Insurance contracts can involve interstate commerce and contain arbitration agreements, thereby triggering the application of the FAA. When an insurance company becomes insolvent and the relevant contract provides for the arbitration of liquidation matters, a conflict can emerge between state law provisions on liquidation that require exclusive judicial recourse and the arbitral clause.

There is no United States Supreme Court precedent directly on point. In *United States Department of Treasury v. Fabe*, 508 U.S. 491 (1993), the Court reversed a Sixth Circuit opinion on the status of an Ohio liquidation statute, but failed to clarify the relationship between the FAA and the MFA. The circuits are split on the question. The Second and Ninth Circuits have held that the MFA does not preclude the application of the FAA, while the Fifth, Sixth, and Tenth Circuits have held that the Act "reverse preempts" the FAA.

In *Hamilton Life Insurance Co. of New York v. Republic National Life Insurance Co.*, 408 F.2d 606 (2d Cir. 1969), the Second Circuit held that the MFA does not exempt the business of insurance from other federal statutes unless such compliance would conflict with state laws regulating insurance. The court stated that "[t]he plain and unambiguous statutory language is persuasive evidence that the McCarran–Ferguson Act was not intended to preclude the application of these federal statutes to insurance unless they invalidate, impair or supersede applicable state legislation regulating the business of insurance." Accordingly, the court refused to find the FAA was reverse preempted by operation of New York law regulating the business of insurance.

Similarly, in *Bennett v. Liberty National Fire Insurance Co.*, 968 F.2d 969 (9th Cir. 1992), the Ninth Circuit held that Montana's insolvency statute did not regulate the business of insurance and, therefore, did not preclude the application of the FAA. The court based its decision on the view that the plaintiff sought to enforce rights primarily derived from the insolvent insurer's contract rather than from Montana's regulation of insolvency matters. Because the underlying dispute between the parties was one of contract, and not one involving the insurance policyholders' rights, the parties were compelled to arbitrate their dispute pursuant to the FAA. The court rejected the argument that the public policy interest underlying the regulation of insolvent insurers outweighed the federal interest in compelling arbitration. Finding no harm to the liquidator, but merely an alternative forum for resolution, the court rejected the reverse preemption effect of the MFA.

In contradistinction, the Fifth Circuit held that a dispute between Munich American Reinsurance Company, NAC Reinsurance Corporation, and the Oklahoma Insurance Commissioner over the insolvency of Employers National Insurance Corporation (ENIC) should go forward in Oklahoma receivership court and should not be resolved through arbitration. The court further concluded that the Oklahoma laws governing insurance company delinquency proceedings preempted the FAA under the MFA. *See Munich Am. Reinsurance Co. v. Crawford*, 141 F.3d 585 (5th Cir.), *cert. denied*, 525 U.S. 1016 (1998). According to the court, "Ordinarily, federal law pre-empts conflicting state law by virtue of the Supremacy Clause.... The McCarran–Ferguson Act reverses that effect in the narrow range of cases involving state regulation of the insurance industry." The court, therefore, concluded that the FAA was reverse preempted by Oklahoma law under the MFA and that the dispute was one for the State of Oklahoma to resolve.

The Tenth Circuit has also held that the stay of proceedings against an insurer in liquidation under the MFA trumps the FAA. *See Davister Corp. v. United Republic Life Ins. Co.*, 152 F.3d 1277 (10th Cir. 1998), *cert. denied*, 525 U.S. 1177 (1999). The appellate court considered the question of whether the district court erred by abstaining from enforcing an arbitration clause in a dispute between Davister Corporation and the Liquidator of United Republic Life Insurance Company (United), an insurance company domiciled in Utah and in insolvency proceedings in Utah state court. The court ruled that the question should be decided under the MFA.

The Utah statute consolidating all claims against a liquidating insurer was enacted to protect policyholders. The court emphasized that the blanket statutory stay against all proceedings made clear that the policy of the state of Utah was to consolidate in one forum all matters attendant to the liquidation of a domiciled insurance company. Therefore, the court concluded that the Utah statute met the test of having been enacted for the purpose of regulating the business of insurance.

The court ruled that "allowing a putative creditor to pluck from the entire liquidation proceeding one discrete issue and force arbitration contrary to the blanket stay entered by the Utah state court would certainly impair the progress of the orderly resolution of all matters involving the insolvent company." The court contended that the issue was not whether Utah prohibits arbitration, but whether enforcing arbitration invalidates, impairs, or supersedes under the MFA the enforcement of the state process designed to protect the interests of policyholders.

More recently, a California state court of appeal held that the MFA prevented the FAA from preempting a state statute that imposed disclosure requirements on arbitration agreements in health care services plans. *See Smith v. PacifiCare Behavioral Health of Cal., Inc.*, 113 Cal.Rptr.2d 140 (Ct. App. 2001), *cert. denied*, 537 U.S. 818 (2002). The state statute regulated the conduct of parties that were involved in the business of insurance. State law, therefore, regulated the business of insurance and was outside the scope of the FAA.

The MFA and the states' right to regulate the business of insurance within their territory have best withstood the imperative of the federal policy favoring arbitration. This circumstance is largely (perhaps exclusively) due to the MFA's express language; it is hardly conceivable that the state right to regulate the business of insurance exceeds in importance civil liberties, antitrust, or securities regulation for purposes of arbitrability. The Court or courts have simply been unable to find, in all cases, a means of circumventing the text of the statute, although the case law on the FAA's employment contract exclusion could offer some inspiration.

In any event, a large part of the case law has been and remains categorical on the "reverse preemptive" effect of the MFA. The Georgia state Supreme Court, in *Love v. Money Tree, Inc.*, 614 S.E.2d 47 (Ga. 2005), held that an arbitral clause in an automobile club membership form was unenforceable because its application would interfere with Georgia insurance law. The MFA, in the court's view, applied to consumer loan transactions in which the lender financed insurance payments at the same time as making the loan. The Eleventh Circuit, following the Fifth, Eighth, and Tenth U.S. Circuits, held that the MFA overrides the FAA when a state law prohibits arbitration agreements in insurance contracts.

The effect of MFA appears to be neutralized in the treaty context. In *Pinnoak Resources, L.L.C. v. Certain Underwriters at Lloyd's, London*, 394 F.Supp.2d 821 (S.D. W. Va. 2005), plaintiff sued an insurer for failing to compensate it for covered losses in connection with methane explosions at a mining facility. The insurance policy provided for arbitration in London, England. The plaintiff argued that the New York Arbitration Convention, which governed the clause, was reverse preempted by the West Virginia Insurance Act. The latter provides that an insurer that is unadmitted to do business can be sued before state courts regardless of what the policy provides. Moreover, any arbitral proceeding must be held in the state regardless of what the policy provides. The court held that the arbitral clause was enforceable under the New York

Arbitration Convention. 9 U.S.C. §§ 203 and 205 provide that an action under the Convention arises under federal law and establishes original jurisdiction in U.S. district courts regardless of the amount in controversy. The court rightly concluded that domestic rules do not apply to an international arbitration implicating a treaty obligation.

Legal Malpractice

On February 20, 2002, the ABA Committee on Ethics and Professional Responsibility issued Formal Opinion 02–425. *See* ABA Committee on Ethics and Professional Responsibility, Formal Opinion 02–425. In that document, the committee addressed the ethical propriety of retainer agreements between attorneys and clients that contain arbitral clauses or agreements that require fee disputes and malpractice claims to be submitted to arbitration. While the committee concluded that such contract provisions did not violate ethical standards, it conditioned their ethical acceptability upon a number of factors. First, the client's acceptance of the agreement to arbitrate such disputes must be based upon informed consent. Second, the effect of the arbitration agreement cannot be to limit or exclude the lawyer's liability exposure to the client:

It is ethically permissible to include in a retainer agreement with a client a provision that requires the binding arbitration of fee disputes and malpractice claims provided that (1) the client has been fully apprised of the advantages and disadvantages of arbitration and has been given sufficient information to permit her to make an informed decision about whether to agree to the inclusion of the arbitration provision in the retainer agreement, and (2) the arbitration provision does not insulate the lawyer from liability or limit the liability to which she would otherwise be exposed under common and/or statutory law.

In explaining its position, the committee emphasized the distinction between fee disputes and professional malpractice claims. Many, if not most, bar associations have implemented arbitral procedures for addressing fee disputes. Rule 1.5 of the Model Rules of Professional Responsibility (MRPR) authorizes "fee arbitration programs"; in fact, there are ABA Model Rules for Fee Arbitration. The MRPR, however, does not address instances in which the arbitral procedure applies to malpractice claims.

In particular, MRPR Rule 1.8(h) forbids lawyers from limiting their malpractice liability through contract unless such agreements are recognized at law as lawful and the subscribing client is represented independently. Moreover, a lawyer owes a client fiduciary duties that include "a duty to explain matters" under MRPR Rule 1.4(b). In terms of arbitration agreements in a professional services contract, the duty would oblige the attorney to explain effectively what arbitration is and its benefits and drawbacks. The explanation must be sufficient to allow the client to achieve "informed consent."

Finally, the incorporation of an arbitral clause in a retainer agreement also implicates MRPR Rule

1.7(b) that addresses conflict of interest situations. According to the committee, Comment [6] to Rule 1.7 was particularly relevant; it provides, "If the probity of a lawyer's own conduct in a transaction is in serious question, it may be difficult or impossible for the lawyer to give a client detached advice."

Despite all of these misgivings, the committee concluded that agreements to arbitrate malpractice claims were ethically supportable. It aligned its reasoning to the judicial reasoning that ordinarily applies in matters of arbitration. That reasoning usually sustains the recourse to arbitration and is intended to eliminate any obstacles that might stand in the way of the reference to arbitration. For example, the committee stated, "The mere fact that a client is required to submit disputes to arbitration rather than litigation does not violate Rule 1.8(h) [prohibiting the lawyer from limiting liability], even though the procedures implicated by various mandatory arbitration provisions can markedly differ from typical litigation procedures." It is difficult to understand when the evident differences between arbitral and judicial adjudication would be sufficient to trigger restraint in this area. Apparently, the possible unavailability of punitive damages in arbitration (as opposed to court proceedings) would be enough to mandate that the client be "independently represented in making the agreement."

In *Henry v. Gonzalez*, 18 S.W.3d 684 (Tex. App. 2000), Chief Justice Hardberger filed the following dissent:

The legal and ethical implications of arbitration provisions in contracts between attorneys and their clients have been the subject of a number of articles.... The essence of these articles is that whatever public policy may be served by enforcing arbitration agreements is more than offset by the public policy of not allowing attorneys to take advantage of their clients. Trust is the essential ingredient in an attorney-client relationship. The great majority of clients are not even close to being in an equal bargaining position with their attorneys. They go to an attorney so the attorney can tell them what to do, not vice-versa.

In a serious personal injury case,...clients are typically deeply in grief and overwhelmed by the circumstances that have come upon them. Pain and disability have entered their lives, and the breadwinner is no longer able to bring home wages for the family. As bills pour in, with no offsetting income, a true state of desperation exists. Are we then to allow attorneys, who represent such clients, to take away their rights to a jury should legal malpractice occur? I agree with the commentators in the cited articles and with the laws established in other jurisdictions that conclude that such a practice is against public policy. Certainly it should be against public policy in the absence of some additional protections for the client, which do not exist in the case.

The traditional advantages of arbitration may not be so advantageous in the context of a legal malpractice claim. For example, the savings of cost and time would likely be more of a disadvantage to the attorney alleged to have committed malpractice than to the client because the client's new attorney will typically be handling the claim on a contingency basis.... In addition, the ability to pursue the claim in court may provide the client with a bargaining advantage in negotiating with an attorney who seeks to avoid litigation and its potential negative publicity....

More importantly, the fundamental fiduciary nature of the attorney-client relationship dictates against an attorney's ability to impose an arbitration condition on a client. Clients are often in vulnerable positions, requiring them to bestow a large amount of trust in their attorneys. "The client's vulnerability vis-à-vis the attorney is often exacerbated by the client's current legal situation.... He is neither expecting, nor emotionally prepared, to 'do battle' with his chosen attorney to protect his own rights." ...Applying general contractual principles to an arbitration provision in the attorney-client context ignores the practical reality that in most instances the attorney and his or her client are not engaged in an arm's length transaction during their initial negotiations....

Attorneys generally have a greater advantage over their clients in an arbitration setting. Attorneys are trained to conduct arbitration to the best advantage of their clients, in this case themselves.... Since one of the "selling points" of arbitration is the ability to proceed without an attorney, the client with the malpractice claim may not seek additional counsel, leaving the trained attorney with a distinct advantage....

In a profession that is called upon to police itself, how can we justify allowing attorneys to take advantage of those who call upon their services? We cannot. Although the traditional contractual defenses, like unconscionability, may be available to clients who are taken advantage of, such a situation should never be allowed to arise. Clients who are in a weaker bargaining position may not be able to meet the burden of proving unconscionability.... This does not mean that the attorney would not have taken advantage of his or her client. It simply means that the legal definition of unconscionability, created by attorneys, is an uncertain road for an already burdened client.

Recognizing these public policy concerns, other states have prohibited or limited the inclusion of arbitration provisions in attorneys' engagement letters. For example, Pennsylvania has adopted a rule that permits an arbitration provision in an engagement letter only if: (1) the advantages and disadvantages are fully disclosed by the attorney; (2) the client is advised of his right to consult independent counsel and is given the opportunity to do so; and (3) the client's consent is in writing.... Both the District of Columbia and Michigan have taken a more restrictive approach and prohibit arbitration clauses in engagement letters unless the client has the advice of independent counsel.... Finally, Ohio has taken the most restrictive approach and simply prohibits pre-dispute arbitration agreements between attorneys and their clients.... Ohio reasons that requiring a client to hire a lawyer in order to hire a lawyer sends the wrong message....

Public policy mandates that some restrictions must be placed on an attorney's ability to include an arbitration provision in an engagement letter. Because no such restrictions were imposed in this case, I would conclude that the arbitration clause violates public policy and affirm the trial court's ruling. I respectfully dissent.

Despite the divisive nature of the debate on the question of the arbitrability of legal malpractice claims, courts are likely to reach the conclusion that these disputes are arbitrable. Such a conclusion would be in keeping with the general trend in the area and coincide with the determinations of various bar groups on the ethical propriety of arbitration clauses in retainer agreements. It could be argued that the special character of these claims warrant an adapted form of arbitration, the characteristics of which respond to the issues and interests that underlie these matters. While it appears contradictory to allow attorneys to deny their clients the traditional remedies typically available, there seems to be little basis for disallowing the arbitration of legal malpractice claims or for making special accommodations for these controversies inside the arbitration process. Notwithstanding the self-evident double standard, the breach of trust, and the contractual unfairness, this battle on subject-matter inarbitrability grounds appears to be as likely of defeat as all the others.

Recent case law has been hospitable to the subject matter arbitrability of legal malpractice claims and attorney-client fee disputes. Courts do not perceive the provision for arbitration in this context as a breach of the attorney's fiduciary duty to the client. The reference to arbitration, it is said, does not create an advantage for either party. Further, given the federal policy on arbitration, one court commented "it would strike us somewhat anomalous to conclude that parties may not agree in advance that arbitration will be the sole remedy for a dispute about legal fees." The reference to arbitration in the retainer agreement should be "clear and unambiguous." *See Kamaratos v. Palias*, 821 A.2d 531 (N.J. Super. Ct. App. Div. 2003); *Shimko v. Lobe*, 813 N.E.2d 669, 682 (Ohio 2004).

CHAPTER SIX

SECURITIES AND CONSUMER ARBITRATION

Securities Arbitration

The use of arbitration in the securities industry has been a long-standing practice. Stock exchanges and brokerage firms have always favored the recourse to arbitration to resolve industry disputes. What is new is the reference to arbitration to resolve disputes with customers and employees, especially disputes that involve statutory frameworks that provide the disadvantaged party with special protections and which uphold the public interest in a viable financial marketplace and a diverse and accessible workforce. The evolution toward arbitration in these settings was gradual but unmistakable.

In *Wilko v. Swan*, 346 U.S. 427 (1953), an investor lodged an action against a securities brokerage firm, claiming that the firm had violated Section 12(2) of the 1933 Securities Act. The brokerage contract contained a dispute resolution clause providing for the submission of disputes to arbitration. Notwithstanding its view that the FAA embodied a strong Congressional policy supporting arbitration, the Court deemed the arbitration agreement in

Wilko to be unenforceable. It reasoned that the provision for arbitration countermanded the express policy of the 1933 Securities Act, which prohibited investors from waiving certain statutorily-established rights, namely, the right to bring suit in any federal or state court, to select a forum from a wide choice of venue, to take advantage of the nationwide service of process provision, and to dispense with the amount in controversy requirement. Moreover, Section 12(2) of the Act expressly gave investors a cause of action to redress claims of misrepresentation against a seller of securities, requiring the defendant to prove its lack of *scienter*.

Therefore, despite a valid arbitration agreement, securities claims arising under the 1933 Securities Act could not be submitted to arbitration. The Act's nonwaiver of rights provisions, in effect, manifested a congressional intent to create an exception to the FAA's validation of arbitration agreements. The policy imperative underlying the 1933 Securities Act took precedent over its counterpart in the FAA. Ordinarily, however, the FAA would have prevailed:

> When the security buyer, prior to any violation of the Securities Act, waives his right to sue in courts, he gives up more than would a participant in other business transactions. The security buyer has a wider choice of courts and venue. He thus surrenders one of the advantages the Act gives him and surrenders it at a time when he is less able to judge the weight of the handicap the Securities Act places upon his adversary.

Even though the provisions of the Securities Act, advantageous to the buyer, apply, their effectiveness in application is lessened in arbitration as compared to judicial proceedings. Determination of the quality of a commodity or the amount of money due under a contract is not the type of issue here involved. This case requires subjective findings on the purpose and knowledge of an alleged violator of the Act. They must be not only determined but applied by the arbitrators without judicial instruction on the law. As their award may be made without explanation of their reasons and without a complete record of their proceedings, the arbitrators' conception of the legal meaning of such statutory requirements as 'burden of proof,' 'reasonable care' or 'material fact'. . . cannot be examined. Power to vacate an award is limited. While it may be true, as the Court of Appeals thought, that a failure of the arbitrators to decide in accordance with the provisions of the Securities Act would 'constitute grounds for vacating the award pursuant to section 10 of the Federal Arbitration Act,' that failure would need to be made clearly to appear. In unrestricted submission, such as the present margin agreements envisage, the interpretations of the law by the arbitrators in contrast to manifest disregard are not subject, in the federal courts, to judicial review for error in interpretation. The United States Arbitration Act contains no provision for judicial determination of legal issues such as is found in the English law. As the protective provisions of the Securities Act require the exercise of judicial discretion to fairly assure their effectiveness, it seems to us that Congress must have intended § 14 to apply to waiver of judicial trial and review.

[. . .]

Two policies, not easily reconcilable, are involved in this case. Congress has afforded participants in transactions subject to its legislative power an opportunity generally to secure prompt, economical and adequate solution of controversies through arbitration if the parties are willing to accept less certainty of legally correct adjustment. On the other hand, it has enacted the Securities Act to protect the rights of investors and has forbidden a waiver of any of those rights. Recognizing the advantages that prior agreements for arbitration may provide for the solution of commercial controversies, we decide that the intention of Congress concerning the sale of securities is better carried out by holding invalid such an agreement for arbitration of issues arising under the Act.

After *Wilko*, lower federal courts consistently held that claims arising under either the 1933 or 1934 Act were inarbitrable because of the public policy interest in investor protection. This assessment was grounded in the language of the Acts (the nonwaiver provisions), rather than the provisions of the FAA. The content of the FAA simply was not germane (*i.e.*, given its lack of reference to subject-matter inarbitrability or its lack of a public policy defense to enforcement) because its policy imperative was secondary—as a matter of law—to another Congressional objective. The federalism trilogy, however, gave a new direction to the domestic U.S. law on arbitration by seeking to establish a national federal policy on arbitration. *Shearson/American Express, Inc. v. McMahon*, 482 U.S. 220 (1987), reinforced the doctrine born of the federalism trilogy by declaring that claims under the Exchange Act and the RICO statute could be submitted to arbitration.

The Court addressed the issue of the arbitrability of Exchange Act claims (a question which divided the Court 5–4). The majority opinion at the outset asserted that the existence of a claim based upon statutorily-established rights did not disrupt the ordinarily "hospitable" inquiry into the question of arbitrability. To defeat the implied presumption favoring the arbitrability of claims, the regulatory vehicle must contain, either in its language or legislative history, a congressional command mandating exclusive recourse to the courts for the vindication of claims. Moreover, the party opposing arbitration bore the burden of establishing the existence of that congressional intent.

The Court then advanced a technical interpretation of the relevant provisions of the Exchange Act, arguing that the nonwaiver language of the Act applied exclusively to the substantive obligations under the legislation. Because the recourse to arbitration represented merely the selection of a different forum and remedial process, such an agreement—the Court would have us believe—had no impact upon the substantive statutory rights in question. The nonwaiver language, therefore, did not apply to the nonsubstantive provisions of the Act. The Court attributed little significance either to the underlying purpose of the Exchange Act (to protect individual investors from overreaching by securities industry professionals) or to the possibility that arbitrators would construe the applicable law differently from judges, especially in light of the fact that the arbitral procedure was established and directed by the securities industry. In effect, the Court chose to ignore the adhesionary character of the contract and the arbitration agreement, neglecting the evident need for consumer protection generated by the facts.

The majority opinion limited the precedential value of *Wilko*, confining its holding to the 1933 Securities Act, and effectively discredited its reasoning. According to the majority, rather than representing a statement of the importance of the policy of protecting investors from broker overreaching, *Wilko* symbolized a general distrust of arbitration that conflicted with the Court's more recent pronouncements on arbitration. The *Wilko* decision, therefore, only prohibited arbitration in circumstances in which the remedy was inadequate to protect the substantive statutory rights at issue. Rulings involving transborder arbitration had established that, when arbitration was deemed (presumably by the courts) sufficient to protect the rights at issue, there was no bar to a waiver of a judicial forum. *See Scherk v. Alberto–Culver Co.*, 417 U.S. 506, *reh'g denied*, 419 U.S. 885 (1974); *Mitsubishi Motors Corp. v. Soler Chrysler–Plymouth, Inc.*, 473 U.S. 614 (1985). This reasoning and revision of precedent extended the doctrine that the existence of statutory rights did not preclude the recourse to arbitration unless there was a legislative command that mandated judicial disposition of alleged violations. *McMahon*, in effect, ignored the special circumstances, express doctrinal content, and segregation of domestic and international considerations in the prior decisional law.

McMahon similarly reformulated the holding in *Mitsubishi Motors Corp. v. Soler Chrysler–Plymouth, Inc.*, 473 U.S. 614 (1985). *Mitsubishi* provided that antitrust claims were arbitrable in the context of international commerce. According to *McMahon*, however, *Mitsubishi* now stood for the more general proposition that the submission of statutory claims to arbitration did not compromise the affected statutory rights. Arbitral tribunals, like courts, were able to interpret and apply statutes. Resorting to the arbitral rather than judicial adjudication merely represented a choice of dispute resolution forum.

The statutory protection afforded to individual investors did not influence the Court's reasoning or alter its view of the primacy of the federal policy on arbitration. The public interest in the integrity of the financial marketplace, in the Court's perception, could only be enhanced by the submission of investor claims to arbitration. The extension of the dispute resolution process to the individual investor would mean that the securities laws would be enforced and would be more fully integrated into specific transactions. Nor did the unilateral character of the arbitral clause and its imposition on a take-it-or-leave-it basis disturb the Court's endorsement of arbitration for the securities investor. The practice of imposing arbitration on customers was an industry-wide practice. Investors could not participate in the marketplace without agreeing to submit disputes—statutory or otherwise—to arbitration. The "hospitable inquiry into arbitrability" was undeterred by any of these considerations.

Rodriguez de Quijas v. Shearson/American Express, Inc., 490 U.S. 477 (1989), confirmed the arbitrability of statutory claims in domestic arbitration. The *Rodriguez* Court decided that claims arising under the 1933 Securities Act were arbitrable, thereby overruling and reversing *Wilko* because it embodied a would-be "outmoded presumption of disfavoring arbitration proceedings." Like *McMahon*, *Rodriguez* involved allegations of consumer fraud in an investor-broker contract for the purchase of securities. The plaintiffs, who had signed a standard contract containing an arbitration clause, claimed violations of both the 1933 Securities Act and the 1934 Securities Exchange Act. In *McMahon*, the Court ruled that 1934 Act claims could be submitted to arbitration; in *Rodriguez*, the issue of litigation was whether the 1933 Act claims could be submitted to arbitration as well.

In a 5 to 4 decision, the *Rodriguez* Court used the precedent set in *Mitsubishi* and *McMahon* to discredit completely the *Wilko* doctrine. The Court, through Justice Kennedy, made much of the fact that arbitration was "merely a form of trial" that did not have an impact upon substantive rights. Moreover, statutory rights were not privileged; they, like contractual obligations, could be adjudicated through arbitration. Having recourse to arbitration resulted only in a waiver of the Act's procedural guarantees, not the substantive rights it created. Finally, the Act's nonwaiver provision applied only to the legislation's substantive provisions.

Wilko was out of keeping with modern arbitration doctrine: "To the extent that *Wilko* rested on suspicion of arbitration as a method of weakening the protections afforded in the substantive law to would-be complainants, it has fallen far out of step with our current strong endorsement of the federal statutes favoring this method of resolving disputes." *Wilko* was imbued with " 'the old judicial hostility to arbitration' " and did not address the arbitrability question " 'with a healthy regard for the federal policy favoring arbitration' " mandated by the federalism trilogy. The ruling in *McMahon* dictated that *Wilko* could no longer stand as applicable law because the language of the 1933 and 1934 Acts pertaining to judicial remedies was identical: "Indeed, in *McMahon* the Court declined to read § 29(a) of the Securities Exchange Act of 1934, the language of which is in every respect the same as that in § 14 of the 1933 Act,...to prohibit enforcement of predispute agreements to arbitrate." Furthermore, an inconsistent interpretation of the provisions of the two acts would impair the basic harmony of the regulatory scheme for the sale of securities: "[T]he inconsistency between *Wilko* and *McMahon* undermines the essential rationale for a harmonious construction of the statutes, which is to discourage litigants from manipulating their allegations merely to cast their claims under one of the securities laws rather than another."

The dissent in *Rodriguez* grounded its criticism in a separation of powers argument and the need to have the Court respect legislative authority in establishing law. According to Justice Stevens, when the Court's "earlier opinion [has given] a statutory provision concrete meaning, which Congress elects not to amend during the ensuing 3½ decades, our duty to respect Congress' work product is strikingly similar to the duty of other federal courts to respect our work product."

Since the decisions in *McMahon* and *Rodriguez*, the security arbitration business has become well-established. There is an enormous volume of cases and an ever-increasing number of industry personnel—from lawyers to consultants to arbitrators. The exchanges have developed more adapted rules and various institutional agencies exist to administer the proceedings that take place. There is a growing literature on the process and its operation. Customary arbitral practices are emerging and are being examined and codified. The status of the securities laws is less well-known because arbitral awards are not generally published. Parties need to be inside the process to have an accurate and informed sense of how the process works. There is no doubt that the decisions in *McMahon* and *Rodriguez* created an entirely new sector of the service industry attached to the financial markets.

The process of securities arbitration is regulated by private professional organizations under the supervision of a governmental body. The private professional organizations are called self-regulating organizations (SRO) and include the New York Stock Exchange (NYSE) and the National Association of Securities Dealers (NASD). These organizations and others make up the Securities Industry Conference on Arbitration (SICA), which has a Uniform Code of Arbitration. The governmental body that oversees the SROs is the Securities and Exchange Commission (SEC).

Each SRO has its own rules of arbitration, although there is a general customary practice as to how to conduct securities arbitration proceedings. The SEC must approve proposals for changes in the SRO's rules of arbitration. The requests for rule changes are published in the Federal Register and subject to public comment. The NASD handles most of the securities arbitrations because it services the arbitration needs of some nine other SROs. In 2002, the NASD received nearly 8,000 case filings. Many cases—in excess of 50%—settled prior to the arbitration and over 1,000 cases were resolved through mediation under the mediation rules in the NASD Code (Rules 10400–10407). Arbitrators decide the more difficult and complex cases in which the parties are divided by irreconcilable conflict. In 2002, NASD arbitrators awarded $139 million in damages. Punitive damages accounted for $23 million of that figure. NASD dispute resolution can take place in forty-seven official locations throughout the country. In general, a NASD arbitration may last about eighteen months and have four or five days of hearings.

In July 2007, the NASD and the NYSE member regulation and arbitration process were consolidated. The resulting entity was "The Financial Industry Regulatory Authority" or FINRA. The latter is now the "largest independent [or, nongovernmental] regulator" of the securities industry and firms in the United States. According to its website (www. finra.org/index.htm), it supervises 5,000 brokerage firms, 173,000 branch offices, and 656,000 registered securities representatives. Its activities affect almost every aspect of the securities business, from market regulation for the various exchanges to administering a dispute resolution process for investors and registered firms, including elaborating and enforcing rules and registering industry professionals. FINRA has its principal offices in Washington, D.C. and New York City, along with fifteen district offices. It has about 3,000 employees. It promotes investor education. Its central mission is to maintain the fairness and integrity of the financial marketplace. It provides both arbitration and mediation services. It receives several hundred new case filings for arbitration annually.

Consumer Arbitration

Another area in which arbitration is new, and becoming firmly entrenched, is consumer transactions. It is virtually impossible to avoid arbitration as one buys goods or services in the American marketplace. Now, all types of consumer transactions—the use of credit cards, banking services, the purchase of a vehicle or of a mobile home, pest control and securities services, membership in a health maintenance organization, and other activities—involve mandatorily acquiescence to arbitration. Arbitration agreements are present in all facets of the economy. Accepting them is necessary to individual participation in the marketplace.

The widening reach of arbitration has been fostered by United States Supreme Court rulings that have made arbitration agreements nearly impossible to challenge on contract grounds. Despite the express language of FAA § 2, it is unlikely that an arbitration agreement can be nullified because it was imperfectly made as a contract. The United States Supreme Court and the lower federal courts do not generally perceive unilateral agreements to arbitrate disputes as unfair contracts. The burden of proof on this question is quite difficult to satisfy. Therefore, consumers can be forced by sellers and manufacturers to agree to arbitrate disputes. The choice of remedy is not subject to negotiation or bilateral agreement. The controlling presumption appears to be that everyone wins by referring disputes to arbitration.

An early ruling by the Seventh Circuit characterized the standard approach in the federal case law. *See Hill v. Gateway 2000, Inc.*, 105 F.3d 1147 (7th Cir.), *cert. denied*, 522 U.S. 808 (1997). There, consumers purchased a computer by direct-sale over the telephone. The manufacturer included a number of terms and conditions in the box with the computer. The terms and conditions provided that they would govern if the customer did not return the computer within thirty days. They included an arbitral clause. The buyers waited more than thirty days before attempting to return the computer. The plaintiffs filed suit, alleging breach of contract and warranty regarding the product and customer service after the sale.

The court of appeals determined that the conditions of the transaction had been expressly stated and were accepted. Moreover, the buying and selling of goods took place on the basis of adhesionary contracts in all sectors of the economy. Adhesionary transactions limited the costs of selling and thereby made products more affordable in a competitive market. The fact that the terms were unilaterally imposed and not subject to negotiation did not affect the validity of the arbitral clause. The court noted that plaintiffs in this case, like many others, benefited from the price reductions brought about by transactional efficiencies. The buyers had a reasonable opportunity to read the documentation. Merchants—especially those whose profit margins were small—needed to restrict or make more predictable their liability exposure. Keeping the computer more than thirty days constituted acceptance of the terms and conditions of the sale, including the arbitral clause. Finally, in light of the ruling in *Doctor's Associates, Inc. v. Casarotto*, 517 U.S. 681 (1996), the court of appeals concluded that the FAA did not require arbitration agreements to be prominently displayed in order to be enforceable. The United States Supreme Court denied *certiorari*.

Emboldened by the initial "arbitration in the box" litigation, the company attempted to misuse the reference to arbitration by having it, in effect, deny any feasible remedy to consumers. The company began to include documents in the computer box that not only mandated that disputes arising in the transaction be submitted to arbitration, but also that any subsequent arbitration would be administered pursuant to the arbitral institutional rules of the International Chamber of Commerce (ICC). The clause also stipulated that Chicago was the exclusive venue for arbitrations and that a single arbitrator would preside. *See Brower v. Gateway 2000, Inc.*, 676 N.Y.S.2d 569 (N.Y. App. Div. 1998). In all other respects, the arbitration agreement that was included in the "Standard Terms and Conditions" was a straightforward contract for arbitration.

The critical problem with the arbitral clause was the unstated economics of ICC arbitration. The sale contemplated by the parties—that of a standard personal computer—involves a price range of $800–$2000. The ICC charges a non-refundable registration fee of $2500 and there are other fees—also not completely retrievable—that must be deposited at the outset of the process and which can be as much as an additional $2000. In addition, the ICC Rules follow a "loser pays" approach to the allocation of legal fees. The prospect of paying the product manufacturer's legal fees would be likely to "chill" any rational consumer's desire to pursue a claim. The reference to ICC arbitration, in effect, made the recourse to arbitration entirely impractical for the purchaser of the computer. The consumer would pay more than twice the value of the computer merely to initiate the arbitration. By selecting the ICC Rules of Arbitration, the computer manufacturer insulated itself from the customers' dissatisfaction and the reparation of their grievances.

The New York state court found that the arbitration provision was substantively unconscionable. The court ruled that the cost factor of ICC arbitration was unreasonable and would serve to deter the consumer from invoking the dispute resolution process. "Barred from resorting to the courts by the arbitration clause in the first instance, the designation of a financially prohibitive forum effectively bars consumers from this forum as well; consumers are thus left with no forum at all in which to resolve a dispute."

Because of the disparity of position between the parties, courts have begun to supervise more closely the validity of consumer arbitration agreements. Although most courts still subscribe to the discipline of the federal policy on arbitration, there are more frequent deviations from that standard. Some courts engage in a rigorous assessment of consumer arbitration agreements as contracts. Case law demonstrates that unconscionability coupled with adhesion is more likely to defeat the agreement to arbitrate in the context of consumer transactions than in other areas in which arbitration applies. In this setting, arbitration agreements become suspect whenever they have the effect of denying consumers access to a dispute resolution process or remedies guaranteed by the governing statute or when they are imposed to insulate the commercial party from meaningful challenges to its sales practices. In a word, the stronger party engages in a form of overreaching that becomes oppressive and overwhelming to the weaker party to the transaction. The economically stronger party, in effect, makes the deal by looking in a mirror.

There are discernible trends in the case law and institutional practice to avoid patent unfairness and abuse in consumer arbitration. The California state Supreme Court has rendered perhaps the most significant opinions on the question of minimal fairness in consumer [and employment] arbitration. In the landmark case of *Engalla v. Permanente Med. Group, Inc.*, 938 P.2d 903 (Cal. 1997), the California high court made it abundantly clear that HMO companies could not administer their own arbitration systems against the interests of members who filed claims against the company. A neutral outside agency had to be employed to administer the system so that all parties who were involved in the process were treated equally and evenhandedly.

The California state Supreme Court established that arbitration agreements (in the employment and other areas of party disparity) must possess a "modicum of bilaterality" in order to be enforceable. *See Armendariz v. Foundation Health Psychcare Servs., Inc.*, 6 P.3d 669 (Cal. 2000). In circumstances in which the parties are significantly unequal, the contract defense override to the enforcement of arbitration agreements appears to have become somewhat more functional among a number of courts, especially the California state Supreme Court.

Along with employment arbitration, consumer arbitration creates the greatest tension between the function of law and the functionality of arbitration. An informed acquiescence to arbitration may be desirable but it is hardly practical. The unilateral imposition of arbitration in form contracts may well remain necessary if arbitration is to be effective in these types of transactions. The concern for fairness could be addressed in other facets of the process: The appointment and qualification of arbitrators, requiring administering institutions to supply consumers with arbitrator lists and a description of the track record of prospective arbitrators as well as of their professional experience and various leanings; allowing consumers to appoint all sole arbitrators;

imposing an across-the-board fiduciary duty upon arbitrators to make the proceedings fair for the weaker party and obligating arbitrators to award punitive damages for egregious behavior by the commercial party; finally, requiring arbitrators to give detailed written recognition to and resolution of statutory claims and providing for the review of such determinations on the basis of clear error through the courts or by the recourse to an appellate arbitral process. Provisions that reduce rights or adjust the arbitral process to the stronger party's advantage should be excluded and subject the maker to special penalties. In the final analysis, arbitration responds well to both the volume and size of ordinary consumer claims. The adjudicatory mechanism needs to be adapted to the disparity of position between the parties.

The mutuality of the obligation to arbitrate has become a critical aspect of the contemporary law of consumer arbitration. Arbitration agreements in the consumer setting are adhesion contracts—unilateral provisions for the arbitration of disputes. Courts sometimes hold such agreements unenforceable when they determine that the contract does not represent the weaker party's reasonable expectations or when they find the clause to be unduly oppressive and therefore unconscionable or against public policy. *See Kloss v. Edward D. Jones & Co.*, 54 P.3d 1 (Mont. 2002), *cert. denied*, 538 U.S. 956 (2003). A number of courts, however, avoid invalidating arbitration agreements even when they contain inequalities or other positional imbalances.

Consumer arbitration agreements can be challenged on a number of other grounds. The contemporary decisional law has cases that oppose agreements on the basis of unconscionability, costs, and severance; for the way arbitral clauses are integrated into consumer transactions; and for excluding class action relief—so-called class action waivers. For a finding of unconscionability, pursuant to the applicable state law, the courts usually require that both the procedural and substantive components of unconscionability be satisfied. Arbitral clauses contained in consumer transactions are, by definition, procedurally unconscionable. Their terms are unilaterally imposed and presented on a take-it-or-leave-it basis by the economically superior, drafting party. The critical question, therefore, is whether the terms themselves oppress the weaker party. When they do through the deprivation of basic and fundamental legal rights, the arbitral clause is substantively unconscionable and becomes unenforceable.

The Anti–Arbitration Forces

The Court's policy on arbitration avoided serious objections until the development of adhesionary arbitration. The Court itself basically shunned the matter. In several landmark opinions, it provided an oblique response by holding fast to the position that the statutory duty of courts was to enforce arbitration contracts. In effect, the Court was saying that would-be contract unfairness did not alter the "prime directive" of the governing statute.

A trend developed in the U.S. Congress and some state legislatures to enact legislation that opposed arbitration's increasing range of application and its influence upon the protection of legal rights. To the power brokers in society—at least to a vocal minority among them—the privatization of the adjudication of public law rights was an unacceptable development in the law of arbitration. The statutory regulation of commercial conduct in the form of antitrust and securities laws and the guarantees of citizenship in terms of civil rights, equal protection, and due process needed to be addressed in public proceedings by duly designated public servants who rendered published determinations reasoned according to the provisions of well-settled law.

The resistance to arbitration gave rise to annual anti-arbitration bills in the U.S. Congress. The proposed legislation was intended primarily, it seems, to thwart arbitration's infringement upon the public law jurisdiction of courts and its perceived unfairness to traditional political constituencies. An early example of this type of proposed legislation was entitled "The Civil Rights Protections Procedures Act." Such bills were introduced annually in the U.S. Congress for more than a decade. They generally constituted a symbolic protest against the growing impact of arbitration. The bills never came out of committee. They banned the use of arbitration in disputes involving statutory rights. They exemplified a singular and exclusive commitment to a most imperfect judicial process and an unrealistic view of public judicial and legislative jurisdiction as sacrosanct.

The "Arbitration Fairness Act" of 2007 continues this tradition but in a less symbolic way. It was introduced in the 110th Congress as H.R. 3010 and S. 1782. The House and Senate versions of the proposed legislation are identical. The principal sponsors of the legislation appear to be Representative Henry C. "Hank" Johnson, Jr. (Ga.) (along with 103 co-sponsors) and Senator Russell D. Feingold (Wis.) (along with seven co-sponsors). The configuration of sponsorships indicate that the proposed legislation is a Democrat party measure that reflects the interests of its traditional constituencies, especially the American Trial Lawyers Association ("ATLA").

The stated purpose of the bills is to dismantle the process of coerced arbitration in disparate-party transactional circumstances: "[N]o predispute arbitration agreement shall be valid or enforceable if it requires arbitration of: (1) an employment, consumer, or franchise dispute, or (2) a dispute arising under any statute intended to protect civil rights or to regulate contracts or transactions between parties of unequal bargaining power." It also eliminates, apparently in all arbitration circumstances, the jurisdictional or *kompetenz-kompetenz* powers of the arbitrator: "[T]he validity or enforceability of an agreement to arbitrate shall be determined by a court, under federal law, rather than an arbitrator, irrespective of whether the party resisting arbitration challenges the arbitration agreement specifically or in conjunction with other terms of the contract containing such agreement." The latter provision reverses or eliminates the effect of the separability doctrine. It also seems to eliminate any reference to state contract law and to create a federal law of contracts applying exclusively to arbitration agreements. This federal contract law for arbitration propounds the limited validity of arbitration contracts and places particular encumbrances upon their range of application. In effect, if the bill is enacted into law, the U.S. Congress will discriminate against arbitration as a form of contract by placing disabling requirements upon it in certain transactions. By so doing, the Congress will be engaging in conduct that the United States Supreme Court forbade to the states for years through the federal preemption doctrine.

Finally, the proposed legislation "exempts arbitration in collective bargaining agreements" from the regulation established in the legislation. The proponents of the legislation approve of the traditional role of arbitration in achieving industrial self-governance in the unionized workplace. In their view, union representation establishes a sufficient level of protection to guarantee the essential fairness of this application of arbitration. It is again interesting to note that the federal decisional law, especially the rulings of the United States Supreme Court, arrives at a diametrically opposed conclusion. In the latter, the Court believed (until recently) that the union's collective interest prevented

union members from asserting their personal acquiescence to the arbitrability of their individual statutory rights through the union. As a result, the
individual union member needed to affirm personally the arbitrability of disputes involving citizenship
guarantees. In the final analysis, it is difficult to
comprehend why an employee's interests are seen
as advantaged in one form of workplace arbitration
and not the other.

It should be emphasized that the stated purpose
of the proposed legislation not only bans arbitral
clauses in the identified transactional circumstances, but it also prohibits the arbitrability of civil
rights disputes on a subject-matter basis. Both aspects of the bills stand in contradistinction to the
United States Supreme Court's longstanding decisional law on arbitration. The latter provides for a
wide, if not unlimited, rule of arbitrability that is
not constrained by subject-matter considerations or
transactional inequality. The Court's objective in
devising this law was to guarantee citizen access to
a functional and effective process of adjudication.
The proposed law simply bans arbitration without
creating more courts, naming judges to unfilled
positions, or correcting the abuses and dysfunction-
ality of judicial litigation.

The bills contain a section of "findings" about
arbitration, the law, and the need for reform. The
statements made in this section of the proposed
legislation constitute a veritable "manifesto"
against arbitration that distorts the current law and

its impact. The declarations are built upon a set of false and conclusory assumptions about the functioning of the court system, unabashed ideological and political convictions, and an ill-concealed objective of advancing the individual self-interests of favored groups. The alleged contractual unfairness of arbitration proceeds from a misconception about the purpose and reality of dispute resolution. The legislative critique mouths the criticism of arbitration advanced by the ATLA. Regardless of how justice is defined, arbitration undeniably depreciates the business interest, adversarial skills, and the professional necessity of ATLA members by creating a more effective and efficient civil dispute resolution process. Eliminating the option for arbitration is equivalent to relegating American citizens to the emergency room for their health care needs.

These transactions unquestionably represent situations in which the stronger, more sophisticated party imposes the obligation to arbitrate upon the economically weaker and less savvy party unilaterally on an all-or-nothing basis. The adhesionary character of these transactions is undeniable. Whether this circumstance results in unacceptable inequity and whether "consumers and employees [are forced] to give up their right to have disputes resolved by a judge or jury..." is at least a matter of opinion, if not a matter of political predilection, rather than a matter of fact. From the perspective of the United States Supreme Court, the mission of erecting a private civil justice process could not be accomplished if uninformed parties, distrustful of corporate practices, were allowed to reject the arbitral alternative on the basis of misconceptions. The simple lack of familiarity would be sufficient to thwart the overriding goal.

The recourse to arbitration may, in fact, be a more effective remedy for the weaker party and a better vehicle for protecting the weaker party's legal rights. The potential superiority of arbitration becomes manifest when the obligor pays the costs of arbitration, is equally subject to the duty to submit disputes to arbitration, and includes all the forms of relief available in court, including class action litigation, attorneys' fees, and punitive damages. The proposed legislation assumes that there is supreme virtue to participation in the process of judicial litigation and that the affected parties surrender rather than forego their right of recourse to that "mystical" mechanism. The courts are seen as "the one true religion." There is, in fact, a great deal of *trompe l'oeil* to the judicial process; for example, court dockets are overwhelmed by volume, access is difficult and expensive, outcomes are difficult to predict, and the availability of appeal can transform a victory at the trial level into a financially driven defeat through appeal. These disadvantages are accompanied by the foibles of the jury, relentless efforts to forum-shop and argue about jurisdiction, and gaming the system through choice-of-law puzzles and the intricate rules of evidence.

The failures of the court trial, over the years, have been the *raison d'être* of arbitration's success.

The stronger party seems to have the better position in the litigious realities of the judicial process. "Referee" judges can hardly direct the conduct of party-driven proceedings. The litigation process, in fact, was conceived for lawyers, not for advancing the client's interests. In effect, only the mythology of outdated belief systems could sustain the view that coerced participation of employees and consumers in arbitration constitutes a denial of justice. In point of fact, the weaker party should rationally seek to avail itself of a more user-friendly dispute resolution process that provides for acceptable final results. Prospective harm is not actual harm or the negation of actual benefit. The assessment in the proposed legislation ignores (probably, deliberately) the advances and adjustments that have been made to disparate-party arbitration in the case law.

Arbitrators generally have substantial expertise in the field—generally more than judges. Their knowledge may lead them to apply governing legal rules with greater intelligence. Critics of arbitration assume that the law contains objective answers that are susceptible of rigorous scientific application and that judges never construe the law by exercising their personal judgment. The existence of dissents and reversals demonstrate unquestionably that so-called legal rules are extremely variable and that judges are hardly uniform in their appraisal of them. Adjudicators frequently invent rules to achieve resolution in individual cases. This is the bargain for judicial and arbitral justice alike. Arbitrators have a greater incentive to avoid being characterized as arbitrary decision-makers.

When domestic arbitration first began to flourish and the Court instituted its liberal policy on statutory (or subject-matter) arbitrability, few domestic arbitrations resulted in significantly reasoned determinations or published awards. The Court's rulings, however, made arbitral decisions into more significant pronouncements. Arbitrators not only were authorized by contract to resolve the parties' dispute, but now the law regulating arbitration invested them with the power to address and rule upon statutory claims. This wider range of arbitral jurisdiction would apply unless the parties provided otherwise in their agreement. To some degree, therefore, the Court's decisional pronouncement attributed public law-making authority to the arbitrators. They ruled primarily pursuant to contract, but acquired (as a matter of law) some of the responsibility of the public servant because they were performing the same function as a judge.

Given their enhanced jurisdiction, the determinations reached by arbitrators became both more voluminous and significant. As in matters of transborder arbitrations involving large sums of money, domestic arbitrators asked to resolve workplace discrimination claims, issues relating to the public regulation of commerce (like antitrust or securities regulation), or to apply consumer protection legislation (*e.g.*, truth-in-lending) felt obligated to contribute to the *gravitas* of their larger mission by engaging in statutory analysis and consulting the case law. They produced judge-like opinions that were introduced in subsequent proceedings by lawyers and were eventually (in some cases) made available to the public through the internet or publication. Increasingly, the publication of arbitral awards included commentary and assessment by specialists in the field. Disparate-party arbitration has not stunted the discussion of public law issues, but rather shifted the discussion to a more accessible and effective adjudicatory mechanism. On this score as well, the development of arbitration has demonstrated its creative ability to adjust and adapt to its changing mandate.

An adjudicatory process that is efficient, effective, and accessible can hardly be described as incapable of protecting rights. The expense and indecision associated with protracted adversarial proceedings before courts do not protect citizen rights, but rather promote the attorneys' combat and embellish their emoluments. Lawyers, of course, tendentiously assert that using their battleground is synonymous with rights protection. The argument ignores the impact of litigation warfare on the litigants' lives and interests. Sunshine is an invaluable tool to democracy precisely because it promotes accountability and prevents sweetheart deals and self-dealing. Mandating that all consumer and employment arbitrations be open to the public would not hinder the process of disparate-party arbitration. To some degree, the openness of such proceedings is already achieved (albeit in a delayed fashion) by vacatur actions and the periodic publication of awards. The need for confidentiality is much greater in commercial proceedings because of the parties' need to preserve business advantage and reputation. Further, reform of disparate-party arbitration can be readily achieved by altering the governing procedure to provide for written opinions that contain reasons and are published. These are generally facile and innocuous modifications that are responsive to the public law character of the implicated disputes.

The demonization of arbitration ignores the remedy's track record and level of user satisfaction. It is the lawyers and the politicians who favor them that complain. The drafters of the proposed legislation demand absolutely bilateral contract formation; they never entertain any solution or position beyond their initial proposition. The latter establishes both the beginning and end of the drafters' thinking. The realities of disparate-party arbitration are, in fact, much more complex and cannot be summarized in a simple political slogan or a set of ideological falsehoods. As a matter of law, arbitrators can rule upon both statutory and contract claims. Because arbitration actually works, it provides greater protection for the parties' statutory rights than standard court proceedings. In a word, the fate of statutory rights is secure in arbitration. In fact, arbitral proceedings are a more effective guarantor of individual constitutional rights. The Court articulated the federal policy on arbitration in the aim of preserving the due process rights of American citizens.

CHAPTER SEVEN

LABOR AND EMPLOYMENT ARBITRATION

Labor Arbitration

Labor arbitration is a separate and highly sophisticated form of arbitration. It is not governed by the FAA, but rather by Section 301 of the Labor Management Relations Act of 1947. Court rulings on matters of commercial arbitration, however, have borrowed heavily from labor arbitration cases and applied the holdings in these cases as basic principles of arbitration law. The influence of labor arbitration is especially evident in the grounds for vacating or confirming arbitral awards and in the doctrine that describes the role of contract in arbitration.

The *Steelworkers Trilogy* represents the landmark cases on labor arbitration. These celebrated decisions address the arbitrability of labor disputes and the enforcement of labor arbitration awards. They state the essence of the federal judicial doctrine on labor arbitration. They also establish that arbitration is the principal mechanism for resolving disputes that arise from collective bargaining agreements between labor unions and management. Arbitration has been instrumental in shaping U.S.

labor-management relations by providing an effective means for the implementation of collective bargaining agreements. The recourse to arbitration makes the resolution of disputes in the unionized workplace possible. *See United Steelworkers of Am. v. American Mfg. Co.*, 363 U.S. 564 (1960); *United Steelworkers of Am. v. Warrior & Gulf Navigation Co.*, 363 U.S. 574 (1960); *United Steelworkers of Am. v. Enterprise Wheel & Car Corp.*, 363 U.S. 593 (1960).

In *AT&T Techns., Inc. v. Communications Workers of Am.*, 475 U.S. 643 (1986), the United States Supreme Court provided the following summary of the judicial doctrine on labor arbitration:

The principles necessary to decide this case are not new. They were set out by this Court over 25 years ago in a series of cases known as the *Steelworkers Trilogy* . . . . These precepts have served the industrial relations community well, and have led to continued reliance on arbitration, rather than strikes or lockouts, as the preferred method of resolving disputes arising during the term of a collective-bargaining agreement. We see no reason either to question their continuing validity, or to eviscerate their meaning by creating an exception to their general applicability.

The first principle gleaned from the *Trilogy* is that "arbitration is a matter of contract and a party cannot be required to submit to arbitration any dispute which he has not agreed so to submit." . . . This axiom recognizes the fact that arbitrators derive their authority to resolve disputes only because the parties have agreed in advance to submit such grievances to arbitration....

The second rule, which follows inexorably from the first, is that the question of arbitrability—whether a collective-bargaining agreement creates a duty for the parties to arbitrate the particular grievance—is undeniably an issue for judicial determination. Unless the parties clearly and unmistakably provide otherwise, the question of whether the parties agreed to arbitrate is to be decided by the court, not the arbitrator....

[. . .]

The third principle derived from our prior cases is that, in deciding whether the parties have agreed to submit a particular grievance to arbitration, a court is not to rule on the potential merits of the underlying claims. Whether "arguable" or not, indeed even if it appears to the court to be frivolous, the union's claim that the employer has violated the collective-bargaining agreement is to be decided, not by the court asked to order arbitration, but as the parties have agreed, by the arbitrator. "The courts, therefore, have no business weighing the merits of the grievance, considering whether there is equity in a particular claim, or determining whether there is particular language in the written instrument which will support the claim. The agreement is to submit all grievances to arbitration, not merely those which the court will deem meritorious."...

Finally, it has been established that where the contract contains an arbitration clause, there is a presumption of arbitrability in the sense that "[a]n order to arbitrate the particular grievance should not be denied unless it may be said with positive assurance that the arbitration clause is not susceptible of an interpretation that covers the asserted dispute. Doubts should be resolved in favor of coverage." . . . Such a presumption is particularly applicable where the clause is as broad as the one employed in this case, which provides for arbitration of "any differences arising with respect to the interpretation of this contract or the performance of any obligation hereunder . . . ." In such cases, "[i]n the absence of any express provision excluding a particular grievance from arbitration, we think only the most forceful evidence of a purpose to exclude the claim from arbitration can prevail." . . .

This presumption of arbitrability for labor disputes recognizes the greater institutional competence of arbitrators in interpreting collective-bargaining agreements, "furthers the national labor policy of peaceful resolution of labor disputes and thus best accords with the parties' presumed objectives in pursuing collective bargaining." . . . The willingness of parties to enter into agreements that provide for arbitration of specified disputes would be "drastically reduced," however, if a labor arbitrator had the "power to determine his own jurisdiction . . . ." . . . Were this the applicable rule, an arbitrator would not be constrained to resolve only those disputes that the parties have agreed in advance to settle by arbitration, but, instead, would be empowered "to impose obligations outside the contract limited only by his understanding and conscience." ... This result undercuts the longstanding federal policy of promoting industrial harmony through the use of collective-bargaining agreements, and is antithetical to the function of a collective-bargaining agreement as setting out the rights and duties of the parties.

The several hundred thousand collective bargaining agreements in force nationwide generate a multitude of alleged violations on a daily basis. Resolving such disputes through court proceedings would overwhelm the judicial process and require courts to acquire specialized knowledge of the practices of the workplace. The system of labor arbitration provides a corps of professional labor arbitrators who not only dispose of the disputes in an efficient and orderly manner, but also have elaborated a type of *stare decisis* of labor arbitration. There is, for example, a basic consensus among labor arbitrators as to what constitutes just cause for dismissal, who bears the burden of proof in discipline cases, when back pay and reinstatement are in order, and how issues of seniority, promotion, and transfer are to be treated.

There are two types of labor arbitration. First, *interest arbitration* is the more legislative form of labor arbitration. It is used to establish the new

terms and conditions of employment under a collective bargaining agreement. Historically, it was the
original form of labor arbitration and constituted a
substitute for strikes to resolve labor-management
disagreements in the negotiation of new labor
agreements. Second, *rights* or *grievance arbitration*
involves the interpretation or application of the
terms and conditions of employment contained in
the collective bargaining agreement. Rights arbitration is the more recent and more judicial form of
labor arbitration. It is the form of labor arbitration
that usually is referred to in the federal decisional
law. *See* MAX ZIMNY, WILLIAM F. DOLSON, & CHRISTO-
PHER A. BARRECA, LABOR ARBITRATION (1990); C. LACUG-
NA, AN INTRODUCTION TO LABOR ARBITRATION (1988).

In *Textile Workers Union of America v. Lincoln
Mills of Alabama*, 353 U.S. 448 (1957), the United
States Supreme Court provided a definitive interpretation of the content of § 301 of the Labor
Management Relations Act of 1947. The Court saw
§ 301 as the authoritative foundation for making
arbitration the principal means of resolving labor
disputes. The Court further asserted that § 301
enables the federal courts "to fashion a body of
federal law for the enforcement of. . . collective bargaining agreements." Part of that federal law dictates the enforcement of agreements to arbitrate
disputes in the collective bargaining agreements.
Section 301 thereby expressed "a federal policy that
federal courts should enforce. . . agreements [to ar-
bitrate] on behalf of or against labor organizations. . . ." Such a practice was instrumental to the

stabilization and effectiveness of the workplace. The Court also federalized this area of labor law by concluding that "the substantive law to apply in suits under § 301(a) is federal law...." Moreover,

Federal interpretation of the federal law will govern, not state law.... But state law, if compatible with the purpose of § 301, may be resorted to in order to find the rule that will best effectuate the federal policy.... Any state law applied, however, will be absorbed as federal law and will not be an independent source of private rights.

Federal law and federal courts, therefore, governed and they required the arbitration of labor disputes.

The *Steelworkers Trilogy* emphasized the importance of grievance arbitration to the stability of the workplace: "[T]he grievance machinery under a collective bargaining agreement is at the very heart of the system of industrial self-government." *See United Steelworkers of Am. v. Warrior & Gulf Navigation Co.*, 363 U.S. 574, 581 (1960). The Court also underscored the need to maintain the autonomy of the arbitration agreement and the supremacy of the arbitrator's jurisdiction. The federal courts had a very circumscribed gatekeeping function: "[T]he judicial inquiry under § 301 [is]...strictly confined to...whether the reluctant party...agree[d] to arbitrate...." The courts could only screen claims on the basis of whether they were covered by the contract. The courts' triage function could not be accomplished on the basis of an assessment of the merits of the claim. Once deemed to be within the ambit of the parties' arbitration agreement, the claims entered the sovereign domain of the arbitrator.

The province of labor arbitration was to fashion solutions to specific workplace disputes that eluded the general provisions of the collective bargaining agreement and that required a sense of the dynamics of the workplace: "The grievance procedure is, in other words, a part of the continuous collective bargaining process." The labor arbitrator could refer to the "industrial common law—the practices of the industry and the shop" to decide disputes. The arbitrator's judgment took into account the common practice of the workplace and the impact of the decision upon the parties and their relationship—elements which generally were beyond the courts' competence.

While the arbitrator had the exclusive authority to determine whether a breach of the collective bargaining agreement took place, courts were authorized to supervise the results of the grievance arbitration process. An award could reflect knowledge of and experience in a particular trade or workplace, but the arbitrator's ruling could not transcend the collective bargaining agreement itself. In order to be judicially enforceable, an arbitral award must "[draw] its essence from the collective bargaining agreement." *See United Steelworkers of Am. v. Enterprise Wheel & Car Corp.*, 363 U.S. 593, 597 (1960). Moreover, "[A]n arbitrator is confined to interpretation and application of the collective bargaining agreement; he does not sit to dispense his own brand of industrial justice." "[I]nfidelity to this obligation" resulted in the vacatur of the award.

Ambiguity in resolution or a questionable interpretation of the contract were not enough to establish that arbitrators exceeded their mandate or that awards could not be confirmed by a court. To demand that arbitrators construe the relevant contract without approximation or ambivalence would not only discourage arbitrators from revealing their reasoning in the awards, but also invite challenges by disappointed parties: "The plenary review by a court of the merits would make meaningless the provision[] that the arbitrator's decision is final . . . ." In the end:

  [T]he question of interpretation of the collective bargaining agreement is a question for the arbitrator. It is the arbitrator's construction which was bargained for; and so far as the arbitrator's decision concerns construction of the contract, the courts have no business overruling him because their interpretation of the contract is different from his.

In addition, courts could scrutinize labor arbitration awards on the basis of public policy violations. As to public policy, the Court stated that the ground arose from the general authority of the courts to refuse to give legal sanction to "immoral or illegal act[s]" and to police private agreements in the name of the public interest. The public policy exception could be applied to the provisions of a collective bargaining agreement and to the dispositions in an arbitral award. The Court, however, adapted the exception to the context of arbitration and to the federal judicial policy favoring arbitration. An award's breach of public policy must be based upon a notion of public policy that arises from " 'laws and legal precedents,' " not a diffuse sense of what the would-be public interest might command. *See United Paperworkers Intern. Union, AFL–CIO v. Misco, Inc.*, 484 U.S. 29 (1987); *Eastern Assoc. Coal Corp. v. United Mine Workers of Am., Dist. 17*, 531 U.S. 57 (2000).

Employment Arbitration

The United States Supreme Court's decision in *Gilmer v. Interstate/Johnson Lane Corp.*, 500 U.S. 20 (1991), provided the impetus for the creation of a new form of arbitration, known as "employment" arbitration. Employment arbitration differs from traditional labor arbitration in that it applies to unrepresented or non-union employees. The agreement to arbitrate is not part of a collective bargaining agreement negotiated by union officials on behalf of unionized employees. Rather, the employer inserts arbitral clauses in individual employment contracts or simply integrates an arbitration agreement into an at-will employment relationship, usually as a precondition to employment or continued employment. Therefore, the recourse to arbitration is mandatory and dictated by the employer. Such agreements also contain an express and comprehensive enumeration of the statutory claims that the employee agrees to submit to arbitration. This practice reflects, among other things, the employer's desire to avoid court litigation and to achieve an expeditious and final resolution of all types of workplace disputes.

In *Gilmer,* the agreement to arbitrate disputes was not technically part of the employment contract. In order to secure work as a stockbroker, Gilmer signed a U–4 Registration Form with the New York Stock Exchange that required him to submit disputes with his employer to arbitration under the rules of the Exchange. The obligation to arbitrate claims against the employer, therefore, was implied and indirect. Accordingly, the Court in *Gilmer* never directly addressed the question of whether employment contracts containing mandatory, employer-imposed arbitral clauses constituted valid contractual references to arbitration under the FAA. Employers both inside and outside the securities industry nonetheless began inserting such clauses into standard employment contracts, usually as part of a company ADR process instituted to address workplace disputes.

Gilmer represents the "new wave" thinking on the arbitrability of legal rights and conflicts with *Alexander v. Gardner-Denver*, 415 U.S. 36 (1974). *Gardner-Denver* epitomizes the "old time religion" on the sanctity of legal rights. It symbolizes the political thinking that arose with and from the civil rights movement of the 1950s and especially the

1960s. *Gardner-Denver* was decided after the enactment of legislation to safeguard civil rights. The
movement toward racial justice had come at an
enormous price. The advances deserved to be implemented with full effectiveness and guaranteed
through special measures. Allowing for a multiplicity of remedies to protect the integrity of such rights
did not violate legal standards, but rather gave
effect to them.

Gardner-Denver

In *Gardner-Denver*, a black man was hired by a
Denver, Colorado company to do maintenance work.
Within two years, he was promoted to a trainee
position as a drill operator. After a little more than
a year in the new position, he was fired—allegedly
for producing many defective parts that had to be
destroyed or scrapped. Mr. Alexander, the discharged employee, was a member of the union. The
collective bargaining agreement that was in place
provided for a "multistep grievance procedure," the
last step of which was the submission of unresolved
disputes to arbitration. The arbitrator was to be
chosen jointly by the union and the company and
the arbitrator's ruling would be final and binding
upon the parties. Moreover, the arbitrator's award
had to comply with the terms of the collective
bargaining agreement—the arbitrator could not
"amend, take away, add to, or change" its provisions.

After negotiations between the union and the
company failed, but prior to the arbitration, Alexan-

der—in effect—brought an action before the EEOC. There, he claimed that his discharge was based upon racial discrimination because trainees who produced many defective parts ordinarily were transferred rather than fired. Alexander also made his discrimination argument to the arbitrator. The arbitrator ruled that Alexander had been dismissed with "just cause" pursuant to the collective bargaining agreement. There was no mention in the award of Alexander's claim of racial discrimination, although the arbitrator did recommend that the union and the company explore the possibility of transferring Alexander rather than discharging him. The EEOC also was unconvinced by Alexander's argument. It ruled that the circumstances did not create a "reasonable cause to believe that a violation of Title VII...had occurred."

Alexander filed suit, alleging racial discrimination. The federal district court, however, dismissed his complaint—primarily upon jurisdictional grounds. It held that he could not sue his employer in court because the claim had already been decided by the arbitrator: "[H]aving voluntarily elected to pursue his grievance to final arbitration under the nondiscrimination clause of the collective-bargaining agreement, [petitioner] was bound by the arbitral decision and thereby precluded from suing his employer under Title VII." The appellate court affirmed.

The United States Supreme Court reversed the lower court determinations. In holding that the employee was entitled to invoke multiple remedies, the Court emphasized what the controlling statute did and did not do. First, the statute enabled the federal courts to enforce its provisions, including the requirements for a proper filing under the legislation. Second, the statute tolerated the recourse to other frameworks and remedies to combat discrimination. Third, Title VII did "not speak expressly to the relationships between federal courts and the grievance-arbitration machinery of collective-bargaining agreements." Finally, "Title VII's purpose and procedures strongly suggest that an individual does not forfeit his private cause of action if he first pursues his grievance to final arbitration under the nondiscrimination clause of a collective-bargaining agreement."

The Court also provided a critical assessment of the potential role of arbitration in the adjudication of civil rights claims. Like the conditional inarbitrability ruling, this segment of the Court's reasoning represented a substantial departure from the currently applicable doctrine. The modern view not only provides that there are no statutory or subject matter barriers to arbitration, but also that arbitration is a suitable remedy for all types of disputes. It is, after all, a mere form of trial with no impact upon the substantive content of rights. There is no impairment of rights, says the contemporary Court, in the transition from judicial to arbitral proceedings. *See, e.g., Mitsubishi Motors Corp. v. Soler Chrysler–Plymouth, Inc.*, 473 U.S. 614 (1985).

The *Gardner-Denver* Court provided a different assessment of arbitration—one that echoed the now-discredited analysis of *Wilko v. Swan*, 346 U.S. 427 (1953). The courts are better able to protect Title VII rights than arbitral tribunals. The arbitrator's allegiance is to the collective bargaining agreement and the parties, not the statute and its underlying purpose. Arbitration is a "comparatively inappropriate" and "inferior" forum because arbitrators apply "the law of the shop, not the law of the land...." Just as arbitrators have a special aptitude in the application of the "norms of industrial relations," courts have "a primary responsibility" for the "resolution of statutory or constitutional issues...." Finally, the procedures of arbitration—establishing the record, general fact-finding, evidence-gathering, questioning witnesses, and writing awards—are not suited to the adjudication of individual political rights. The efficiency and functionality of arbitration make it "a less appropriate forum for final resolution of Title VII issues than the federal courts."

The *Gardner-Denver* Court reached a conclusion that elevated the policy to promote nondiscrimination above the policy favoring arbitration. Title VII claims, therefore, could be submitted—at the employee's choice—to arbitration, to the courts, or to both types of proceedings. Thus, even though an arbitral determination has been rendered, a court must consider the Title VII suit and the plaintiff's claims anew. Further, the court can attribute whatever evidentiary weight it deems appropriate to the arbitral award.

Gilmer

The *Gilmer* Court advanced a radically different position on the question of the arbitrability of claims based upon statutory civil rights. The statute that was implicated in *Gilmer* was the Age Discrimination in Employment Act of 1967 (ADEA). Interstate had hired Gilmer in 1981 as a manager of financial services. The employment contract required Gilmer to register with several stock exchanges. The registration form at the exchanges required securities representatives to arbitrate claims "arising out of the employment or termination of employment" "between a registered representative and any member or member organization . . . ."

In 1987, Interstate terminated Gilmer. Gilmer was sixty-two years old. He filed a complaint with the EEOC, alleging age discrimination, and later filed suit in federal district court on the same basis. Interstate responded with a motion to compel arbitration. Referring to *Gardner-Denver*, the district court denied the motion, stating that the ADEA prohibited "the waiver of a judicial forum." The Fourth Circuit disagreed. It held that "nothing" in the ADEA framework indicated "a congressional intent to preclude [the] enforcement of arbitration agreements."

The Court addressed the arbitrability question from a doctrinal predisposition that presumed that statutory claims were not an obstacle to arbitration. Once the parties agreed to arbitrate disputes, they should be held to their bargain. Only a congressional directive against the waiver of judicial remedies could defeat the recourse to arbitration. The governing doctrine encouraged findings of arbitrability and the party opposing the arbitration of disputes had the burden of proof.

The *Gilmer* Court acknowledged that the ADEA was intended to promote "important social policies." Unlike the *Gardner-Denver* Court, however, it did "not perceive any inherent inconsistency between these policies...and enforcing agreements to arbitrate age discrimination claims" to the exclusion of judicial relief. A lengthy line of cases established that arbitration was an effective means of vindicating statutory rights and of enforcing the mandate that underlied the enabling statute. The ADEA did not expressly exclude the recourse to nonjudicial mechanisms. Moreover, arbitration could give effect to the statutory purpose of conferring rights and deterring undesirable conduct.

The Court dismissed Gilmer's extensive inventory of objections to the arbitration of his age discrimination claims. Most, if not all, of these objections, the Court noted, had been addressed and rejected in prior cases. Legal remedies and institutional practice as to the selection of arbitrators provided adequate protection against possible arbitrator bias. Moreover, security arbitration proceedings included adequate discovery procedures that permitted the aggrieved party to substantiate its statutory claim. Awards could be rendered with reasoned determinations and could be made public. Arbitrators had wide discretion in ordering relief. Simply put, it was beyond any argument, in the Court's assessment, that arbitration was a fully sufficient means of adjudicating statutory claims. Finally, the Court also summarily dismissed Gilmer's allegation that the contract of arbitration was unenforceable due to the parties' "unequal bargaining power": "Mere inequality in bargaining power, however, is not a sufficient reason to hold that arbitration agreements are never enforceable in the employment context."

Further, the Court asserted that the issue in *Gilmer* was distinguishable from, and could not be controlled by, the ruling in *Gardner-Denver*. Gilmer's "reliance" on *Gardner-Denver* to buttress his contention that employment discrimination claims were inarbitrable was "misplaced." To the Court, the two cases differed significantly: *Gardner-Denver* "did not involve the issue of the enforceability of an agreement to arbitrate statutory claims.... [It] involved the quite different issue [of] whether [the] arbitration of contract-based claims precluded subsequent judicial resolution of statutory claims." Moreover, in *Gardner-Denver*, there was a "tension between collective representation and individual statutory rights." In *Gilmer*, union representation was not a factor. Finally, *Gardner-Denver* did not implicate the "liberal federal policy favoring arbitration" because it was not decided under the FAA.

The Court held that Gilmer failed to meet his burden of proof. He failed to show that Congress intended to preclude the arbitration of ADEA claims. In his dissent, in which he argued for inarbitrability of ADEA claims, Justice Stevens observed that the majority failed to address the significance of the "employment contract exclusion" to the determination in *Gilmer*. Presumably, because Gilmer's job involved interstate commerce, the language of FAA § 1 excluding employment contracts applied. Therefore, arbitration provisions in employment contracts did not benefit from the favorable policy of the FAA and could be defeated more readily or given secondary standing to other policy objectives. Eventually, in later litigation, the lower federal courts and then the United States Supreme Court would rule that the employment contract exclusion only applied the contracts of workers who were directly involved in the interstate transport of goods and services. *See McWilliams v. Logicon, Inc.*, 143 F.3d 573 (10th Cir. 1998); *O'Neil v. Hilton Head Hosp.*, 115 F.3d 272 (4th Cir. 1997); *Asplundh Tree Expert Co. v. Bates*, 71 F.3d 592 (6th Cir. 1995); *Circuit City Stores, Inc. v. Adams*, 532 U.S. 105 (2001).

Additionally, Justice Stevens emphasized that no agreement to arbitrate employment disputes existed between Gilmer and Interstate, his employer. Gilmer had agreed to arbitrate disputes in his application to be a registered representative on the exchange. The contractual obligation was owed to the exchange, not Interstate. Interstate was a third-party beneficiary to the agreement between Gilmer and the exchange. Therefore, there was arguably no arbitration agreement underlying the litigation in this case.

Finally, the dissent joined the rationale of *Gardner-Denver* and asserted that "compulsory arbitration conflicts with the congressional purpose animating the ADEA...." Arbitration could cripple the antidiscrimination goal of the statute because it did not provide "broad, class-based injunctive relief" and it enabled those who practiced discrimination "to contract away the right to enforce civil rights in the courts."

Wright

The cases that followed *Gilmer* emphasized the contrast between its holding and the result in *Gardner-Denver*. For example, the Fourth Circuit, in *Austin v. Owens–Brockway Glass Container, Inc.*, 78 F.3d 875 (4th Cir.), *cert. denied*, 519 U.S. 980 (1996), argued that the *Gilmer* opinion "reject[ed] the principal concern in...*Gardner-Denver*...that arbitration is an 'inappropriate forum' for the resolution of Title VII statutory rights...." Other federal courts refused to take such an unequivocal position. They acknowledged the disparity between the results in *Gilmer* and *Gardner-Denver*, but found a means of allowing them to coexist. In any event, other federal courts held the view that *Gardner-Denver* was still good law, particularly in light of the pains the United States Supreme Court took to distinguish it from *Gilmer*.

In 1998, the United States Supreme Court appeared ready and willing to resolve the schism in the doctrine. In *Wright v. Universal Maritime Service Corp.*, 525 U.S. 70 (1998), Justice Scalia delivered an opinion for a unanimous bench. The Court decided to reverse a Fourth Circuit ruling that emphasized the reasoning in *Gilmer*. The lower court had held that a worker must first bring his ADA claim to collective bargaining arbitration before filing a lawsuit for alleged violations of his statutory rights. The Court's opinion, however, did not reconcile or resolve the tension between *Gardner-Denver* and *Gilmer*.

The Court avoided the confrontation between *Gilmer* and *Gardner-Denver* by focusing upon the statutory nature of Wright's claim. Because Wright's claim was statutory and not contractual, the "presumption of arbitrability did not come into play." It only applied to claims that arose under the labor contract, "not federal statutes relating to workplace rights." The arbitration clause in *Wright* was very general, providing for arbitration of "matters under dispute." Statutory claims would be compelled to CBA arbitration only when the requirement to arbitrate statutory claims was "particularly clear" in the labor agreement. The CBA had to include statutory anti-discrimination protections expressly and "a clear and unmistakable waiver of the covered employee's right to a judicial forum for federal claims of employment discrimination." The Court acknowledged the "tension" between *Gilmer* and

Gardner-Denver, but found it unnecessary to resolve the differences between the two cases.

The lower federal courts seem to have followed the *Wright* holding precisely. For example, the Second Circuit has held that a union-negotiated collective bargaining agreement, under which an employee had purportedly waived her right to a federal forum, was not enforceable. The arbitration provision did not constitute a clear and unmistakable waiver of the employee's right to bring an action before a federal court. *See Rogers v. New York Univ.*, 220 F.3d 73 (2d Cir.), *cert. denied*, 531 U.S. 1036 (2000).

In the Second Circuit case, Susan Rogers began working for New York University (NYU) as a clerical employee. The terms and conditions of her employment were governed by a CBA. The CBA contained a standard arbitration clause providing "that disputes arising under the agreement shall be arbitrated." Allegedly because Rogers' FMLA medical leave time had expired, NYU terminated her employment. Rogers filed a complaint with the EEOC. The EEOC issued a right-to-sue letter to Rogers, informing her that she could bring an action against NYU in federal court. NYU asked the court to stay the proceedings pursuant to FAA § 3. The court denied the motion. NYU appealed. The Second Circuit affirmed the district court's holding, reasoning that: (1) under *Gardner-Denver*, an individual employee's right to a federal forum could not be waived in a CBA; and (2) the narrow *Wright* exception to *Gardner-Denver* did not apply.

In its reasoning, the Second Circuit emphasized that *Gardner-Denver* had established that a "discharged employee whose grievance had been arbitrated pursuant to an arbitration clause in a CBA was not precluded from bringing an action in federal court." While *Gilmer* allowed "an employee who had agreed individually to waive his right to a federal forum [to] be compelled to arbitrate an age discrimination claim[,]" *Gardner-Denver* applied, in the court's view, when "the arbitration provision ha[d] been negotiated by a union in a CBA." Therefore, under "*Gardner-Denver*, to which this Court and a majority of others adhere, such provisions [providing for a waiver of a federal forum] are not enforceable."

Secondly, the court found that the facts before it were not governed by the *Wright* exception to *Gardner-Denver*. *Wright* "suggest[s] that, under certain circumstances, a union-negotiated waiver of an employee's statutory right to a judicial forum might be enforceable." The court, however, pointedly reasoned that "*Wright* may have called *Gardner-Denver* into question, [but] it did not overrule it." A union-negotiated CBA provision to submit disputes to arbitration and waive a judicial forum could be enforced under *Wright* only if the provision contained a "clear and unmistakable" waiver of the judicial forum for resolving statutory rights. Further, such a waiver must be "explicit." According to the United States Supreme Court's holding in *Wright*, the CBA must "specifically incorporate pertinent statutory requirements and make compliance therewith a contractual commitment."

Following *Wright*, according to the Second Circuit, "other courts have determined that a waiver of statutorily conferred rights contained in a CBA is sufficiently clear and unmistakable if either of two conditions are met." First, "a waiver is sufficiently explicit if the arbitration clause contains a provision whereby employees specifically agree to submit all federal causes of action arising out of their employment to arbitration." The court, however, found the arbitration clause in the instant case to be too broad and general to satisfy this condition. The clause encompassed only "any dispute concerning the interpretation, application, or claimed violation of a specific term or provision of this Agreement."

Second, a waiver can be sufficiently clear and unmistakable if the "CBA contains an explicit incorporation of the statutory anti-discrimination requirements in addition to a broad and general arbitration clause." According to the Second Circuit, "specific incorporation requires identifying the anti-discrimination statutes by name or citation." The court also emphasized that *Wright* had held that "the CBA should make compliance with the named or cited statute a contractual commitment that is subject to the arbitration clause."

The court found that the CBA in the instant case contained "both a general arbitration clause and a nondiscrimination provision," but that it failed to "incorporate anything explicitly." The court, therefore, refused to compel the arbitration of the matter because the CBA did not meet the requirements for a clear and unmistakable waiver of a judicial forum, as required by *Wright*.

The Demise of Gardner–Denver

On April 1, 2009, in *14 Penn Plaza LLC v. Pyett*, 129 S.Ct. 1456 (2009), the United States Supreme Court held that "a collective-bargaining agreement that clearly and unmistakably requires union members to arbitrate ADEA claims is enforceable as a matter of federal law." The ruling was a 5 to 4 decision and authored by Justice Thomas. Although it does not officially reverse *Alexander v. Gardner–Denver, Co.,* the decision emasculates that prior determination in every other respect, leaving it with little precedential significance or value. The unresolved "tension" the Court perceived in *Wright* between *Gardner-Denver* and *Gilmer* has disappeared as the Fourth Circuit predicated in *Austin v. Owens–Brockway Glass Container, Inc.*, 78 F.3d 875, *cert. denied*, 519 U.S. 980 (1996). As long as the National Labor Relations Act (NLRA) authorizes the union to negotiate on behalf of the employees, the union can agree to submit their discrimination claims to arbitration, just as it would barter about any other aspect of the workplace relationship.

The circumstances of *14 Penn Plaza* are straightforward and dwarfed by the doctrinal significance of the ruling they produce. Under the NLRA, the union is the exclusive bargaining representative of building services employees in New York City. 14 Penn Plaza is a member of the Realty Advisory Board (RAB), an organization of employers in the New York City real estate industry. The relevant CBA contained a standard nondiscrimination clause and required that all claims of employment discrimination be submitted to binding arbitration. During the course of the contract, 14 Penn Plaza decided with union approval to secure licensed security guards to staff its office buildings in New York City. As a result, the prior staff was reassigned by its employer to other jobs (*e.g.*, night porters and cleaners) in the building. The workers were unhappy with the reassignments, contending that the shift resulted in a loss of income, overtime, and seniority, and was generally undesirable. They asked the union to file a grievance on their behalf, claiming—in part—that the reassignments targeted disproportionately older employees. Eventually, after a number of procedural developments during the arbitration, the union members filed suit in federal court on the basis that the reassignments affected primarily old workers and violated the ADEA.

The opinion in *14 Penn Plaza* declares that the rule of arbitrability reaches civil rights and implies that these rights are secondary to the federal policy on arbitration and its aims. The discussion reiterates many of the doctrinal staples that have emerged in the line of subject-matter arbitrability cases (*Mitsubishi, McMahon, Rodriguez,* and *Gilmer*). Federal statutes that create rights of citizenship can be divided into procedural and substantive components. Altering available remedies does not affect substantive guarantees, especially when the modification refers to arbitration. According to well-settled Court doctrine, arbitration is nothing more than another form of trial that has no impact upon the substantive content of rights. Arbitration does not diminish the content of rights. As a result, the "clear and unmistakable" or "knowing and voluntary" standard applies to waivers of the substantive rights guaranteed by statutes, not the procedural choice of alternative remedies. Moreover, a perception that arbitration is a lesser form of adjudication than court litigation or ill-suited to undertake the resolution of complex statutory or other legal claims is evidence of a hostile and prejudicial view of arbitration that is not conversant with governing doctrine. The FAA's primary objective is to eradicate judicial hostility to arbitration, an aim to which the Court is merely giving effect in its rulings.

Gardner-Denver is barely recognizable in the description it receives at the hands of majority. It is not depicted as a thunderous defense of the constitutional sanctity of civil rights, but rather as a narrow ruling that generated a questionable progeny that is far out-of-keeping with the modern view of arbitration and arbitrability. The gravamen of the case was not the inviolability of civil rights, but rather the pedestrian question of contract scope. *Gardner-Denver* does not represent a clash of theologies that can only be resolved through ecumenical understanding, but rather—in its *dicta* about the

public policy significance of discrimination claims—
a heretical departure from the tenets of established
faith on arbitration. In *Gardner-Denver*, the CBA
did not, according to Justice Thomas, address the
question of whether statutory rights were arbitrable. It did no more than state that, when the
parties' agreement fails to provide for the arbitrability of statutory claims, the arbitrator is simply
precluded from ruling on such matters: "*Gardner-
Denver* and its progeny thus do not control the
outcome where, as is the case here, the collective-
bargaining agreement's arbitration provision expressly covers both statutory and contractual discrimination claims."

Even *Wright* has been misconstrued and needs
adjustment. There is no "tension" and no real
distinction between private employment contracts
and CBAs. In both settings, the arbitrator is "the
proctor of the bargain" and the arbitrator's task is
"to effectuate the intent of the parties." The rule of
arbitrability can only be thwarted by Congress in
the express language of the enacted statute. Otherwise, statutory rights, including those arising in the
1964 and 1991 Civil Rights Acts, can be submitted
to arbitration by party agreement. The resolution of
statutory claims in arbitration does not compromise
or alter the rights at issue.

As it has done throughout its rulings on arbitration, the Court anchors its determination in fealty
to legislative texts. By constructing a federal judicial policy on arbitration, the Court is giving effect

to the congressional directive in FAA § 2 to enforce arbitration contracts as written by the parties. In *14 Penn Plaza*, the Court is merely applying the provisions of the ADEA, which do not contain any bar to arbitrability. There is no "policy favoring arbitration" that explains the ruling. The "preferences" of individual Justices are irrelevant in the face of the governing statute's actual language. "This Court is not empowered to incorporate such a preference into the text of a federal statute.... It is for this reason, and not because of a "policy favoring arbitration" ... that the Court overturned *Wilko v. Swan....* And it is why we disavow the antiarbitration dicta of *Gardner-Denver* and its progeny today." "The timeworn 'mistrust of the arbitral process' harbored by the Court in *Gardner-Denver* thus weighs against reliance on anything more than its core holding." "*Gardner-Denver* is a direct descendant of the Court's decision in *Wilko v. Swan....*" In that sense, it is purveyor of opinions on arbitration that are untenable.

The *Gardner-Denver dicta* demeans the adjudicatory capabilities of arbitration and unnecessarily emphasizes the conflict of interest that could emerge from the union's collective responsibilities. By attributing a special status to civil rights and discrimination claims, *Gardner-Denver* suggests that arbitration may be an insufficient form of adjudication for some claims, rights, and legal issues. This "misconception," of course, is anathema to the emphatic (now formidable) federal policy on arbitration, which the majority reaffirms unequivocally. The Court, as a matter of law, has every confidence in the adjudicatory capability and professionalism of arbitration. Contrastive views expressed in *dicta* or in judicial reasoning are simply out-of-step with the controlling doctrine and, if found to have a decisive impact, illegal.

By the same token, concern about the union's influence in CBA arbitration is not a reason or justification for depreciating the value and role of arbitration. "Until Congress amends the ADEA to meet the conflict-of-interest concern identified in the *Gardner-Denver* dicta. . ., there is 'no reason to color the lens through which the arbitration clause is read' simply because of an alleged conflict of interest between a union and its members." "[T]his attribute of organized labor does not justify singling out an arbitration provision for disfavored treatment." Finally, "It was Congress' verdict that the benefits of organized labor outweigh the sacrifice of individual liberty that this system necessarily demands. Respondents' argument that they were deprived of the right to pursue their ADEA claims in federal court by a labor union with a conflict of interest is therefore unsustainable; it amounts to a collateral attack on the NLRA." Union members with this grievance can file suit on the basis that the union breached its duty of fair representation to older workers. The judicial policy favoring arbitration remains intact and is even more impervious to exceptions or limitations. Party agreement to arbitrate disputes is a fail-safe jurisdictional command no matter the parties, their relationship, or the issues in question.

An Assessment

The case law on employment arbitration also affects the use of arbitration in other areas. The overlap is particularly marked between employment and securities arbitration. In the latter, claims by stockbrokers or other brokerage employees that they have been mistreated or discriminated against on a gender or racial basis by fellow employees, supervisors, or the management of the firm (in violation of Title VII and the 1964 and 1991 Civil Rights Acts) can be classified as matters involving either securities or employment arbitration or both. Such cases nonetheless retain a primarily employment character by raising the question of the arbitrability of statutory workplace rights. In effect, arbitration is used to resolve workplace civil rights claims that happen to arise in the securities industry.

Two critical questions are repeatedly brought before the courts in employment arbitration cases. These questions essentially represent two sides of the same coin. First, are contract provisions providing for employment arbitration enforceable as arbitration agreements? Many, if not most, of these "agreements" are imposed unilaterally upon employees as a precondition to employment or continued employment. Their existence and content are generally non-negotiable, thereby bearing the essential characteristics of an adhesion contract—which, under the express language of FAA Section Two, could render them unenforceable as contracts.

Second, the rights an employee may seek to vindicate can be based upon federal statutory provisions. When the rights involved implicate the application and interpretation of federal statutes, are the employee's claims arbitrable? The public law character of these rights could make the claims unsuitable for private, non-judicial adjudication. Arbitration was intended to resolve disputes in the application and interpretation of contracts, not to provide the adjudicatory machinery for debating the implementation of civil liberty issues. Nonetheless, the rule that all types of statutory claims are arbitrable—even those involving guarantees of basic political rights—appears to be firmly established among the federal courts.

The processing of such claims through privatized adjudicators raises a host of concerns. Despite the judicial confidence in arbitration, at a basic level, should these cases, given their public law content, be adjudicated before public adjudicatory bodies? Can an employer validly require employees to waive their right to the judicial resolution of such claims? Is there any meaningful difference between a waiver of judicial relief and a waiver of rights? What does the arbitrability of statutory claims do to the legislative scheme? Is the arbitrability doctrine merely a device to achieve the ends of judicial management? Is civil liability solely a matter of private interest? In the opposite vein, are courts able to respond to these claims in any meaningful fashion? Does every case involve the integrity of the U.S. Constitution? Is private resolution not fully sufficient in the vast majority of cases? These concerns essentially restate the overt and underlying opposition between *Gilmer* and *Gardner-Denver*.

Costs

In *Cole v. Burns International Security Services*, 105 F.3d 1465 (D.C. Cir. 1997), a federal district court made the allocation of arbitration costs essential to the validity of an arbitration agreement in an employment relationship. The court reasoned that requiring employees to pay all or part of the arbitrators' fee would amount to a "*de facto* forfeiture of employee's statutory rights." In *Shankle v. B–G Maintenance Management of Colorado, Inc.*, 163 F.3d 1230 (10th Cir. 1999), the court ruled that an arbitration agreement was unenforceable when it functioned as a condition of employment or of continued employment and required the employee to pay an unaffordable amount for the costs of arbitration. As written, the agreement effectively deprived the employee of any remedy by barring access to the courts and by making the recourse to arbitration prohibitively expensive.

In a subsequent case, a federal district court in Colorado rendered a cost-sharing provision void but distinguished its case from *Shankle* and upheld the reference to arbitration in an employment discrimination case. Invoking the severance clause in the agreement, the court removed the cost-sharing clause from the agreement and enforced the remaining provisions. *See Fuller v. Pep Boys—Manny, Moe & Jack of Del., Inc.*, 88 F.Supp.2d 1158 (D. Colo. 2000). The district court held that *Shankle* did not render the fee-splitting provisions or payment-of-costs clauses void *ab initio*. Moreover, the severance clause (which had not been present in *Shankle*) allowed the reference to arbitration to take place despite the invalidity of the stipulation for cost-sharing. Given the policy in support of arbitration, voiding the entire agreement would have been too drastic a measure.

In late 2000, the United States Supreme Court rendered its decision in *Green Tree Financial Corp.-Alabama v. Randolph*, 531 U.S. 79 (2000). In its opinion, the Court—speaking through the late Chief Justice Rehnquist—addressed the impact of arbitral costs upon the validity of arbitration agreements. In contrast to the ruling in *Cole* and *Armendariz,* the Court held—in a divided segment of its opinion—that the fact that a consumer bears some of the costs of the arbitral process ''alone is plainly insufficient to render [the arbitration agreement] unenforceable.... To invalidate the agreement would undermine the 'liberal federal policy favoring arbitration agreements'...[and] would conflict with [this Court's holdings, for example,]...that the party resisting arbitration bears the burden of proving that Congress intended to preclude arbitration of the statutory claims at issue.... Thus, a party seeking to invalidate an arbitration agreement on the ground that arbitration would be prohibitively expensive bears the burden of showing the likelihood of incurring such costs. Randolph did not meet that burden.''

Subsequent lower court cases indicate that the *Green Tree* ruling has influenced the federal courts' approach to the assessment of costs upon the validity of arbitration agreements. For instance, the Fourth Circuit has held that a fee-splitting provision which divided the cost of arbitration between all parties did not *per se* render an arbitration agreement unenforceable. *See Bradford v. Rockwell Semiconductor Sys., Inc.*, 238 F.3d 549 (4th Cir. 2001). Determining whether such a provision had an impact upon the validity of the arbitration agreement required a case-by-case analysis that focused upon the claimants' ability to pay arbitration fees and costs.

At the end of its analysis, the court acknowledged that the federal circuits were divided on whether fee-splitting provisions were *per se* invalid. Both the Eleventh Circuit and the D.C. Circuit had concluded that ''fee-splitting provisions render arbitration agreements unenforceable because the cost of fee splitting deters or prevents employees from vindicating their statutory rights in arbitral forums.'' The First, Fifth, and Seventh Circuits, however, have refused to espouse that position. These courts prefer to assess the validity of fee-splitting provisions on a case-by-case basis.

By contrast, the Sixth Circuit, in *Morrison v. Circuit City Stores, Inc.*, 317 F.3d 646 (6th Cir.

2003), held that the cost-splitting provisions in two separate employment arbitration agreements were unenforceable. In so doing, the court articulated a new standard by which to address the cost issue when a case involved federal antidiscrimination statutes such as Title VII. The Sixth Circuit held that "potential litigants must be given an opportunity, prior to arbitration on the merits, to demonstrate that the potential costs of arbitration are great enough to deter them and similarly situated individuals from seeking to vindicate their federal statutory rights in the arbitral forum." In the court's view, the focus should be upon a group of similarly situated individuals, rather than solely upon the plaintiff, in order to further the federal anti-discrimination statutes' goal of deterring discrimination.

The Epitome of Unfairness

The Seventh Circuit ruled in *Penn v. Ryan's Family Steak Houses, Inc.*, 269 F.3d 753 (7th Cir. 2001), that an arbitration agreement entered into by an employee (at the behest of his employer) with an arbitration service-provider was unenforceable because it contained an illusory promise under state contract law. In the court's assessment, "[t]he contract [was]...hopelessly vague and uncertain as to the [service's] obligation.... For all practical purposes, [the service's] promise under this contract 'makes performance entirely optional with the promisor.' " The contract also lacked consideration and mutuality of obligation and was, therefore, un-enforceable.

Penn, the employee, was a waiter in the Ryan's chain and had been fired after a few years of employment. He alleged that he had been fired in "retaliation for his complaints about...harassment" in the workplace. He filed a lawsuit against Ryan's, claiming a violation of the Americans with Disabilities Act (ADA) to which Ryan's responded with a motion to compel arbitration. The facts of the case are an eloquent statement of the extraordinary lengths to which some business entities will go to deprive their lower-level employees of their basic legal rights. Ryan's entered into an agreement with Employment Dispute Services (EDS), a specialized arbitration service-provider. The purpose of the contract was "to have EDS provide an arbitration forum for all employment-related disputes between Ryan's and its employees." Ryan's then required its prospective employees to enter into a contract with EDS to use its services exclusively to resolve any employment disputes that arose with Ryan's. The contract language emphasized that the contracting parties were the employee and EDS; Ryan's was described as "a third-party beneficiary of the contract." The "triangulation" presumably would make it more difficult for employees to challenge the fairness of the employer's ADR practices.

EDS appeared to be an entrepreneurial outgrowth of the judicial rulings that have favored arbitration and, in particular, fostered the development of employment arbitration. The company attempted to create a niche for itself in the dispute resolution industry by providing arbitration services exclusively in the employment area. Employers were its clients, paying for EDS' professional services. Employees apparently paid no fees for arbitration.

Despite a testimonial of EDS' Chair and co-owner describing the company's services as fair and neutral, the district court concluded that the EDS system "was inherently biased against employees." Employers not only constituted EDS' sole revenue stream, but they were "repeat players" who were familiar with the process and the arbitrators and the system administrators. The court denied EDS' petition to compel arbitration partly on this basis.

The lower court also expressed concern about EDS' ability to control and manipulate the arbitration process, particularly with respect to arbitrator lists and the applicable institutional rules. It viewed with equal circumspection the process' limited right of discovery (allowing essentially only one deposition per side in the proceeding) when most employment cases are fact-sensitive. Finally, the district court believed that the employee had not "knowingly waived" his right to a court hearing.

The Seventh Circuit upheld the district court's basic conclusion that the arbitration contract Penn had signed was unenforceable, but had different reasons for its determination. Judge Diane Wood emphasized that her decision complied with the judicial policy that favors the recourse to arbitration.

The district court was mistaken in its unbalanced critique of the EDS arbitral system: "we are concerned that the district court placed too much weight on certain specifics of this system that, in and of themselves, do not distinguish it from many others that have passed muster...." The presumption in favor of the recourse to and adequacy of arbitration was very difficult, if not impossible, to rebut.

For Judge Wood, the issue did not center upon the merits of the EDS system, but rather upon the legal enforceability of the arbitration agreement between EDS and the employee, Penn. In her view, "Penn never entered into an enforceable contract to participate in [the EDS arbitral system]." The relationship between the appellate and district court approach in *Penn* was reminiscent of the litigation in *Rosenberg v. Merrill Lynch, Pierce, Fenner & Smith, Inc.* as well as *Hooters of America, Inc. v. Phillips. See generally Rosenberg v. Merrill Lynch, Pierce, Fenner & Smith, Inc.*, 995 F.Supp. 190 (D. Mass. 1998), *aff'd*, 170 F.3d 1 (1st Cir. 1999); *Hooters of Am., Inc. v. Phillips*, 173 F.3d 933 (4th Cir. 1999).

The court then embarked upon a well-crafted doctrinal explanation of why the arbitration agreement that Penn had signed with EDS was not an enforceable agreement under the state's governing contract law. The court concluded that there was a lack of mutuality of obligation between the parties, that EDS had agreed only to "an unascertainable, illusory promise," and that the contract lacked any basic detriment on EDS' part and was, therefore, devoid of consideration.

Judge Wood reached the right result, but did not challenge the basic components of the federal judicial doctrine on arbitration. Her approach, however, minimized one aspect of the litigation. She did not address the questionable character of Ryan's and EDS' behavior. By private action, they had undertaken to deny powerless people any possible access to justice. Judge Harlington Wood, Jr. refers to this in his concurring opinion:

> Penn was being hired as a waiter in a chain restaurant, not as a corporate executive. His employment was only to be "at will." Likely a substantial share of his income would be from tips. The agreement, the rules, the relationships between the parties, and the ramifications of the arbitration arrangement have now reached this court to sort out. Above his signature this agreement states that Penn signed it "knowingly and voluntarily." We doubt it could have been "knowingly" in view of its complexities, or even "voluntarily." Had he questioned its meaning and its complexities, it is doubtful Penn would have been hired. However, the agreement provided that Penn had the right to consult an attorney, but even if Penn could have afforded an attorney, the appearance of any attorney on the scene would

doubtless have foreclosed any job opportunity. In Ryan's eyes, Penn would look like a troublemaker. If he wanted the waiter's job, he would be trapped in an unfair situation until a court could unravel it.

There have been a number of Ryan's Family Steak House cases, all involving the provision of arbitration services by Employment Dispute Services, Inc. (EDSI). *Walker v. Ryan's Family Steak Houses, Inc.*, 400 F.3d 370 (6th Cir. 2005), is the latest opinion in this line of decisional law; it was resolved in keeping with the prior cases. When employees contract directly with the arbitration service-provider as a condition of employment or continued employment, the arbitration agreement is invalid and unenforceable. It lacks mutuality in the obligation to arbitrate; the employer, in effect, retains the right to bring disputes to court because it is not a party to the arbitration agreement, but rather its third-party beneficiary. The circumstances also exhibit structural bias in the arbitral process; arbitrator selection, for example, appears to disfavor the employees' interest. Such agreements breach a number of basic contractual requirements: Lack of consideration, structural bias in the contract formation and arbitral process, lack of neutrality in the contemplated arbitral forum, and pervasive and profound fundamental unfairness in the making of the contract and in the established arbitral forum and process.

CHAPTER EIGHT

THE ENFORCEMENT OF ARBITRAL AWARDS

Introduction

Once the arbitral tribunal renders an award and the administering arbitral institution delivers it to the arbitrating parties, a number of events can occur. The losing party can comply fully with the terms of the award—in which case no compulsory enforcement process is required. A party can file an action to modify or correct the award to rectify evident clerical mistakes. Also, when there is an alleged ambiguity or confusion, the court can remand an award to the arbitrators for clarification. In the absence of voluntary compliance, an action to confirm or vacate the award can be undertaken within the one-year time limit. The confirmation or vacatur of the award is the final step in the process of arbitral adjudication.

Federal court practice regarding the enforcement of domestic arbitral awards is in keeping with the dictates of the emphatic federal policy favoring arbitration. Most courts acknowledge a strong presumption in favor of enforcement. In fact, the presumption is so strong that it is nearly irrebuttable. It can be defeated only in exceptional circumstances of extreme procedural unfairness or arbitrator incompetence. As a consequence, the courts do not generally apply the FAA § 10 grounds for the judicial supervision of awards with any rigor. Vacatur will be ordered only if the arbitrators are corrupt, exceed their powers, or ignore the parties' fundamental adjudicatory rights or the material terms of the arbitration agreement.

A party opposing the enforcement of an arbitral award cannot use the confirmation proceedings to introduce new issues into the litigation by making counterclaims. The content of any counterclaims is restricted to the issue of confirmation itself. Three common law grounds supplement the statutory list: Enforcement can be denied if the award reflects a manifest disregard of the law, is arbitrary and capricious or irrational, or violates public policy. Somewhat paradoxically, the elaboration of additional grounds for review in the case law has not created a greater likelihood of vacatur. *See Advest, Inc. v. McCarthy*, 914 F.2d 6 (1st Cir. 1990).

The FAA does not govern matters of labor arbitration. The absence of a statutory regime to regulate the determinations reached in the labor arbitration process created a need for articulating standards that took into account the fact that labor arbitrators interpreted collective bargaining agreements and federal labor statutes. "Manifest disregard of the law," along with the two other common law grounds for review, achieved that objective. They created a basis upon which the courts could supervise the substantive rulings of labor arbitrators. The level of intended scrutiny, however, remained relatively unintrusive and superficial. The courts policed labor awards on the merits for gross deviations from and misunderstandings of the underlying labor contract or applicable statutory law on labor relations. *See, e.g., Eastern Assoc. Coal Corp. v. United Mine Workers of Am., Dist. 17,* 531 U.S. 57 (2000).

The courts, however, did not maintain a proper boundary between collective bargaining arbitration and FAA arbitration. They began to apply the grounds for reviewing labor awards indiscriminately to all arbitral awards. This practice created confusion about the intended purpose and function of the nonstatutory grounds for the supervision of arbitral awards. It, however, had little consequence upon the enforceability of awards except to increase the costs of the final phase of the process. The courts construed "manifest disregard" and the other nonstatutory grounds for review so narrowly that they generally had little impact upon the enforcement of awards. For example, "manifest disregard" existed when arbitrators deliberately ignored what they had determined to be the applicable law in the case. Also, the nonstatutory grounds began to converge in the case law with the statutory basis for review. "Manifest disregard," for instance, overlapped with "excess of arbitral authority," and courts sometimes referred to both grounds to express the same basis for supervision.

Finally, the common law grounds authorize the courts to review the merits of arbitral determinations. Judicial review of awards on the merits is not contemplated under FAA § 10; in fact, such a practice contradicts the gravamen of the legislation and the judicial policy that underpins it. While a scrutiny of the merits may be a necessary feature of labor arbitration, it is completely inapposite for regulating the enforcement of commercial awards. Moreover, from a practical perspective, the judicial scrutiny of the merits of commercial arbitration awards is difficult, if not impossible, to accomplish.

The commonplace practice (until recently) is for domestic arbitrators to render such awards without opinions. In addition, a verbatim transcript of the arbitral proceedings usually is not available. Further, the case law demonstrates that, when courts have given effect to challenges to the enforcement of awards on a common law basis, they simply have disagreed with the conclusions reached by or the reasoning of the arbitrators. These courts have been critical of the arbitrators' assessment of the record or their use or construction of a legal doctrine. This type of supervision infringes upon the arbitrators' decisional sovereignty.

Despite the incongruity in the enforcement framework, the general judicial practice is to uphold the results of the arbitral process no matter the ground for recourse, the nature of the complaints, or the substantive arbitral determination. Divisions, however, exist among the various federal circuits on some issues of doctrine: For example, whether a common law ground applies and, if so, what restraints it places upon the arbitral process. Moreover, in recent decisions, some courts have adopted a more exacting standard for arbitrator impartiality and, albeit to a lesser extent, for establishing conformity to the public policy requirement. By and large, however, clients in arbitration get finality and only "one bite at the apple."

The current enforcement regime is subject to another general criticism. The lodging of an action to vacate an award brings into play the discovery of the arbitral proceedings that resulted in the award. The defendant's objections to the award need to be supported by evidence as do the plaintiff's responses. These circumstances not only allow the losing party to compromise the arbitration's confidentiality, but also have the courts intrude upon the arbitrators' procedural and decisional mandate. Further, such a procedure makes the award more expensive to secure and may result in discounting the defendant's liability by pressuring an exchange of immediate recovery for desisting from challenge. These aspects of the action for vacatur should result in a reconsideration of the procedure for enforcement. One solution may be to provide automatic judicial enforcement of arbitral awards. Another approach may be to limit court scrutiny to a facial examination of the basic documents. Under current law, any extensive rehearsing of the arbitral proceedings before the court of enforcement, in effect, constitutes a breach of the federal policy favoring the unobstructed recourse to arbitration.

It should also be noted that the practice of reviewing awards on the merits through the common law grounds may have a new use in the law of arbitration. The expansion of arbitral jurisdiction to include statutory claims may have created a need for merits review in statutory arbitrations as well as in collective bargaining arbitration. Arbitrator rulings in employment and consumer arbitration that implicate statutory rights should be underscored in the award and accompanied by reasons and then subject to some level of review by the courts (or by a second arbitral tribunal) for the benefit of the public interest.

Finally, there are questions about what sort of judicial authority and process take place at the award enforcement stage. Are the courts, that are requested to confirm or vacate an arbitral award, asked to supervise the process or review the determination or both? How are these standards of review distinguished from one another? Which one is more apposite in the arbitral context? What evidentiary standards should apply at this stage of the proceedings for lodging motions? Must the party opposing enforcement buttress allegations by convincing evidence or simply by a preponderance of the available evidence? The existing practice is to sublimate these considerations in a perfunctory standard of review that yields a positive enforcement result in the overwhelming majority of cases.

The incongruity of that practice—not its conclusions—should be revisited and altered.

The Basic Policy

Judicial deference in the circumstances of enforcement is linked to maintaining the functionality of arbitration as a mechanism for dispute resolution. In *Fine v. Bear, Stearns & Co., Inc.*, 765 F.Supp. 824, 827 (S.D.N.Y. 1991), the court stated: "It is well-settled that a court's power to vacate an arbitration award must be extremely limited because an overly expansive judicial review of arbitration awards would undermine the litigation efficiencies which arbitration seeks to achieve...." The court in *Remmey v. PaineWebber, Inc.*, 32 F.3d 143 (4th Cir. 1994), *cert. denied*, 513 U.S. 1112 (1995), provided a more extensive description of the general approach and its rationale:

We must underscore at the outset the limited scope of review that courts are permitted to exercise over arbitral decisions. Limited judicial review is necessary to encourage the use of arbitration as an alternative to formal litigation. This policy is widely recognized, and the Supreme Court has often found occasion to approve it....

A policy favoring arbitration would mean little, of course, if arbitration were merely the prologue to prolonged litigation. If such were the case, one would hardly achieve the "twin goals of arbitration, namely, settling disputes efficiently and avoiding long and expensive litigation." ...Opening up arbitral awards to myriad legal challenges would eventually reduce arbitral proceedings to the status of preliminary hearings. Parties would cease to utilize a process that no longer had finality. To avoid this result, courts have resisted temptations to redo arbitral decisions. As the Seventh Circuit put it, "[a]rbitrators do not act as junior varsity trial courts where subsequent appellate review is readily available to the losing party."...

Thus, in reviewing arbitral awards, a district or appellate court is limited to determining " 'whether the arbitrators did the job they were told to do—not whether they did it well, or correctly, or reasonably, but simply whether they did it.' " ...Courts are not free to overturn an arbitral result because they would have reached a different conclusion if presented with the same facts....

Despite the adoption of a straightforward unitary standard, the enforcement process for awards also evidences an increasing sophistication and complication. In *Green v. Ameritech Corp.*, 200 F.3d 967 (6th Cir. 2000), the Sixth Circuit upheld an arbitral award despite claims that it did not satisfy the requirements established by the arbitration agreement. According to the plaintiffs, the arbitral award failed to set forth a full explanation as to each theory of the complaint as required by the arbitration agreement.

The parties proceeded to arbitration on a set of discrimination claims. All of the plaintiffs, except

Green, settled within a few days. After the arbitral hearing, Green and Ameritech filed post-arbitration briefs. The arbitrator indicated that he hoped to meet with counsel for each party separately and that he wanted the parties to settle. The parties did not settle. The arbitrator never rendered an award and did not contact the parties for almost a year. At the end of the year, Green filed a motion to replace the arbitrator or to reinstate the case in federal court, arguing that the arbitrator's failure to rule breached the submission agreement.

Before the district court ruled on the motion, the arbitrator rendered an award in favor of Ameritech. The award described the plaintiff's claims, provided an account of the allegations of discrimination, and reached conclusions on each claim. The arbitrator asserted that the plaintiff had not met his burden of proof under any of his three theories of recovery. Green filed an action to vacate the arbitral award because it failed to follow the parties' agreement, was untimely, and in excess of the arbitrator's authority. In particular, the award failed to adhere to the contractual requirement for an explanation of the decision.

The district court vacated the award for excess of the arbitrator's authority because the arbitrator did not provide an explanation for the results as required by the arbitration agreement. The appellate court disagreed. The Sixth Circuit emphasized the precise character of the agreement's requirement as to the award. The agreement provided that the award "explain[] the arbitrator's decision with respect to each theory advanced by each Plaintiff." Because the language was so general, the court reasoned that it was "left with little guidance as to how to determine whether the arbitrator explained his decision so as to meet the requirements of the agreement."

Ruling that the plaintiff failed to meet his burden of proof, the court concluded that the arbitrator had "explained" the result in the award. "If parties to an arbitration agreement wish a more detailed arbitral opinion, they should clearly state in the agreement the degree of specificity required. In addition, the use of familiar legal terms would serve to ensure that reviewing courts have a standard to guide their analysis." The parties needed to state with greater clarity and definiteness their desire to have a formal judicial discussion of the facts and law by employing terms like "conclusions of law" and "finding of facts." That terminology would require the arbitrator to set forth the record and explain systematically the application of the law to the stated facts.

Errors made as to the application of law and the assessment of the record generally are not a proper basis for the vacatur of arbitral awards. *See Rodriguez v. Prudential–Bache Sec., Inc.,* 882 F.Supp. 1202, 1207 (D. P.R. 1995) (*quoting Advest, Inc. v. McCarthy,* 914 F.2d 6, 8 [1st Cir. 1990]). According to one court,

> The statute does not allow courts to roam unbridled in their oversight of arbitral awards.... The statute contains no express ground upon which an award can be overturned because it rests on garden variety factual or legal bevues.... Even where [the factual or legal] error [by an arbitrator] is painfully clear, courts are not authorized to reconsider the merits of arbitration awards.

In an early case, the Second Circuit asserted that vacatur on a common law basis could only take place if at least one of the statutory grounds had been violated. The party opposing enforcement had the burden of establishing the basis for objecting to the award. *See Barbier v. Shearson Lehman Hutton, Inc.,* 948 F.2d 117, 120 (2d Cir. 1991).

Some federal circuits recognize all three grounds, while other circuits adopt only one or two of the common law grounds. Some circuit courts fashion special rules of application for the statutory and common law grounds. For example, the basis of review can vary if the award contains a reasoned opinion. Providing reasons for the ruling gives the supervising court a record to review. It may be more advantageous to enforcement to prohibit arbitrators from rendering an opinion with the award. While such a practice would limit judicial supervision, it creates an incentive for arbitrators to rule without giving an explanation of their determination, a feature of arbitral adjudication that may or may not be desirable.

Public Policy

The public policy exception to the enforcement of arbitral awards, like the other common law grounds for vacatur, was elaborated in the context of labor arbitration. *United Paperworkers International Union, AFL–CIO v. Misco, Inc.*, 484 U.S. 29 (1987), is the landmark case. The *Misco* doctrine was recently reaffirmed by the U.S. Supreme Court in *Eastern Associated Coal Corp. v. United Mine Workers of America, District 17*, 531 U.S. 57 (2000). In *Misco*, "The United States Supreme Court has made clear that a court's refusal to enforce an arbitrator's interpretation of a contract is limited to situations where the contract as interpreted would violate some explicit public policy that is well defined and dominant, and is to be ascertained by reference to the law and legal precedents, and not from general considerations of supposed public interests." The ruling in *Misco* further established that "a broad judicial power to set aside arbitration awards as against public policy" did not exist.

Misco involved a labor arbitration, but its holding has been generalized, like the public policy exception itself, to cover all forms of arbitration (labor, maritime, commercial, trade-sector, and consumer). *Misco* provided that the public policy exception could not be applied lightly or on the basis of some diffuse judicial notion of the exigencies associated with the public interest. Although this interpretation was not expressly confirmed by the *Misco* formulation, the public policy exception, it seems, must emanate from and be embedded in a statute and articulated in express statutory language. Vacatur of the award would require the arbitrator to ignore conduct that specifically contravened a well-defined and identifiable congressional mandate expressed in a federal statute. Not surprisingly, attesting to the labor specificity of the common law ground, the examples used by the court to illustrate the application of public policy to the enforcement of awards are drawn from the circumstances of labor arbitrations. They involve arbitrator reinstatement of employees despite a legal prohibition to the contrary (*e.g.*, reinstating a pilot who had piloted airplanes while intoxicated).

Be that as it may, the public policy exception, like the other common law grounds, appears difficult to establish. There is no "broad judicial power to set aside arbitration awards as against public policy" and it seems that the courts afford arbitrators every benefit of the doubt. *See Brown v. Rauscher Pierce Refsnes, Inc.*, 994 F.2d 775 (11th Cir. 1993). Nonetheless, the practice has its dangers. It invites greater judicial scrutiny that might not always result in a superficial examination of awards. Some courts have used the public policy exception ingeniously and amalgamated the public policy underlying several statutes into a new public policy hybrid. Addressing whether the arbitral reinstatement of an employee with alcohol abuse problems to a "safety-sensitive" position was binding, the court in *Exxon Shipping Co. v. Exxon Seamen's Union*, 11 F.3d 1189 (3d Cir. 1993), examined the Clean Water Act, the Oil Pollution Act, and various coast guard regulations. Thereafter, the court stated, "While we are aware of no statute or regulation that directly prohibits the owner or operator of an oil tanker from continuing to employ a crew member who is found to be intoxicated on duty, there can be no doubt that the statutes and regulations we have noted convey the unequivocal message that such an owner or operator should take every practicable step to ensure that an intoxicated crew member does not cause or contribute to an oil spill."

Clearly violating the *Misco* directive, the court held:

Accordingly, based...on the statutes, regulations, and expressions of congressional policy previously noted, we conclude that there is a well-defined and dominant policy that owners and operators of oil tankers should be permitted to discharge crew members who are found to be intoxicated while on duty. An intoxicated crew member on such a vessel can cause loss of life and catastrophic environmental and economic injury. Some of this injury may not be reparable by money damages. Moreover, because of limitations on liability under the Clean Water Act and the Oil Pollution Act, it is entirely possible that much of the cost resulting from a major oil spill may fall on taxpayers and those who are injured by the accident. While the federal labor laws undoubtedly embody a strong policy favoring the settlement of labor disputes by arbitration, that policy must yield in the present context to the public policy favoring measures designed to avert potentially catastrophic oil spills. In *Exxon Shipping I*, we held that this policy precluded the reinstatement of a seaman who tested positive for marijuana. Consistency with this precedent dictates a similar result here.

The appellate opinion in *Westvaco Corp. v. United Paperworkers International Union, AFL–CIO*, 171 F.3d 971 (4th Cir. 1999), demonstrates a more ordinary application of the public policy exception. The Fourth Circuit recognized that "the very purpose of arbitration procedures is to provide a mechanism for the expeditious settlement of industrial disputes without resort to strikes, lockouts, or other self-help measures." Additionally, "labor-management relations law 'reflects a decided preference for private settlement of labor disputes without the intervention of government'.... [E]ffective arbitration serves as 'the means of solving the unforeseeable by molding a system of private law for all the problems which may arise and to provide for their solution in a way which will generally accord with the variant needs and desires of the parties.'" Courts have recognized that arbitration "must be final to be effective.... Permitting judicial second-guessing of arbitral awards 'would transform a binding process into a purely advisory one, and ultimately impair the value of arbitration for labor and management alike.... Absent the most unusual of circumstances, courts must uphold and enforce arbitral awards.'"

The court rejected Westvaco's argument that reinstatement violated public policy by hindering

Westvaco's ability to remedy sexual harassment in the workplace. "All of the protections of a labor arbitration process would go for naught if they could be undone by a broad and amorphous public policy exception." There is no "broad judicial power to set aside arbitration awards as against public policy.... If the contract as interpreted by [the arbitrator] violates some explicit public policy, [the court is] obliged to refrain from enforcing it. Such a public policy, however, must be well-defined and dominant, and is to be ascertained by reference to the laws and legal precedents and not from general considerations of supposed public interests."

In *Eastern Associated Coal Corp.*, the United States Supreme Court affirmed the authority of arbitration and of arbitrators in the collective bargaining dispute resolution context. In particular, the Court confirmed the vigor of the doctrine it established in *Misco*, namely, that an arbitral award could be vacated on a public policy basis only if it violated an "explicit, well-defined, and dominant" public policy. Such a public policy is to be "ascertained by reference to the laws and legal precedents and not from general considerations of supposed public interests." In other words, vacated awards must contravene an express statutory provision that is identified by the legislature as having a public policy character.

Manifest Disregard of the Law

This is perhaps the best known of the three common law grounds for the vacatur of arbitral awards. It is invoked with greater frequency than the other grounds to challenge the enforcement of awards and reflects a party's disagreement with the arbitrator's application of the law. It also has generated a great deal of debate about its meaning. As with its companion grounds, a precise definition of manifest disregard of the law remains elusive. The courts have not settled upon a clear meaning because to do so would encourage the vacatur of awards and undermine the federal policy in favor of arbitration. The ground has a clear mission in labor arbitration determinations. It requires them to comply with the governing collective bargaining agreement. Manifest disregard was first noticed in *Wilko v. Swan*, 346 U.S. 427 (1953), a case involving the arbitrability of security act claims. Like the other grounds for vacatur, it overlaps with other nonstatutory bases for review. It is then simultaneously elusive, narrow, and redundant. Finally, it may develop a new role in the supervision of awards as arbitrators address a greater number of statutory claims. The possibility assumes that arbitrators will commit their reasoning and determinations to writing.

The standard view is that there is manifest disregard of the law when the arbitrator recognizes the applicable law but ignores it in deciding the case. *See Merrill Lynch, Pierce, Fenner & Smith, Inc. v. Bobker*, 808 F.2d 930 (2d Cir. 1986). The elements of the ground make it difficult to invoke: (1) there must be a record, and (2) that record must indicate clearly that the arbitrator (a) recognized the law, and (b) disregarded it in reaching a determination. None of these elements is readily established in the arbitral context. The award may not be accompanied by an opinion and usually there is no transcript of the proceedings. Few arbitrators are likely to provide a written statement of the applicable law and then reach a determination that completely ignores it as a guiding principle. Commercial arbitrators may describe the law or apply it in a judicially erroneous manner, but they are not likely to dismiss it once it has been presented and argued, unless they are authorized by the parties to rule as amiable compositors. Outside the context of labor or maritime arbitration, "manifest disregard" appears to be misplaced and to have no real function.

One court has stated that manifest disregard can only occur when the arbitrator's error was "capable of being readily and instantly perceived by the average person qualified to serve as an arbitrator." *See Fine v. Bear, Stearns & Co., Inc.*, 765 F.Supp. 824, 827 (S.D.N.Y. 1991). The integration of a reasonable arbitrator standard makes an already complicated determination even more complex. It also makes an already nebulous concept even more difficult to grasp. The supplemental language does not clarify the concept, but rather proposes another tortured and emblematic definition of it. At least, the determination is made by reference to arbitral practice, not judicial standards.

The Seventh Circuit provided the most critical yet persuasive assessment of manifest disregard of the law:

Th[e] formula is dictum, as no one has found a case where, had it not been intoned, the result would have been different. It originated in *Wilko v. Swan*,...a case the Supreme Court first criticized for mistrust of arbitration and confined to its narrowest possible holding...and then overruled.... Created *ex nihilo* to be a nonstatutory ground for setting aside arbitral awards, the *Wilko* formula reflects precisely that mistrust of arbitration for which the Court in its two *Shearson/American* opinions criticized *Wilko*. We can understand neither the need for the formula nor the role that it plays in judicial review of arbitration (we suspect none—that it is just words). If it is meant to smuggle review for clear error in by the back door, it is inconsistent with the entire modern law of arbitration. If it is intended to be synonymous with the statutory formula that it most nearly resembles—whether the arbitrators "exceeded their powers"—it is superfluous and confusing.

Baravati v. Josephthal, Lyon & Ross, Inc., 28 F.3d 704, 706 (7th Cir. 1994) (citations omitted).

The Second Circuit recently vacated an arbitral award on the basis that the arbitrators presumptively disregarded the law or the evidence presented or both. In *Halligan v. Piper Jaffray, Inc.*, 148 F.3d 197 (2d Cir. 1998), *cert. denied*, 526 U.S. 1034 (1999), a salesman of equity investments submitted his ADEA and other claims against his employer, Piper Jaffray, Inc., to arbitration as required by the

NASD U–4 Registration Form. During the arbitration, Halligan presented evidence and testimonials of instances of age-based discrimination he allegedly suffered.

Halligan testified that the new senior management at Piper often made discriminatory comments based on his age prior to his resignation. Halligan's view that he was forced out of the firm because of his age was buttressed by notes he took after his discussions with senior management and by the testimony of other Piper employees. Halligan stated that he was unable to find employment after he left Piper in 1992. Since 1990, Halligan suffered from oral cancer and underwent several surgeries for the condition. He passed away while the arbitration was pending.

In response to these allegations, Piper asserted that Halligan had chosen to retire from the firm. Moreover, Piper management questioned the quality of Halligan's performance as a salesman, arguing that his accounts had a large built-in potential and that other Piper employees contributed substantially to Halligan's success. Piper management also criticized Halligan's ability to develop new accounts and to use firm research. In effect, Piper contended that Halligan had taken the "option" of retirement because of his poor performance and health problems.

The arbitral tribunal rendered an award that rejected Halligan's claims. The award restated the parties' allegations and arguments and contained the arbitrators' determination, but it did not provide any explanation or reasons for the result reached by the tribunal. The district court confirmed the award, concluding that there was "factual as well as legal support for the Panel's ultimate conclusion" and rejecting arguments that the arbitrators had "manifestly disregarded the law." The district court also noted that evaluating evidence for possible indications of discrimination was a not easy and that "[c]rediting [the testimony of] one witness over another does not constitute manifest disregard of the law...." Finally, subscribing to the basic judicial position in matters of enforcement, the court stated that its "role is not to second-guess the fact-finding done by the Panel."

On appeal, the Second Circuit emphasized that "mandatory pre-dispute arbitration agreements [that] resolve statutory claims of employment discrimination ... ha[ve] caused increased controversy [and] engendered greater [judicial] scrutiny...." According to the court, greater recourse to arbitration to resolve Title VII claims apparently modified the standard law governing arbitration. Courts and organizations were creating new means of protecting statutory rights within the arbitral process. In *Halligan,* the Second Circuit joined these efforts by articulating a new interpretation and definition of the "manifest disregard" standard.

The court found that the arbitrators were presented with convincing evidence of age discrimination and were correctly informed by the parties of the applicable legal standards. Because they did not reach a result that the court believed was commanded by the record, the court concluded "that [the arbitrators] ignored the law or the evidence or both." Moreover, the failure of the arbitrators to include reasons with the award also appeared to be fatal to the enforceability of the award. The court recognized that arbitrators were not legally compelled to provide reasoned determinations. It nonetheless stated that the holding in *Gilmer* regarding the arbitrability of statutory rights imperiled the continued viability of that practice in employment discrimination cases. The Second Circuit concluded that it was "left with the firm belief that the arbitrators here manifestly disregarded the law or the evidence or both."

As a result of the reasoning in *Halligan*, the "manifest disregard" standard now appears to be more flexible (at least, in employment discrimination cases) and to include a new element, *i.e.*, possible disregard of the evidence presented during the proceedings. Moreover, it seems that arbitrators ruling in Title VII employment discrimination cases should include reasons with their award whenever they hold against the plaintiff. The absence of reasons, it seems, creates a presumption of bias on the part of the arbitrators and of the misapplication of the law or misassessment of the record. The articulation of reasons by the tribunal, it appears, would have the effect of confirming what the court believes to be arbitrator bias, misapplication, and misassessment.

In *Wallace v. Buttar*, 378 F.3d 182 (2d Cir. 2004), the Second Circuit held that arbitral awards could not be vacated for "manifest disregard of the evidence." The latter standard appeared as *dicta* in *Halligan* and was not a recognized ground for vacatur in the circuit. "To the extent that a federal court may look upon the evidentiary record ... at all, it may do so *only* for the purpose of discerning whether a colorable basis exists for the panel's award so as to assure that the award cannot be said to be the result of the panel's manifest disregard of the law."

The recent United States Supreme Court ruling in *Hall Street Associates, LLC v. Mattel*, 128 S.Ct. 1396 (2008), has generated even more uncertainty and, therefore, debate about manifest disregard. On the one hand, the majority opinion proclaimed the statutory grounds for vacatur to be "exclusive," but it then described the common law grounds perhaps under state law or state law itself as an example of alternative recourse to the FAA setting. The ambivalent ruling has led courts to reach contradistinctive conclusions. For example, several courts asserted that *Hall Street Associates, LLC* eliminated manifest disregard as a basis for the supervision of awards, while an equal number of other courts see it as unaffected by the ruling. For the latter, it remains a viable basis for the vacatur of awards.

Excess of Arbitral Authority

It is well-settled that excess of arbitral authority refers to circumstances in which the arbitrators rule on matters not submitted. They have no authority to rule on disputes that have not been placed before them. Rulings on matters not submitted can be severed from the other parts of the award and the validly decided parts of the award can be enforced. In theory, excess of arbitral authority can cover a multitude of would-be sins— from overbearing procedural decisions to manifest disregard of the law. The overlap between the various types of infractions is considerable and undercuts the specificity of any particular ground. This and other problems hardly have much practical significance because so few awards are opposed on this basis and even fewer are vacated. Moreover, the professionalism of arbitrators generally leads to an avoidance of mistakes on the basis of excess. The aggressive judicial pursuit of infringements by arbitrators of their jurisdictional mandate would overly adversarialize the reference to arbitration.

Even though it is part of the FAA, the use of excess of authority has a special function in labor arbitration. There, arbitrator misconstruction of or addition to the collective bargaining agreement can constitute excess of authority. In *Major League Baseball Players Ass'n v. Garvey*, 532 U.S. 504 (2001), the United States Supreme Court stated that "[c]ourts are not authorized to review the arbitrator's decision on the merits despite allegations that the decision rests on factual errors or misinterprets the parties' agreement." The Court noted that the prevailing decisional law regarding the judicial review of labor arbitration decisions makes clear that such review is very limited. The Court reiterated its recent holding that, if an arbitrator is even arguably construing or applying the contract and acting within the scope of his authority, the fact that a court is convinced he committed serious error does not suffice to overturn the decision. Only when the arbitrator strays from the interpretation and application of the agreement and effectively "dispense[s] his own brand on industrial justice" does his decision become unenforceable.

The increasing recourse to arbitration—whether through adhesion or voluntary agreement—has resulted in greater formalization and sophistication of the process. Some parties have sought to integrate features of judicial litigation into arbitral procedure in order to secure certain rights in the arbitral trial. The integration of these mechanisms are often intended to limit the arbitrator's discretion and to avoid the arbitrary exercise of power.

One of the emerging limitations is to require that the arbitrator render reasons with the award. There is some question about what such a requirement entails. Does it require the arbitrator to write a judicial opinion as if s/he were a judge? Is there a prototypical judicial opinion? How much analytical detail and intellectual sophistication are requisite? What sanction should apply if the arbitrator fails to give reasons or provides only modest, even elementary reasoning? The case law needs to address these issues as they arise and arbitration agreements should supply reasonably precise instructions as to this feature of the arbitral process.

Arbitrator Misconduct

Arbitrator misconduct sufficient to cause the vacatur of an arbitral award is difficult to establish. The arbitrators are sovereign in the conduct of the arbitral proceedings; their procedural decisions, therefore, are basically unassailable. Denying a request for discovery does not constitute procedural misconduct. Fundamental fairness in arbitration consists of "notice, an opportunity to present relevant and material evidence and arguments to the arbitrators, and an absence of bias on the part of the arbitrators." *See Nationwide Mutual Ins. Co. v. The Home Ins. Co.*, 278 F.3d 621 (6th Cir. 2002).

The exclusion of relevant evidence must be truly prejudicial; it must "so affect [ ] the rights of a party that it might be said that he was deprived of a fair hearing." Even the failure to render a timely award does not constitute actionable misconduct: If the parties failed to make "time of the essence" in their arbitration agreement, a delay in rendering the award could not subject a party to the "harsh penalty of forfeiture or rescission" of the arbitral award. *See Hasbro, Inc. v. Catalyst USA, Inc.*, 367 F.3d 689 (7th Cir. 2004).

City of Bridgeport v. Kasper Group, Inc., 899 A.2d 523 (Conn. 2006), involves elaborate factual circumstances, the interplay between criminal and arbitral proceedings, and an aggressive judicial ruling on an arbitrator's decision on evidentiary matters. It is the type of judicial disposition and result that could eventually impair the independence and autonomy of arbitration. Fortunately, it is a case that can be readily confined to its exceptional circumstances and deemed an anomaly. If not, it should be subject to preemption under FAA § 2 because it clearly contravenes the parties' agreement to have recourse to arbitration.

The Kasper Group was awarded a contract by the City of Bridgeport to build an elementary school. The city apparently never signed the contract. Two years later, it informed Kasper that it was retracting the contract and beginning the submission process for proposals all over again. The parties filed various court actions, but they eventually agreed to submit their disputes to arbitration. The arbitration became entangled with criminal proceedings when the majority shareholder of Kasper entered into a plea agreement with the U.S. Attorney. In the plea agreement, he admitted to having engaged in a scheme of bribes and kickbacks with the mayor. The city sought to have the shareholder testify in the arbitration and to introduce evidence from the ongoing criminal trial against the mayor. The arbitrator ruled against the city's motions to link the arbitration to the criminal proceeding. The arbitrator did not want to delay the arbitration. The arbitrator eventually rendered an unreasoned award in favor of Kasper.

Lower courts concluded that the arbitrator's ruling prejudiced the city's right to a fair hearing. In reviewing the vacatur determinations, the Connecticut state Supreme Court recognized the need to minimize judicial intervention in arbitration and that arbitrators possessed "substantial discretion" with regard to the admissibility of evidence. Moreover, the moving party bore the burden of proof to establish prejudice. The court nonetheless concluded that the exclusion of the transcript of the testimony at the criminal trial made it more likely the arbitrator would find that the construction contract was procured illegally. The court concluded that the city was substantially prejudiced because the evidence "was highly probative and very likely would have altered the outcome of the arbitration had it been introduced." It affirmed vacatur.

The result may have been influenced by the public impact of the case and political circumstances. It may have been untenable for the court to reach any other conclusion. Nonetheless, it is clear that the judicial determination intruded upon the sovereignty of the arbitrator's procedural authority and the autonomy of the arbitral process. The matter at issue represented a disagreement between the court and the arbitrator on the admissibility of evidence. Unless the arbitrator was himself corrupt or legally incapacitated, his determination should have prevailed. The ruling, therefore, violates the essential protocol between the courts and the arbitral process.

Finally, the Seventh Circuit articulated the generally applicable standard on this question. It upheld an arbitration award when the lack of evidence was the sole basis for challenging the award. The court explained that the FAA limits judicial review to improper arbitrator conduct enumerated in the FAA or that is violative of the parties' agreement.

In *Wise v. Wachovia Sec., LLC*, 450 F.3d 265 (7th Cir. 2006), the Wises were Wachovia clients who had agreed to arbitrate any dispute arising from their dealings with the firm. Months later, the Wises alleged that Wachovia was responsible for fraud when their investment advisor took their money through a sham investment. During arbitration, Wachovia moved for summary judgment without submitting any evidence and the arbitrators granted the motion without explanation.

On appeal, the Wises argued that the award must be vacated because "there was not even an atom of evidence to support summary judgment for Wachovia." After reciting the grounds for vacating an award under the FAA, the court concluded that the absence of evidence did not trigger any of those grounds. Noting the Seventh Circuit's narrow definition of "manifest disregard of the law," the court explained:

It is tempting to think that courts are engaged in judicial review of arbitration awards under the [FAA], but they are not. When parties agree to arbitrate their disputes they opt out of the court system, and when one of them challenges the resulting arbitration award he per force does so not on the ground that the arbitrators made a mistake but that they violated the agreement to arbitrate, as by corruption, evident partiality, exceeding their powers, etc.—conduct to which the parties did not consent when they included an arbitration clause in their contract.

The case law illustrates the difficulty of challenging the enforcement of an arbitral award on the statutory basis that the arbitrators engaged in "misconduct" in their handling of the proceedings. The courts are reluctant to find procedural irregularities because informality is one of the hallmarks of arbitration and part of the bargain for arbitration. To require conformity to the requirements of the judicial trial would not only undermine arbitration's systemic autonomy, but also rewrite the arbitration contract *post facto* and impose unrealistic demands upon the arbitral process.

Arbitrators have substantial authority to conduct the arbitral proceedings. They have broad discretion to grant adjournments and to hear witnesses and to undertake the making of a record. They are not bound to gather all of the possible evidence, but they can entertain evidence that would not be admissible in court. Their procedural decisions, however, cannot prejudice a party's right to a fair trial.

In *Gruntal & Co., L.L.C. v. Maharaj*, 13 F.Supp.2d 566 (S.D.N.Y. 1998), the Maharajs alleged that their broker made excessive, unauthorized, and unsuitable trades on their account. The parties submitted the dispute to a National Association of Securities Dealers, Inc. (NASD) arbitral tribunal. Gruntal demanded thirty-nine categories of documents and information from the Maharajs. They refused to provide most of the documents.

Gruntal petitioned the arbitral tribunal to compel discovery and to grant a three-month adjournment. In response, the tribunal directed the Maharajs to produce the requested information, adding that a noncompliance would result in barring the information later. In addition, Gruntal could draw negative inferences about the unrevealed information. The tribunal, however, refused to grant the requested adjournment.

Arguing that the information was potentially exculpatory on its behalf, Gruntal asked the tribunal to reconsider its request for adjournment. The tribunal agreed to postpone the hearing for a week. Gruntal then filed an action before the U.S. District Court for the Southern District of New York, seeking to stay the arbitral proceedings. The court dismissed the motion, stating that it lacked authority to hear "an interlocutory appeal of a non-final, case-management order of an NASD arbitration panel." Gruntal had failed to show the irreparable harm necessary for injunctive relief.

Gruntal argued that FAA § 10(a)(3) and the case law gave a district court the authority to entertain an interlocutory application to stay an arbitral proceeding on the ground that adjournment was unreasonably denied. Assessing the precedent to apply at the vacatur stage of the process, the court reasoned that judicial action and authority should seek to preserve the expedition and efficiency of arbitration. It stated that "[u]ndue judicial intervention would inevitably judicialize the arbitration process." Finally, the court found that § 10(a)(3) afforded Gruntal adequate post-award relief for any injury caused by the arbitral tribunal's refusal to grant the adjournment.

Similarly, in *Shamah v. Schweiger*, 21 F.Supp.2d 208 (E.D.N.Y. 1998), Shamah, a broker, sought to vacate an arbitral award. During the arbitral proceeding, Shamah's attorney withdrew from representation and requested a six-month adjournment. Shamah was allegedly in financial distress and could not retain new counsel. When the arbitral tribunal refused to adjourn the proceedings, Shamah informed the NASD he would testify over the telephone. The tribunal rejected the request. The hearing was held in Shamah's absence.

The three-member arbitral tribunal unanimously awarded Schweiger, the investor-client, compensatory and consequential damages as well as prejudgment interest for the litany of complaints against Shamah (including breach of the brokerage agreement, breach of fiduciary duty, misappropriation and conversation of funds, misrepresentation, and negligence). The tribunal also awarded Schweiger punitive damages because of Shamah's egregious willful and malicious conduct. Further, Shamah was assessed costs for the arbitration.

In his motion to vacate the arbitral award, Shamah made the following allegations: (1) the arbitral tribunal engaged in misconduct by refusing to grant a six-month adjournment; and (2) notice of the proceedings was not properly served pursuant to CPLR § 7506. The court deferred to the findings of the arbitral tribunal. It stated that adjournment was within the appointed arbitrators' discretionary powers and did not amount to misconduct under FAA § 10(a)(3). The court found that Shamah had received due notice but simply failed to appear. Under the NASD Code of Arbitration Procedure, Section 10318, if any party fails to appear after due notice, the arbitral tribunal shall render all awards as if each party had entered an appearance in the proceeding. The court also rejected the argument that punitive damages were improper. The court confirmed the arbitral award and denied motions for vacatur or modification.

Evident Partiality

At first blush, the ground of evident partiality appears to be as narrow and restrictive as the other grounds for vacatur. It, too, is applied with due regard for the federal policy favoring arbitration. For example, in *Austin South I, Ltd. v. Barton–Malow Co.*, 799 F.Supp. 1135, 1142 (M.D. Fla. 1992), the court ruled that:

> A trivial relationship does not create the appearance of impropriety necessary to violate 9 U.S.C. § 10(b); there must be a substantial relationship between the arbitrator and a party in order to establish 'evident partiality' under the statute. . . .

"Evident partiality" exists "where a reasonable person would have to conclude that an arbitrator was partial to one party to the arbitration"; a mere "appearance of bias" is insufficient to vacate an arbitration award. . . .

The burden of demonstrating facts which would establish a reasonable impression of partiality is on the party challenging the award. . . . The possibility of bias must be "direct, definite, and capable of demonstration rather than remote, uncertain and speculative." . . .

The ground of "evident partiality," however, can be much more rigorous and demanding. Referring to the United States Supreme Court's landmark opinion in *Commonwealth Coatings Corp. v. Continental Casualty Co.*, 393 U.S. 145 (1968), the courts have defined "evident partiality" to include situations in which there is no "actual bias," but where the arbitrators' failure to disclose information creates an "appearance of bias."

More recently, the Texas state Supreme Court followed the exacting standard established in *Commonwealth Coatings* but applied it to a neutral arbitrator. It held in *Burlington Northern Railroad Co. v. TUCO, Inc.*, 960 S.W.2d 629 (Tex. 1997), that a neutral arbitrator exhibited "evidential partiality" by failing to disclose information which could create a reasonable impression of partiality to the objective observer. Such partiality can be established from nondisclosure alone and need not be accompanied by actual partiality or bias.

The Texas court reaffirmed the policy that, in order to choose a neutral arbitrator intelligently, each party must have access to any and all information which "might reasonably affect the arbitrator's partiality." "This allows the parties to evaluate any potential bias at the outset." In this case, it was irrelevant that the potential conflict arose in the midst of the arbitral proceedings. The arbitrating parties were entitled to know of any potential conflicts or biases that arose during the course of the proceedings because they could exercise their right to remove the arbitrator.

Thus, the court held that the referral could have created an impression of partiality, and that "an objective observer could still reasonably believe that a person in [the arbitrator's] position, grateful for the referral, may have been inclined to favor" one party over the other. The court held that "a prospective neutral arbitrator selected by the parties or their representatives exhibits evident partiality if he or she does not disclose facts which might, to an objective observer, create a reasonable impression of the arbitrator's partiality. We emphasize that this evident partiality is established from the nondisclosure itself, regardless of whether the nondisclosed information necessarily establishes partiality or bias."

In so ruling, the court noted that this standard of evident partiality only applies to arbitrators who are chosen to act as the neutral. The duty of disclosure does not extend to party-designated arbitrators. Additionally, the court did not find any actual bias or partiality on the part of the arbitrator in question. Its ruling was grounded on "the fact that a reasonable person could conclude that the referral might affect [the arbitrator's] impartiality" and that factor "triggers the duty of disclosure."

Recent litigation indicates cooling enthusiasm for enforcing the *Commonwealth Coatings* standard. For example, in *JCI Communications, Inc. v. International Brotherhood of Electrical Workers, Local 103*, 324 F.3d 42 (1st Cir. 2003), the court held that the mere fact that business rivals of one of the arbitrating parties are members of the arbitral tribunal does not constitute evident partiality or bias. The litigants were on notice that the arbitrators would be drawn from their industrial *milieu*. Moreover, the court stated that a party waives its right to object when it fails to inquire about the backgrounds of the arbitrators either before or during the hearing. The court relied on a Fifth Circuit case in which that court held that the unconditional submission of an issue to arbitration, without raising any jurisdictional objection, ceded authority to the arbitrator and represented party consent to arbitrate that issue.

In *Sphere Drake Insurance Ltd. v. All American Life Insurance Co.*, 307 F.3d 617 (7th Cir. 2002), the Seventh Circuit held that a party-appointed arbitrator need not be disqualified because he served as full-time legal counsel for the appointing party in an unrelated insurance arbitration that occurred four years earlier. In evaluating the "evident partiality" standard, the court relied upon the rules that apply to the disqualification of federal judges. The Seventh Circuit found *Commonwealth Coatings* inapplicable because, there, the neutral was engaged in an *ongoing* business relationship with one of the parties. That relationship even included the rendition of services on the very projects that were part of the matters being arbitrated.

In the court's view, the standard expectation was that party-appointed arbitrators were *supposed* to advocate for the appointing party. The court also contended that *Commonwealth Coatings* did not hold that disclosure was compulsory for its own sake or that a failure to disclose was fatal when the arbitrator satisfied judicial standards for impartiality. The lack of disclosure might sully the arbitrator's reputation for candor, but it did not demonstrate "evident partiality," and, therefore, did not warrant the vacatur of the award.

In summary, courts that favor arbitration and unequivocally sustain the federal policy on arbitration will not find evident partiality unless actual bias can be established. Instances of actual bias can be demonstrated by the arbitrator's procedural conduct, prior relationships, or by personal financial interest. From this perspective, evident partiality is meant to eradicate blatant abuse and corruption in the process. Moreover, courts that favor this approach will apply strict impartiality standards only to the neutral, presiding arbitrator of a three-member panel or to a sole arbitrator. They hold party-designated arbitrators to a lesser impartiality standard; in fact, the general expectation is that such arbitrators will favor the appointing party's position.

Other courts—also favorable to arbitration—require at least a "reasonable appearance of bias," facts indicating a likelihood of arbitrator bias because of undisclosed conflicts. The appearance of bias standard provides that "evident partiality is established when the arbitrators fail to disclose 'any dealings that might create an impression of possible bias.'" Undisclosed material information about possible conflicts generally creates a "reasonable impression of partiality."

Another group of courts follows the plurality reasoning in *Commonwealth Coatings* and holds that the mere appearance of bias is sufficient to establish evident partiality and bring about the vacatur of the award. The appearance of bias standard provides that "evident partiality is established when the arbitrators fail to disclose '*any* dealings that might create an impression of possible bias.'" (Emphasis added.) "An arbitrator has an affirmative duty to disclose any dealings that might create an impression of possible bias."

In a ruling that refines current trends, the Wisconsin state Supreme Court held that a presumption of neutrality applies to arbitrators, but that presumption can be overcome by the parties' express agreement. Furthermore, the court held that evident partiality is not overcome simply by having the arbitrator disclose the relationship and then declaring himself impartial.

In *Borst v. Allstate Ins. Co.*, 717 N.W.2d 42 (Wis. 2006), Borst arbitrated a claim against Allstate in connection with an underinsured motorist claim against his policy. One of the arbitrators that rendered the award routinely served as Allstate's attorney. Nothing in the arbitration agreement prohibited the arbitrator from being non-neutral, and the arbitrator refused to recuse himself. He disclosed the relationship and assured Borst that he could be neutral. Borst was dissatisfied with the award and moved to vacate it. The lower court confirmed the award and Borst appealed.

Although not a decisive issue in the case, the court first addressed whether parties could explicitly contract for non-neutral arbitrators. It found that there is a presumption of impartiality that applies to the designation of the arbitrators, but that parties could explicitly contract for a non-neutral arbitrator. Because many arbitration agreements do not specifically state that an arbitrator must be neutral, the court issued its ruling so that "confusion will be lessened ... by prescribing presumptive impartiality as the appropriate role for the party-appointed arbitrator."

The court continued, holding that evident partiality cannot be avoided by simply disclosing the relationship that would cause the partiality. The court found it unreasonable to assume that evident partiality simply disappears once the relationship is disclosed. The court recognized, however, that the more difficult issue to determine is what a party may be entitled to when it objects to a party's arbitrator at the beginning of an arbitration.

The court noted a split in authority regarding whether an arbitrator can be removed before an award is rendered. Aligning Wisconsin with New Jersey and New York, the court held that a party can enter a pre-arbitration challenge against an arbitrator. The court reasoned that this was the best way to "reduce the likelihood of potentially wasteful post-arbitration challenges" and promote the efficiency of the arbitration process.

Sanctions for Frivolous Appeals

A point about the enforcement of arbitral awards under the FAA that has never been made with sufficient conviction is that vacatur proceedings breach the presumed confidentiality of the arbitral process. No matter what ground serves as the basis of the action, vacatur generally entails the development of a full judicial record regarding the underlying arbitration. Any of the statutory or common law grounds for vacatur can justify an extensive adversarial confrontation about whether the necessary elements are constituted under the evidence. Moreover, the parties can engage in a definitional contest about the exact significance of the ground and can further debate the impact of that result upon the specific circumstances of the case. In effect, many vacatur proceedings result in a complete re-enactment of the arbitral proceedings on a public record before a court. Once the court ruling is made available, the arbitration has been completely exposed. An attempt to vacate the award will, therefore, result in destroying the confidentiality of arbitral proceedings.

Disgruntled parties who refuse to comply voluntarily with an award can also use the vacatur procedure to delay the day of reckoning or discount their liability. They can expose the existence and content of the arbitral proceedings and thereby eliminate—*post facto*—a major business benefit of arbitration. Parties might argue that they have a due process right to some form of *de minimus* appeal against awards, that they should be protected against the possible corruption and fundamental unfairness of the process, as well as flagrant arbitrator abuse. Appeal, however, ceases to be *de minimus* once it thwarts a vital benefit and the essential attractiveness of the arbitral process. While absolute confidentiality of the arbitral proceedings cannot be guaranteed, enforcement actions should not allow the losing party to exact the proverbial "pound of flesh" or to inflict damage on the winner by rehashing the entirety of the proceedings. Participants in the arbitral process must recognize that their abuse of right can deprive society of a workable and fair adjudicatory process. Accordingly, should FAA § 10 vacatur actions be altered and, if so, how and by whom?

Desiring to ensure that parties in arbitration get the benefits of a faster and less expensive procedure than litigation, the Eleventh Circuit issued a stern warning that it was "ready, willing, and able to consider imposing sanctions" on those considering appealing arbitration decisions without a strong justification under the manifest disregard of law standard. The parties in *B.L. Harbert Int'l, LLC v. Hercules Steel Co.*, 441 F.3d 905 (11th Cir. 2006), litigated about the length of time Hercules, a subcontractor, required to finish work for Harbert, a general contractor. The parties arbitrated the dispute; the arbitrator rendered an award in favor of Hercules.

Harbert appealed to the district court and to the Eleventh Circuit asserting that the arbitrator, who was a former federal judge, manifestly disregarded the law. The court reviewed the facts and found "no evidence that the arbitrator manifestly disregarded the law." Clearly annoyed by the appeal, the court stated, "the only manifest disregard of the law evident in this case is Harbert's refusal to accept the law of this circuit which narrowly circumscribes judicial review of arbitration awards." The court continued:

If we permit parties who lose in arbitration to freely relitigate their cases in court, arbitration will do nothing to reduce congestion in the judicial system; dispute resolution will be slower instead of faster; and reaching a final decision will cost more instead of less. This case is a good example of the poor loser problem and it provides us with an opportunity to discuss a potential solution.

The court's "potential solution" would sanction parties on the losing end of arbitration who bring baseless vacatur litigation over arbitration awards. Harbert was spared sanctions in the case because "it did not have the benefit of the notice and warning this opinion provides."

From the outset, the court perceived the systemic implications of the case: "The laudatory goals of the FAA will be achieved only to the extent that courts ensure arbitration is an alternative to litigation, not an additional layer in a protracted contest...." The Eleventh Circuit ruling echoes the practical concerns expressed by Justice Breyer in *Kaplan*, that the litigation relating to arbitration should be held to a minimum in order to preserve the benefits of arbitral adjudication.

In an adversarial system, it is unlikely that the parties and their counsel will engage in self-discipline. It is, therefore, the courts' responsibility to discourage post-award litigious representational conduct and to limit the appeal procedure to absolutely fundamental abuse. The law—namely FAA § 10—could assist in maintaining the posture of arbitral appeal by recognizing and enforcing a procedure of internal arbitral appeal.

In arbitrations between merchant parties, cases that do not involve any significant disparity between party positions, due process concerns must cede to the effectiveness and functionality of the adjudicatory process. The parties must respect the finality of arbitrator determinations that resulted from an essentially fair proceeding. It is simply too easy for talented advocates to foist a laundry list of objections before the courts on behalf of their losing clients.

Opt-in Judicial Review

Practice created "opt-in" provisions for enhanced judicial supervision of arbitral awards. These contract stipulations represented the use of contract freedom to achieve greater rights protection in arbitration at the expense of its functionality and efficiency. In effect, the "true sovereigns" in the process—the parties—could command courts to scrutinize arbitrator determinations if they deemed such protection necessary or warranted in their arbitration.

The federal circuit courts were divided on the enforceability of opt-in provisions. The First, Second, Sixth, Seventh, Eighth, Ninth, and Tenth Circuits opposed opt-in provisions to some degree. Some of these courts denied the very existence of the contract right (*i.e.*, the Seventh and Ninth Circuits); others were more tentative and allowed parties to set the standard of review if the contract language was clear and unmistakable (*i.e.*, the First, Eighth, and Tenth Circuits).

Whether by contract or statute, allowing courts to intervene in the arbitral process is a bad idea that threatens the core attributes of arbitration. While courts and arbitral tribunals both engage in adjudication, they do so in different ways and pursuant to distinct mandates. Each has its own purpose and function. They respond to and satisfy different social needs. The judicializaiton of arbitration is a perilous creation because it not only sullies arbitration's basic character, but it also invites the process' deterioration and eventual elimination.

In arbitration, rights protection is always at odds with the functionality of adjudication. The provision of *de novo* review of arbitrator rulings integrates the right of appeal into the arbitral process and renders it much closer, on a fundamental way, to judicial proceedings. Disgruntled parties, therefore, are given an opportunity to express their opposition to the arbitrators' determinations beyond complaining about would-be procedural irregularities in vacatur. Instructing the court of enforcement to undertake a full review of the substance of the award expresses distrust of the arbitrators and of their ability to interpret and apply the law.

It also raises serious questions about the parties' motivation for choosing arbitration. The addition of an opt-in provision alters a material term in the standard and long-standing bargain for arbitration. It is difficult to conceive of contemporary arbitration as a mere fact-finding procedure. Opt-in provisions also give judicial proceedings a mythical and unrealistic glow. Finally, they significantly compromise the finality and effectiveness of arbitration.

Like the misguided common-law grounds, the availability of opt-in judicial merits review contradicts the express language of the governing statute. FAA § 10 contains no mention of, and thereby excludes, the judicial supervision of the merits of awards. The FAA is the enacted governing law. It is not merely a "default" framework, meant to supplement the exercise of freedom of contract. Barebones legal regulation is not insignificant because of its economy. It states basic regulatory principles, important to society and to the law, that are not secondary to party contract discretion—unless the legislation itself so provides.

Moreover, if a contract can be used to increase judicial supervision, logic demands that it can also be used to lessen or eliminate it. Parties could demand that courts automatically enforce their awards. Such an approach is likely to generate chaos and confusion. Contract negotiations would establish the law of arbitration in a completely *ad hoc* fashion.

The United States Supreme Court decision in *Hall Street Associates, LLC v. Mattel, Inc.*, 128 S.Ct. 1396 (2008), ended (it seems) the contractual possibility of entering into an opt-in arrangement. The Court declared that the grounds in FAA § 10 were "exclusive" and, presumably, could not be altered or modified by private contract. Although it left some sort of state law or nonstatutory door open, the Court appears to have firmly eliminated the prospect of opt-in provisions in the context of the FAA. Despite its vitality at the front end of and during the process, contract freedom ends with the conclusion of the arbitration and the enacted law, at that point, becomes the sole source of governing rules.

The Action to Clarify Awards

In U.S. arbitration law, the development of a right to seek a clarification of an award arose through judicial rulings rather than statute. For example, FAA § 11, the relevant provision in the governing statute, does not authorize such an action and, in fact, implies that it is unavailable and even unlawful.

The action to clarify an award has a number of unresolved problems of application: For example, when and by whom is the action triggered? If because of ambiguity, who defines ambiguity and how much ambiguity is necessary? Must affected arbitrators agree with a court's determination of ambiguity? Can arbitrators ignore or refuse to comply with the court order? Can they reach an independent determination? When is their correction or clarification of an award sufficient? Are there one, two, or several awards at the end of an action to clarify?

Allowing clarification also raises larger systemic concerns. It is undeniable that an opportunity to challenge the meaning of arbitrator rulings on the substance invites a judicial practice of merits review and greater and more sustainable adversarial confrontation among advocates at the enforcement stage of the process. It thereby lessens arbitration's finality and, as a consequence, its effectiveness.

Such a procedure may have been sensible in a circumscribed process founded upon consensus and trust, but—in contemporary arbitration—enormous sums are in play and sophisticated advocates do battle. Such an action, therefore, is likely to be shaped by and to service adversarial adjudication. For its part, FAA § 10 has an answer to "incomprehensible" arbitrator rulings: The vacatur of awards that are not "mutual, final, and definite." U.S. courts, however, have rarely vacated awards on this basis, perhaps because they view the statutory rule as too draconian and disruptive of the process.

By proclaiming a common-law right to request that arbitrators clarify an award, U.S. courts—in all probability—are simply seeking to do better and more effective justice in regard to arbitration. They perceived a potential problem and created a workable pragmatic solution to it—at least, in theory. While the action to clarify may not be in the best interests of the arbitral process, it does not necessarily exhibit hostility to arbitration. An unsympathetic judiciary could invoke almost any legal basis to create barriers to arbitration. The action to clarify an award, in fact, fits well into the contemporary scheme of judicial supervision. It promotes the enforceability of awards.

Despite this arguably "seamless" integration into the present framework for enforcement, the creative additions of the decisional law demand that basic questions be revisited. What is the proper role of courts and of the law in the evaluation of arbitral proceedings and awards? Should courts become more activist in matters of arbitration and take liberties with existing legal rules and adapt them to the accomplishment of a particular end? What ends should be pursued?

Private adjudication—if it is to have any standing at all—must be effective. Otherwise, judicial jurisdiction should be exclusive. Having courts police awards on the basis of ambiguity may not provide any true protection from ill-considered arbitrator rulings. The aggressive pursuit of ambiguity could allow adversarial representation to intrude upon, and eventually undermine, the functionality of arbitral adjudication.

The ruling in *Hardy v. Walsh Manning Securities, L.L.C.*, 341 F.3d 126 (2d Cir. 2003), illustrates the inter-relationship between vacatur for manifest disregard of the law and the action to clarify an award. The *Hardy* court's reasoning exhibits how misguided both actions are and how antagonistic their underlying rationale is to the autonomy and functionality of arbitration. The *Hardy* circumstances represent nothing more than the majority's disagreement with the arbitrator's application of law.

The majority opinion makes abundantly clear that the court believes that the implicated securities arbitration tribunal misconstrued and thereby misapplied New York state law. It also makes clear that the court invoked its "authority to seek a clarification of . . . [the tribunal's] intent" in order to avoid vacating the award on the basis of manifest disregard of the law. In reaching its determination, the court's objective appears to have been two-fold: (1) to "afford" the arbitral tribunal "an opportunity" to avoid vacatur on the basis of manifest disregard ("We are reluctant to announce that the Award is void outright as written."); and (2) to avoid imposing a "substantial financial liability ... upon an individual without a clear basis in law." Seeking to uphold the federal policy in favor of arbitration and to enforce a would-be legally accurate award, the court seems in the end to have achieved neither objective.

The dissent, however, provided the most persuasive and accurate interpretation of the facts:

> In this case, the disputed portion of the arbitrators' decision simply states: "Walsh Manning and Skelly be and hereby are jointly and severally liable...based upon the principles of respondeat superior." The majority's interpretation, while conceivable, ignores the fact that the critical phrase "based upon the principles of respondeat superior" may simply explain the basis for Walsh Manning's joint and several liability, without referring to the basis for Skelly's primary liability. Indeed, the phrase may indicate Walsh Manning's liability for *Skelly's* actions, not just Cassese's wrongful conduct, based upon the theory of respondeat superior. In other words, the award may specify the form of liability, joint and several, while remaining completely silent as to the un-

derlying claims on which Skelly was actually found liable.

Not only is this a *plausible* interpretation of the decision, but also a completely *probable* one, for Hardy presented substantial evidence during the arbitration hearing that Skelly, who was Cassese's direct supervisor, failed to properly supervise Cassese, that Skelly was personally aware of Cassese's unauthorized trading, and that Skelly violated federal securities laws by engaging in direct market manipulation.

It would seem that the judicial policy favoring arbitration would require that courts view the arbitrators' ruling in the light most favorable to the enforcement of the award. Because it is, in fact, quite likely that the reference to respondeat superior only applies to the brokerage firm, the award could not be challenged on the basis of manifest disregard of the law or remanded by the court to the arbitrators for clarification. The firm was liable to its customer because its agents/employees had overreached and violated their fiduciary obligations by failing to properly supervise and by pushing the customer to buy house stocks. It is indeed difficult to accept the majority's conclusion, that "[i]n our case, we have crossed the line from confusion to inexplicability, and we can discern no reading of the Award that resolves its apparent contradiction with the law of respondeat superior."

The dissent properly evaluates the majority's distorted reasoning: "By remanding to the arbitration panel for clarification as to the underlying legal basis for liability, the majority ... disregards the well-settled precedent establishing our severely limited review of arbitration awards." Further, "in 'wishing for more clarity,' the majority's decision overlooks our limited role in reviewing arbitration decisions...." It underscores how the majority opinion deviates from well-settled standards: "[M]ere ambiguity in the award itself is not a basis for denying confirmation, so long as the award can be interpreted as having a colorable factual or legal basis." Also, "an ambiguous award may be confirmed, so long as any plausible reading of the award is legally sustainable." In responding specifically to a point made by the majority, the dissent describes the long-standing judicial practice in terms of arbitration: "Our goal, then, is not to discern the actual subjective intent of the arbitration panel, but only to determine if the award can be sustained under any plausible reading."

The dissent also criticizes the majority's muddled view of the interaction between the action to clarify awards and manifest disregard of the law. If a court determines that the arbitrators' ruling constitutes a manifest disregard of the law, the award is unenforceable. The governing legal provisions do not give the arbitral tribunal another chance to get it right. The majority's position trivializes both the role of the court and the remedial integrity of arbitration. It also fosters protracted litigation about arbitration. It ignores the parties' expectations as to their bargain for arbitration and substitutes a misguided activism for the deference that has characterized the courts' relationship with arbitration for so long. The dissent usefully emphasizes that the action to clarify an award does have a place in the legal regulation of arbitration. It is available when the court of enforcement simply does not understand what the arbitrators in fact held. The lack of understanding does not express disagreement with the arbitrators' legal reasoning, but applies to the holding. A failure to clarify would result in the impossibility of enforcement. According to the precedent, "such a remand is appropriate 'so that the court will know exactly what it is being asked to enforce.'"

CHAPTER NINE

INTERNATIONAL COMMERCIAL ARBITRATION

Introduction

Because business transactions cannot take place without a functional system of adjudication, international commercial arbitration (ICA) has enabled parties to engage in and pursue international commerce. As a result, it has had an enormous impact upon the international practice of law, the structuring of a *de facto* international legal system, and the development of a world law of commerce. In a word, ICA has been a vital engine in the creation of a transborder rule of law. Furthering this design, the arbitral "method" has even been applied to the unruly political problems that attend international trade and the implementation of international trade policy.

At the very least, a transborder contractual dispute can raise choice-of-forum, venue, jurisdictional, choice-of-law, proof and interpretation of foreign law, and enforcement of judgment problems. Once a dispute arises, the fear of foreign law and of foreign judicial bias, compels the parties to file suit in their respective national jurisdictions, to pursue parallel actions in the two fora simultaneously, and to arrive at the costly stalemate of having two judgments that are equally unenforceable. The conduct of business across national boundaries already involves a high level of risk: Compliance with customs regulations, obtaining government permissions and licenses, the hazards of international transport, the special labor law regimes in foreign countries, and the variability and complexity of national import-export regulation. It is unlikely, therefore, that transborder commerce would take place at all if there were no effective adjudicatory mechanism for resolving the basic problems of commercial contracts (defining breach, establishing performance, enforcing delivery, and other requirements).

In addition to its service to the wealth-creating ambition of the international business community, ICA also represents an idealistic experiment in transborder understanding and cooperation. The early and present-day architects of the process faced head-on the challenge of diversity. They confronted a wide variety of cultural, historical, religious, national, regional, economic, and political dispositions in erecting and then maintaining the process. The founders of ICA engaged in and demonstrated an abundance of creativity, ingenuity, and resourcefulness of a technical, legal, and political kind in order to establish a workable process of adjudication that spanned the range of international commercial disputes and the breadth of world laws and legal cultures. A bold and steadfast yet tolerant intelligence needed to prevail at every stage of elaboration.

Sovereign State cooperation was indispensable to instituting the process. States needed to approve ICA so it could benefit from the support of municipal courts and function effectively as a transborder system. State approval was facilitated by the fact that the political or human rights of individual citizens were not directly implicated by the development of a private transborder system of adjudication—although the State's power to regulate commercial conduct was at play, might have to be delegated in whole or in part to arbitrators, and could eventually be substantially eroded. States needed to be persuaded to delegate the public function of adjudication to a group of private actors and organizations. Moreover, the delegation of sovereign authority had to be unequivocal and unqualified. Once undertaken, the deregulation of transborder adjudication could not be altered or abandoned. It needed to be continuous to avoid disrupting commerce and the marketplace.

Moreover, after it had been conferred, State approval needed to be self-effacing. The transborder arbitral process had to operate on its own and serve exclusively commercial objectives. In addition, a variety of professionals—ranging from judges and lawyers to prospective arbitrators and the commercial users of the process—needed to become unflinchingly loyal to a private system of adjudication to which they owed neither political nor social allegiance.

Finally, a synthesis of highly disparate national approaches to law and legal adjudication needed to be achieved in order to make the process work. In matters of trial procedure, for example, it is well-settled that the United States adversarial, party-driven model of trial differs greatly from its civilian, judge-centered counterpart. In fact, the opposition can be so radical on some matters that just results reached under one system are deemed illegal in the other. Therefore, would the envisaged transborder arbitral proceedings include pretrial discovery and cross-examination or *l'expertise judiciaire* and *le contradictoire*?

Divergences in national substantive law also needed to be accommodated. For instance, would a party reference to ''the basic law of contract'' include the doctrine of mitigation of damages, the good faith obligation, and clear rules on the passing of title? National laws contain variegated positions on these issues. Which version of the law should prevail? Would party choice always govern the resolution of such conflicts? Was party choice a sufficient basis for decision? Should it always provide the final word in commercial litigation? Also, in a more technical sense, would a contractual reference to a law of arbitration—in addition to the reference to a law to govern the merits—create a concurrent governing law? If so, how would the dual designation operate? Would the law of arbitration dislodge the other law and be controlling or would it act as a default mechanism—in all or some circumstances? What if the reference to the law of arbitration was the only party designation? Would the substantive law of that jurisdiction apply to the merits?

Many of the challenges that arose from the diversity of national laws were successfully addressed within the process. A large number of States endorsed ICA, thereby shielding international arbitral agreements and awards from national divergences and opposition. Currently, 141 States have ratified the New York Arbitration Convention. The presumption of the enforce-ability of awards under the Convention generally is respected and applied by the national courts of the ratifying States. National court judges seem to have understood well the lesson that the enforcement of arbitral awards is essential to the viability of ICA, which, in turn, makes national participation in international business possible.

The Convention's success reflects the breadth and depth of the world community perception that transborder commerce is vital to national interests and that arbitration is indispensable to the operation of international business. The New York Arbitration Convention replaces several prior international instruments on arbitration and is intended to function as the "universal charter" on international commercial arbitration. To some extent, the New York Arbitration Convention has superseded its own content and legislative history. It has become a juridical vehicle for the elaboration of a transborder law on international commercial arbitration.

Moreover, the elaboration of a model arbitration law and rules through the UNCITRAL (United Nations Commission on International Trade Law) framework attests to the greater civilization of the process. A basic consensus exists as to the applicable regulatory predicate and acceptable hearing procedures. Finally, there are strong indications that arbitral awards are creating a substantive transborder law of commerce that is likely to be controlling in most arbitrations.

The New York Arbitration Convention

The New York Arbitration Convention is an exemplary treaty—a model of modern arbitration legislation. The force of its authority is based upon its codification of the international consensus on arbitration. Also, rather than attempt to regulate all aspects of the arbitral process, the New York Convention focuses directly upon two vital elements of arbitral procedure (the validity of arbitration agreements and the enforcement of arbitral awards), leaving a more comprehensive regulatory scheme to be implied from its express principles.

The Convention's objective is to unify national laws on the enforcement of foreign arbitral awards and to establish a transnational rule of law that favors the recourse to arbitral adjudication. For example, Article II(1) provides that the Contracting States shall recognize an agreement to submit disputes to arbitration. The purpose of this provision is to eradicate systemic hostility to arbitration—hostility stemming from the view that arbitration amounts to a usurpation of judicial adjudicatory authority. Consequently, by adhering to the Convention, Contracting States agree to recognize the arbitral process as a legitimate means of resolving disputes. Under Article II(3), a motion to compel arbitration can be defeated only by establishing that the arbitration agreement was null and void, inoperative, or incapable of being performed. Decisional interpretations of the Convention demonstrate that these grounds were meant to function as ordinary contract defenses to the enforcement of an agreement. Arbitration agreements, therefore, are valid contractual arrangements and do not, *per se*, violate principles of public policy. They symbolize party use of contractual rights—rights the assertion of which can be defeated only by a deficiency in contractual intent, capacity, or language. Accordingly, courts in the Contracting States are under a legal obligation to enforce arbitration agreements if they meet the ordinary requirements of contractual validity.

The text of the Convention proposes a unified transnational rule of law not only in regard to the validity of arbitration agreements, but also concerning the enforcement of foreign arbitral awards. The systemic viability of any nonjudicial adjudicatory process is dependent both upon the legal system's recognition of the validity of agreements to enter into such processes and its willingness to give binding effect to its determinations. The seven grounds for the judicial supervision of awards contained in Article V can be grouped into two broad categories. The first category encompasses the procedural requirements that dictate compliance with basic adjudicatory standards. The parties must have had the contractual capacity to enter into an arbitration agreement; they must have been afforded proper noticePROPER NOTICE of the proceeding; the arbitrators must not have exceeded the jurisdictional authority conferred upon them by the agreement; the composition of the arbitral tribunal and the appointment of arbitrators must reflect the provisions of the agreement; and the award must have been binding in the jurisdiction in which it was rendered.

Second, national courts can deny recognition and enforcement to a foreign arbitral award upon the basis of two broad substantive law grounds. The dispute which the award settles must be arbitrable under the law of the requested jurisdiction; moreover, recognition and enforcement of the award must not be contrary to the requested jurisdiction's public policy. To some extent, the inarbitrability defense and public policy exception overlap. For example, as a general rule, disputes relating to the status and capacity of persons are inarbitrable. An award relating to a person's status and capacity, if recognized and enforced, would also be contrary to the public policy of the requested jurisdiction.

The Convention's truly international stature and law-making capacity are built upon two factors. First, it functions to codify an existing and emerging international consensus on arbitration. Second, its widespread endorsement by national legal systems gives legal credibility to its normative content.

Traditional analysis would argue that national courts must apply the provisions of the Convention as written. Subsequent developments and schools of thought cannot repeal or amend the content of an international treaty. The Convention expressly refers to national law and its application. Therefore, the law of the place of arbitration, the parties' national law, and the law of the place of enforcement should play a significant role in validating arbitration agreements and awards. Private international adjudications are still dependent upon national legal authority. Coercive enforcement cannot be achieved without invoking the laws of the requested territorial jurisdiction.

There is, however, another view of the Convention's law-making status—one that relies upon a sense of the realities of litigation practices and which ignores, rightly or wrongly, the legal considerations of territory and institutional hierarchy. The provisions of the Convention are not static, but rather reflect law-in-the-making. They are primarily responsive to the policy imperative that underlies the Convention. The references to the application of national law within the Convention may have been necessary to create an international movement toward ratification. Events, however, have outpaced that original purpose. International commercial arbitration has become an "anational" phenomenon. Although transborder adjudication can acquire the force of law only through national legal authority, arbitration—once the Convention gained universal adherence—transcended the need for continued national legal approval.

National courts and legislatures surrendered their authority to regulate arbitration and permitted it to function autonomously. As a result, factors such as the parties' national law, the law of the place of arbitration, and even the law of the place of enforcement are relevant only to the extent that they converge with the norms generated by the process of "anational" arbitration.

The movement toward uniform national laws on arbitration has undercut much of the debate about the impact of national sovereignty and national law in the implementation of the Convention. In fact, the continuing global ratification of the Convention has reversed the traditional tendency of States to make local exceptions to an agreed-upon international regime. Moreover, States appear to be competing to enact the most liberal laws on international commercial arbitration. The UNCITRAL Model Law and Model Rules on arbitration also indicate a trend toward "anational" uniformity. Parties seeking to enforce arbitration agreements and awards, of course, are always subject to the particularities of their case and a given national law and judiciary. By and large, however, national laws are no longer a constraint upon arbitration. States understand the international commercial importance of arbitration and actively promote themselves as venues for international arbitral proceedings. The "deregulatory" movement and the State acquiescence to the rise of arbitration are motivated in large measure by the desire to sell professional and infrastructure services to the international business community.

The Convention has created an effective and functional rule of law in the international community. Its textual provisions are neither numerous nor complex. The economy of the Convention's text is as remarkable as its international force. Of the sixteen articles that constitute the Convention, only Articles I, II, III, and V have law-making content; other articles deal with formal procedural requirements. Articles II and V are the central law-making provisions.

Article II establishes the legal obligations of ratifying States in regard to arbitration. By ratifying the Convention, States agree to recognize the submission and the arbitral clause as valid contractual undertakings and to enforce them as they would ordinary contracts. Article II(2) defines the "in writing" requirement broadly and by reference to commercial practices rather than legal requirements. This provision reveals aspects of the underlying ideology of the Convention, namely, that it is meant to codify the dispute resolution practices of the international commercial community rather than establish a legal regime for its governance. Courts have recognized that new technological means of communication also satisfy the "in writing" requirement.

Finally, Article II(3) establishes the duty of national courts in the ratifying States to compel arbitration in the appropriate circumstances. The obligation is triggered upon the request of a contracting party when it can establish that an arbitration agreement exists. The motion can be denied only if the court finds that the agreement to arbitrate is deficient as a contract. Moreover, the parties' right to enter into arbitration agreements can be defeated only when the requirements of contractual validity are not satisfied.

Article V is a critical provision. It outlines the grounds upon which a national court in a contracting State can deny recognition and enforcement to an international, nondomestic, or foreign arbitral award. There are five procedural grounds and two other grounds based upon substantive law considerations. According to the Convention, an award can be challenged on the basis of the contractual deficiency of the arbitration agreement, lack of notice or of an opportunity to be heard, excess of arbitral authority (with a severance caveat), and failure to abide by the agreement in matters of procedure. Article V(1)(e) adds a traditional private international law consideration to the enforcement regime under the Convention, namely, *res judicata* and the conflict of judgments. This provision forcefully puts into play the national law question and brings the text of the Convention into direct conflict with the tenets of "anational" arbitration. It provides that an award can be denied recognition or enforcement if it is not final or has been set aside by a court in another jurisdiction with contacts to the arbitration. The courts having jurisdiction to set aside an award are courts at the place of arbitration or courts in the jurisdiction the law of which governed the making of the award. This part of the provision, in effect, restates the problem of the "double *exequatur*" in a diluted form. Double *exequatur* refers to the requirement that an award be made enforceable both at the place of rendition and then at the place of enforcement. It was a problem in arbitration practice at the beginning of the twentieth century, at the time of the Geneva Convention (1927) and Protocol (1923) on arbitration. Although an award need not be enforceable both at the place of rendition and at the place of enforcement, it must not have been rendered unenforceable at the place of rendition in order to be legally enforceable at the place of enforcement.

In *Chromalloy Aeroservices*, 939 F.Supp. 907 (D.D.C. 1996), an ICC arbitral tribunal—sitting in Egypt and applying Egyptian law pursuant to the directive in the parties' contract—rendered an award against the Egyptian Air Force and in favor of a U.S. company for the unilateral rescission of an equipment maintenance contract. The Cairo Court of Appeal set aside the award on the ground that the arbitrators erroneously applied Eygptian law. The U.S. party then brought an action before the federal district court in Washington, D.C. to enforce the nullified award. The court granted the request, reasoning that the Article V grounds were conditional and Article VII of the Convention mandated the preservation of a party's rights of enforcement under domestic arbitration law.

The approving view of *Chromalloy* asserts that it adds to the autonomy of international commercial arbitration by insulating it from arbitrary national idiosyncrasies on arbitration. The disapproving view criticizes the U.S. court's disregard of treaty obligations and its creation of potential inconsistencies in enforcement. Another commentator sees *Chromalloy* as providing support for the position that the New York Arbitration Convention establishes a permissive set of guidelines for enforcement matters.

The unusual federal court action was not an isolated event; at least one major European arbitration jurisdiction had already achieved the same result. The Paris Court of Appeals upheld a lower court decision granting enforcement to the *Chromalloy* award in France. The court reasoned that, under the 1982 Franco–Egyptian Treaty of Judicial Cooperation, domestic French law applied pursuant to Article VII of the New York Arbitration Convention. In matters of enforcement, French law (which does not include foreign annulment of the award as a ground for nonenforcement) is less restrictive than the Convention.

In related litigation, the U.S. District Court of the Southern District of New York refused to enforce an arbitral award rendered in Italy because the award had been nullified by an Italian trial court, and the nullification had been upheld by Italy's highest court. The trial court ruled that the arbitrators exceeded their authority because they conferred a "bonus" on the petitioner that had not been authorized by the parties' contract. The petitioner sought to enforce the award in the district court in New York while his opponent challenged the award before the Italian courts. The district court deferred judgment until after a decision by the Italian court, at which time the petitioner renewed his petition. The district court denied the petition. The court stated that, under the New York Arbitration Convention, the State (in this case, Italy) in which an award is rendered is free to set aside an arbitral award in accordance with its own law. Moreover, a foreign court decision setting aside an award should not be ignored simply because a national court would have reached a different result with respect to the enforcement of the award under an application of domestic law. *See Spier v. Calzaturificio Tecnica, S.p.A.*, 77 F.Supp.2d 405 (S.D.N.Y. 1999).

The district court's opinion is in line with the standard approach to the application and interpretation of the New York Arbitration Convention on the question of the effect of a setting aside of an award at the place of rendition. It is difficult—if not, impossible—to reconcile the district court's reasoning with its counterpart in *Chromalloy*. Under *Chromalloy*, the U.S. policy favoring arbitration overrides the express provisions of the Convention and the decisions of parallel foreign tribunals. The district court's attempt to distinguish the cases is neither persuasive nor responsive to the clash of doctrine that separates the decisions. In addition, it is not necessarily true that vacatur would have resulted under an application of U.S. domestic arbitration law in these or similar facts. The Italian courts appear to have scrutinized the arbitrator's determination with an abundance of judicial zeal. In any event, the district court decision provides for the unwholesome result of allowing national law to block the enforcement of an international arbitral award on the basis of a judicial review of the merits of the arbitrator's determination. Despite its foibles, *Chromalloy* established a much sounder policy on the enforcement of awards under the New York Arbitration Convention.

Article V(1)(e) squarely places the enforcement of international, nondomestic, or foreign arbitral awards under the Convention into a complex choice-of-law framework. It contradicts the liberal policy on arbitration that animates the other provisions of the Convention and undermines the effort to establish a functional transborder regime for the enforcement of arbitral awards. In particular, it invites lawyers to engage in forum-shopping strategies to protect the interests of their award-averse clients by using disparate national laws to frustrate the process of international commercial accountability and justice. Article V(1)(e) is expressly at odds with the central premise of "anational" arbitration that the only national law of any consequence in an enforcement action is the law of the place of intended enforcement (where assets exist to satisfy the award). Laws or venues selected for transactional or contractual convenience should not impinge upon the legitimacy of awards. Considerations of territoriality have little relevance to global commerce.

Moreover, the emerging view of "anational" arbitration is that the local law of the place of intended enforcement should have a bearing on the award only to the extent that it conforms to the "anational" transborder norms on arbitration.

Article V(2)(a) and (b) establish the substantive law grounds for opposing the enforcement of an award under the Convention: (1) substantive inarbitrability (ground a) and (2) public policy (ground b). Both concepts expressly rely upon the local law of the enforcement jurisdiction for their content; according to the Convention, it is the national law version of inarbitrability and public policy that governs. There is some unavoidable overlap between the two grounds: More than likely, a subject area will be deemed inarbitrable because its importance to the State makes it part of national public policy. The public policy exception to enforcement, however, can include matters that have no linkage to the inarbitrability defense. An award could violate local public policy for reasons of trial procedure or for its conflict with other fundamental legal norms of the jurisdiction. A vigorous application of the public policy exception to enforcement could come close in some instances to a judicial review of the merits of the award.

The deference to national law in Article V(2)(a) and (b) again points to the danger of acknowledging the role of national law in the regulation of international commercial arbitration and of inviting choice-of-law considerations to have a bearing upon the operation of a transborder regime for arbitration. Practice under the Convention since 1958 has largely eliminated the possibility of national law interference. In applying the Convention, national courts have responded to the underlying spirit rather than the technical letter of the Convention and Article V(2)(a) and (b). In fact, they have devised the notion of an "international" public policy that applies under Article V(2)(b) and which replaces the application of domestic notions of public policy to guard against unwarranted national law intrusion upon the transborder regime of arbitration.

Also, through the efforts primarily of the United States Supreme Court, the inarbitrability defense has waned considerably in significance and operation. The emerging position under many national laws of arbitration is that international arbitrators have the right, if not the obligation, to rule upon disputes that involve rights created by statute rather than through contract. Both of these developments attest to the fact that, through its application before national courts, the Convention has generated legal norms that transcend the specific language of its provisions, and that it stands as the foundation of a transborder law on arbitration in constant adaptation.

9 U.S.C. §§ 202–208 implement the Convention in U.S. law. Section 202 defines the scope of application of the Convention or its jurisdictional reach in U.S. law. Section 203 establishes that the application of the Convention raises federal-question juris-

diction that cannot be defeated by the amount in controversy requirement. Section 206 gives U.S. courts extraterritorial powers to sustain the reference to arbitration. Section 207 establishes both a three-year statute of limitation period for bringing an enforcement action under the Convention and an obligation upon courts to confirm awards that do not violate the grounds for enforcement. The three-year limit tolls from the date of the award's rendition. 9 U.S.C. § 15 is also relevant to the present considerations. Under Section 15 of the FAA, the Act of State doctrine cannot be invoked to frustrate the enforcement of arbitration agreements or arbitral awards.

The disposition of the federal courts toward the New York Arbitration Convention and the enforcement of international arbitral awards has generally been very favorable. To a large degree, the favorable judicial attitude is mandated by the "emphatic federal policy" that sustains the recourse of arbitration. A number of technical problems, relating primarily to the liability of foreign States under arbitral determinations, have arisen. They, however, have not altered the positive judicial posture on the question of enforcing international arbitral awards. *Chromalloy* best reflects the judicial pragmatism that supports both international commercial arbitration and international commerce. It is a characteristic attitude. In the vast majority of cases, the federal courts appear to see their mission as the elimination of legal obstacles to arbitration.

U.S. Supreme Court Rulings on ICA

Although the Court has never ruled on the Convention itself, the U.S. ratification of the New York Convention in 1970 inspired the United States Supreme Court to elaborate a set of decisional principles on international commercial arbitration. The series of cases, ranging from *The Bremen v. Zapata* through *Scherk* and *Mitsubishi* and ending with *Vimar v. Sky Reefer*, initially seeks to fashion legal rules that accommodate the process of international commercial arbitration. They eventually establish a broad legal deference to arbitral jurisdiction in international matters, and lead to a merger of the domestic and international case law. In the end, the rulings create a unitary U.S. judicial policy on arbitration.

The Bremen v. Zapata Off–Shore Co., 407 U.S. 1 (1972), is not, strictly speaking, an arbitration case. It deals with forum-selection clauses in international contracts. The agreement to arbitrate, however, is a type of forum-selection clause in that it designates not only the place of adjudication, but also the form of adjudication (arbitration instead of court proceedings). Therefore, the doctrine in *The Bremen* also is relevant to arbitration agreements. In fact, *The Bremen* Court's reasoning regarding party autonomy and the needs of international commerce reverberates through *Scherk* and *Mitsubishi* as well as other cases on transnational litigation (*e.g.*, *Carnival Cruise Lines, Inc. v. Shute*, 499 U.S. 585 (1991), and *Asahi Metal Industries Co., Ltd. v.*

Superior Court of California, Solano County, 480 U.S. 102 (1987)).

In *The Bremen*, a company, which was based in Houston, Texas, contracted with a German company to tow a drilling rig from Texas to the Adriatic Sea. The executives for the Houston company reviewed the contract submitted by the German company. They did not object to a forum-selection clause that placed any litigation under the contract before a would-be English court and to exculpatory clauses that eliminated the towing company's liability for certain damages. They did, however, make other modifications to the contract. The forum-selection clause was a cryptic and rudimentary statement that contained a variety of interpretative difficulties. Nonetheless, apparently believing that substantial difficulties would not arise, that lawyers were meddlesome, or that greater protection was unaffordable, Zapata went ahead with the transaction with Unterweser.

Unexpected or at least unwanted difficulties did arise due to a violent storm in the Gulf of Mexico during the initial stage of transport. Zapata initiated litigation before a federal district court in Florida. The loss occasioned by the storm was substantial. When The Bremen was arrested in Tampa, it was released upon Unterweser's provision of $3,500,000 as security. Although Unterweser's bid included an offer to arrange for insurance coverage, Zapata decided to self-insure. This was Zapata's general policy regarding all of its rigs. Relief for

Zapata was less likely or perhaps unavailable in England. The exculpatory clauses probably would be enforced by English courts, resulting in a dismissal of the action against Unterweser. Moreover, even if Unterweser were held liable, the limitation fund in England was modest. Additionally, the incident occurred near a U.S. jurisdiction, involved directly the business assets of a U.S. company, and generally implicated U.S. interests. Why should English courts and law have exclusive jurisdiction over a matter that has no connection or proximity to England or English interests?

The United States Supreme Court disagreed with a parochial analysis. It emphasized that the implicated transaction involved an international commercial contract. Therefore, a special policy, designed to further the development of international commerce, was applicable. Domestic strictures on judicial jurisdiction and the enforceability of contract provisions had to yield to the parties' bargain. In the international arena, the only real law was supplied by the contract. Allowing parties to skirt their agreement through the shield of a domestic law would destabilize the international marketplace and render it chaotic. Parochialism and protectionism had to yield to a more all-encompassing view that truly promoted American interests in international commence. Moreover, sophisticated business parties, equal in measure, should not be heard to complain after they knowingly entered into a transaction. The protection of nationals was not a factor of consideration once these parties had entered the international marketplace.

The Court emphasized new global commercial realities and asserted that legal doctrine should be made to respond to them in a nonsectarian fashion. In matters of transborder litigation, the function of domestic courts is not to create juristic roadblocks or to compete for jurisdictional primacy. As long as duress or fraud are not involved, national courts should give effect to the intent of transborder parties. Predictable outcomes are essential to the conduct of business transactions. That type of stability in matters of international commerce can only emanate from contract provisions.

The majority opinion in *The Bremen* acts as the foundation for the Court's progressive articulation of a judicial policy on transborder litigation and international arbitration. *The Bremen* is the first case in which the Court establishes a marked boundary between law for domestic and international matters, holding that domestic rules may be inapposite in the international sector and that they need to be disregarded or amended for application in that sector. With *The Bremen*, the Court begins the process of elaborating normative rules of private international law that generally reject the extraterritorial application of domestic law as a source of law for transborder commercial ventures.

Scherk v. Alberto–Culver Co., 417 U.S. 506 (1974), and *Mitsubishi Motors Corp. v. Soler Chrysler–Plymouth, Inc.*, 473 U.S. 614 (1985), further elaborate the law that began in *The Bremen*. These cases, however, are true arbitration cases. They involve deciding whether national courts or international arbitrators have jurisdiction to rule on claims involving domestic statutory law. In each case, there was an arbitration provision in the contract; moreover, domestic precedent indicated that claims made under the relevant statutes were inarbitrable. The statutes were significant legislative enactments that directly implicated key economic features of American society: Securities regulation and antitrust. In each case, the Court emphasizes the transnational dimension of the transaction and insulates the determination from the effect of the existing domestic case law.

A special regime emerges for international business contracts that allow international arbitrators to rule upon claims based upon U.S. regulatory law. The authority of the international arbitrator, the court appears to believe, cannot be compromised without undermining transborder commerce itself. Once it is agreed upon, the provision for arbitration must be absolutely enforced in all circumstances. Moreover, these transactions are individual deals that are generally devoid of systemic consequence and have little, if any, bearing upon the domestic development of the law. Because there is no transborder legal process or binding rule of law, the parties' agreement is the primary and the exclusive source of stability in international commerce.

The consistency and unequivocal character of the Court's policy on international arbitration, as well as its eventual merger with the policy on domestic arbitration, perhaps can best be explained by the Court's need to manage judicial dockets and the federal judicial system. Because transnational litigation imposes an additional and more complex burden upon the federal courts, it is critical to make arbitration agreements and awards effective to avoid placing inordinate demands upon national judicial resources. The same "managerial" rationale explains the compromise of rights that occurred in the federalization of domestic U.S. arbitration law and the extension of domestic arbitration to statutory conflicts.

The admonition against parochialism, the need to avoid the uncertainty of resolution that proceeds from the entanglements of conflicts and forum-shopping strategies, and the rejection of extraterritoriality in transborder litigation appear to have little to do with whether claims arising under the 1934 Securities and Exchange Act can be submitted to arbitration. Federal statutory law was applicable because Scherk chose to engage in a business transaction with a U.S. party covered by the provisions of the statute. The facts involve not only a breach of contract, but also implicate directly the regulation of commercial conduct for the benefit of American society. It is not the character of the contract that is at issue, but rather how the behavior of the parties affected larger U.S. juridical interests.

The *Mitsubishi* opinion contains a more direct focus upon the subject-matter inarbitrability question. Also, the Court in *Mitsubishi* begins to commingle its rulings on domestic and international arbitration. The majority makes significant reference to the federalism trilogy in supporting its conclusions on the question of arbitrability. Although the ruling is still couched in terms of the needs of transborder commerce, a unitary policy on arbitration begins to emerge. Eventually, the Court forgets the international uniqueness of the rule of statutory arbitrability once it decides *McMahon* and *Rodriguez*.

Vimar Seguros y Reaseguros, S.A. v. M/V Sky Reefer, 515 U.S. 528 (1995), is a recent expression of the Court's policy on arbitration. It is a decision on international commercial arbitration in that it involves a maritime transaction, the application of maritime statutory law (COGSA) to the transborder transport of goods, and treaty law. It is also characteristic of the litigation on domestic arbitration in that it involves an alleged conflict between the legislation on arbitration and another regulatory statute. Given the merger of arbitral judicial policy, the precise character of the litigation, however, may not be very significant: What applies internationally also governs purely domestic arbitral matters.

In *Vimar*, the majority eventually concludes that COGSA and the FAA are not in conflict because the reference of a COGSA dispute to arbitration is permissible under Section 3(8) of the treaty. The dissent asserts that the contractual reference to arbitration in the bill of lading violates the letter and spirit of Section 3(8) and is, therefore, invalid. The majority takes exception with "the reasoning" and "the conclusion" of the Second Circuit in *Indussa Corp. v. S.S. Ranborg*, 377 F.2d 200 (2d Cir. 1967) (*en banc*), by drawing a distinction between the substantive obligations under the legislation and the procedure for the enforcement of these obligations. The Court took extensive pains to eliminate any conflict between the recourse to arbitration and legislative schemes so that the reach of arbitration would not be confined in any litigious circumstance. The availability of arbitration continues to be essential to the functioning of transborder (and domestic) justice.

ICA in the World Community

ICA has a wide, but uneven, standing in the world community. It originated in Europe and initially reflected the continental civilian procedural approach to adjudication. The International Chamber of Commerce (ICC), which is headquartered in Paris, was a significant force during the 1950s in drafting and fostering the widespread acceptance of the New York Arbitration Convention. The French government ratified the Convention within months of its being opened for signature, attesting to the importance it attached to the international arbitration process. Moreover, French courts progressively elaborated a judicial policy that heavily favored the recourse to and the effective operation of ICA. France was the principal proponent of transborder arbitration at the outset of its contemporary devel-

opment. Once the United States government ratified the Convention in 1970 and the United States
Supreme Court began to issue rulings on transborder litigation and arbitration, the doctrinal center of
gravity shifted from Europe to the United States.

As noted earlier, when Wall Street lawyers finally
accepted the primacy of arbitration in transborder
commercial litigation, an even greater volume of
international commercial litigation migrated from
domestic courts to transborder arbitral tribunals.
The influence of the Anglo–American legal profession extended to the structure of arbitral proceedings, which began to mirror the basic characteristics
of a U.S. common law trial. In effect, the coexist-
ence of two influential centers of legal doctrine on
arbitration instituted a struggle between the European civil law and the Anglo–American common law
for dominance in the conduct of arbitral proceedings. This tension persists in contemporary arbitral
practice.

Accordingly, despite a few reservations regarding
the process, Northern, Western countries accepted
ICA as necessary and professed support for the
process. In recent times, ICA has become more
popular in formerly inhospitable regions like Latin
America. Mexico's adhesion to the consensus on
ICA is a good example. Historically, from the perspective of the Mexican government, the settlement
of boundary and other disputes through international claims commissions in the nineteenth and
early twentieth centuries made any recourse to in-

ternational adjudicatory processes suspect. The commissions were seen (not inaccurately, in most instances) as an ill-disguised mechanism by which the United States imposed its will upon its weaker, southern neighbor and furthered its own interests. Accordingly, Mexico refused, by and large, to participate in such proceedings and embraced the rationale of the Calvo Clause, providing for the national treatment of foreign investors and the exclusive reference to local remedies for the resolution of foreign investment disputes. In response to the emergence of globalization, Mexico revised its position on arbitration.

In 1993, Mexico became one of the first Latin American countries to adopt a modern arbitration statute based upon the UNCITRAL Model Law. The Mexican endorsement of ICA symbolized a desire and willingness to participate in world commerce on transborder terms. A number of other Latin American countries, including Brazil (1996), Bolivia (1997), Colombia (1996), Costa Rica (1997), Ecuador (1997), Guatemala (1995), Panama (1999), Peru (1995), and Venezuela (l998), followed the Mexican example. These countries enacted modern, UNCITRAL-inspired arbitration statutes. The new legislation, along with the ratification of major international conventions on arbitration (the Inter–American Conventions, the ICSID Convention, and the New York Arbitration Convention), at least created the impression of a favorable national posture toward arbitration.

The depth of commitment to ICA in the individual countries, however, is difficult to gauge accurately, especially in circumstances in which the enforcement of an international arbitral award might be antagonistic to local interests or favor a national or corporate entity from a country with a well-developed economy. Despite the adoption of a modern statutory framework, courts in some of these countries might be reluctant or refuse to enforce such international arbitral agreements and awards. They could use procedural delay to thwart enforcement indirectly or invoke the public policy exception to express direct opposition. The days of the Calvo Clause appear to be a bygone era. There also seems to be a great enthusiasm among Latin American countries for mediation (known there as conciliation). It is difficult to ascertain whether mediation has become an effective competitor to arbitration in the Latin American setting and whether the current economic decline and episodic political instability will have a substantial impact upon the stature of ICA in the area.

National resolve in favor of ICA in some Latin American countries may be precarious. For example, on December 13, 2001, the Supreme Court of Panama ruled, with one dissenting vote, that the doctrine of *kompetenz-kompetenz* was unconstitutional under Panamanian law. The court reasoned that arbitrators had no legal standing to decide the propriety of their jurisdiction. Only courts, using their publicly-conferred authority, could rule on such questions. As the earlier European history on arbitration illustrates with unmistakable clarity, such a ruling (despite its formal conceptual rectitude) is highly antagonistic to the effective operation of arbitration. As a result of the opinion, every arbitral proceeding held in Panama or subject to Panamanian law is vulnerable to a jurisdictional challenge before a court either at the head or at the back end of the proceeding. This opportunity for dilatory obfuscation can easily result in a two-year or longer delay and the possible nonenforcement of the award. This development could have hindered considerably the recourse to arbitration in Panama. It was reversed in recent legislation.

By comparison, ICA has a mixed standing in Asian countries, such as Japan, Singapore, the new Hong Kong, and India. The Japanese endorsement of ICA is limpid and unenergetic. Institutional centers for the conduct of international arbitrations have existed in Japan for years, but the volume of cases has never been substantial and a strong international arbitration community has never been established. Nonetheless, Japan is a party to all of the major international conventions on arbitration, including the New York Arbitration Convention. Arbitral awards generally have the same effect in Japan as the final and binding judgments of a court of law. The Japanese Chamber of Commerce and Industry maintains a Commercial Arbitration Association. The Japan Commercial Arbitration Association (JCAA) is one of Japan's best known arbitral institutions; established in 1953, it resolves disputes arising from international and domestic business transactions. The JCAA has cooperative agreements with thirty-three major arbitral institutions, including the American Arbitration Association (AAA) and the London Court of International Arbitration (LCIA).

The protracted arbitral procedure described in *Fotochrome, Inc. v. Copal Co.*, 517 F.2d 512 (2d Cir. 1975), attests to the strong cultural preference in Japan for negotiated dispute settlement rather than adjudication. In fact, private, unofficial adjudication is seen as the worst form of adjudication. While participation in court proceedings may constitute a public humiliation under Japanese concepts, the authority of the judge at least results from public laws. By contrast, the arbitrator's mandate emerges merely from a private agreement. Some commentators have ascribed the static state of arbitration in Japan to the fact that few Japanese attorneys speak English. Linguistic insularity contributes to the lack of outreach.

Also, the Japanese code provisions on arbitration are dated. In 1979, a law group was commissioned to draft a new arbitration law. In 1989, the group completed a draft law that contained modern provisions and modern principles of arbitration law. The Diet enacted the Revised Draft Law on July 25, 2003. The new Japanese law on arbitration came into force in March 1, 2004. In any event, the Japanese misgivings about arbitration are not shared by the other major players in international trade and commerce. Finally, these characteristics of the Japanese position on arbitration indicate that Japan is not ready to assume a role of regional leadership in ICA.

Singapore differs significantly from Japan in its approach to ICA. It appears eager to become the Asian center for ICA. Recently, it adopted new laws that favor arbitration. There also is an administrative center for arbitration that actively supports the recourse to arbitration in Singapore and the international marketplace. In seeking to assume a dominant position, however, Singapore must contend with the new Hong Kong. Prior to the historic reunification in 1999, Hong Kong was a bustling center of capitalism and could serve as a meeting place for East–West business interests. Its present-day ability to act as a venue for international business and commercial adjudication is uncertain. Historically and geographically, it is an ideal setting for achieving such intermediation. Ultimately, its status within the global commercial community will be decided by the vicissitudes of both internal Chinese and international politics. Moreover, with the formation and development of CIETAC arbitration, China as a whole is attempting to become a player in the area.

Other members of the Asian communist world seem to be embracing arbitration and international commerce. Despite some long-standing difficulties, Vietnam has demonstrated of late a genuine willingness to comply with the *quid pro quos* of ICA. In late 2001, the Lam Dong People's Court confirmed an arbitral award rendered by the International Chamber of Commerce and Industry (ICCI) in Geneva, Switzerland against a Vietnamese company and in favor of a South Korean company. The arbitrators ruled that the Vietnamese company, the Vietnam Sericulture Corporation (Viseri), breached its contract with the South Korean Kyunggo Silk Company. The award required Viseri to pay (U.S.) $425,891 to the Korean enterprise. The court rejected Viseri's arguments opposing the enforcement of the award. Remarkably, it held that the award "conformed to international practices, the Vietnam Trade Law, and the ordinance on international arbitration in Vietnam."

The willingness to accept both the losses and gains associated with international commercial activity is instrumental to a country's effective integration into the stream of international business. Courts and national legislation cannot simply pursue the protection of nationals or national economic interests in transborder economic exchanges, but must uphold the universal role of contract and embrace the practices of the international commercial community. Constraining business by State-controlled systems cannot result in meaningful national economic growth and development. In this case, Vietnam has exhibited a desire to accept the discipline of the international marketplace and of the transborder rule of law.

Finally, in the last several years, India has endeavored to revise its position on ICA. Its previous reservations may have stemmed from geo-political positioning and been grounded in political ideology. In any event, in 1996, India adopted the Arbitration and Conciliation Ordinance based upon the UNCI-TRAL Model Law on Arbitration. The purpose of the legislation was to stabilize the arbitration system in India and to encourage foreign investment. The then-Prime Minister told Indian lawyers that it was necessary to bring Indian laws on the settlement of disputes in line with international standards because the economy was undergoing substantial reforms.

Previous arbitration acts required court decrees to enforce arbitral awards, and courts were given wide latitude to vacate awards. The new ordinance made several improvements to the prior law. It allows arbitral tribunals to promote the use of conciliation during the arbitral proceeding in order to encourage the parties to settle the dispute. If the parties settle during the arbitral proceeding, their agreement is recorded and given the same effect as an arbitral award. An arbitration award or settlement pursuant to conciliation is automatically deemed a decree of an Indian court, thereby expediting the enforcement of the determination. There are fewer grounds for setting aside an award, thereby creating an implied presumption of the enforceability of awards. Finally, the ordinance requires a party challenging a domestic award to deposit the amount of the award in court prior to filing its challenge.

Moreover, parties are given the freedom to control many aspects of the arbitration process through the arbitration agreement. Among other things, the parties can make a provision for the number and selection of arbitrators, the procedure of the arbitration, the presentation of evidence, and the use of experts. There are, however, mandatory requirements regarding the conduct of the arbitral proceedings. If the arbitration takes place in India, and the conflict being adjudicated is not an international commercial dispute, the tribunal has to decide the dispute in accordance with Indian laws. When the dispute is international, the arbitral tribunal decides by reference to the rules of law designated by the parties. If the parties did not select an applicable law, the tribunal applies the rules of law it considers appropriate in the circumstances.

Under the ordinance, an arbitral award can be set aside if: (1) an arbitrating party is under some incapacity; (2) the agreement is null under the applicable law; (3) a party is not given proper notice of the appointment of the arbitrator or of the proceedings; (4) the award deals with a dispute outside the scope of the arbitration agreement; or (5) the composition of the arbitral tribunal or the arbitral procedure violates Indian public policy. Parties are obligated to file an action to set aside the award within three months of the date of rendition. Domestic awards become effective as a decree of the court three months after being rendered. Enforcement of a foreign award can be refused only if, in addition to the reasons for vacating a domestic award, the award has not yet become binding on the parties, or the subject matter is not capable of settlement by arbitration under Indian law.

In addition, the Indian Supreme Court, in several recent rulings, interpreted the newly-enacted legislation favorably for arbitration. Although there have been clear efforts to establish India as a jurisdiction that is supportive of international arbitration, attempts to promote arbitration and ADR domestically have generally been met with less success. The crowded court dockets make such alternative processes a virtual necessity, but the establishment of centers and programs has not yet persuaded the legal profession and the public. Recent ecomonic strides and legal developments, however, indicate a reversal of attitudes.

The Business of Arbitration

A number of traditional service providers have a virtual lock upon the transborder arbitration service industry. It is difficult for newcomers to establish a foothold in the area. There is also intense competition among the existing institutions for clients. The American Arbitration Association (AAA) is the only entity that has made a new institutional inroad into the business of ICA. Previously, the AAA administered international arbitrations on a small scale. It has, however, a long-standing history as a domestic arbitral service provider. In June 1996, the AAA created the International Center for Dispute Resolution. Since its inception, the Center has administered more than

1,000 cases, and its annual caseload is approaching 400 cases. In 2001, the AAA also opened a European Office of the International Arbitration Center in Dublin, Ireland. The Irish International Arbitration Centre represents the AAA's second institutional incursion into the highly territorialist domain of ICA. It is too early to determine whether the second venture is likely to be as successful as the first.

The International Chamber of Commerce (ICC), headquartered in Paris, France, is the most well-established and well-known international arbitral institution. Despite recent attempts to lower costs, ICC administration of transborder arbitration remains expensive. The ICC charges a percentage of the amount in dispute, which decreases as the disputed amount increases. The ICC, however, provides highly professional arbitration services. Given its long-standing presence in the field, some international lawyers (with or without ties to the ICC) maintain that ICC arbitral awards have greater credibility before national courts than awards from other arbitral institutions. They believe that a stronger presumption of enforceability attaches to ICC awards on a worldwide basis. Be that as it may, the ICC has administered more than 12,500 arbitrations since the mid-1920s. It administers approximately 650 arbitrations annually, and usually at least half of these arbitrations represent very significant cases in terms of the amount in dispute and the stature of the parties.

The London Court of International Arbitration (LCIA) is also an important entity in the provision of arbitration services to international commercial parties. It, too, is an experienced service provider and benefits from an impeccable professional reputation. Because it charges an hourly rate rather than a fee based on a percentage of the amount in controversy, LCIA arbitration is regarded as less expensive than ICC arbitration. The LCIA, however, does less business than the ICC—approximately 150 cases per year. The LCIA Rules of Arbitration are more accessible than their ICC counterpart, which seems to be mired in the *franglais* foibles of French-to-English translation and composition. Among international lawyers, LCIA arbitration has generally been perceived as English arbitration and linked to English court supervision of the merits of arbitral awards. The organization added "international" to its corporate title and created a number of regional councils throughout the world to alter this perception. That effort, however, has met with mixed success. The 1996 UK Arbitration Act, like its predecessor in 1979, improved England's standing as a venue for transborder arbitration. The further liberalization of English arbitration law accompanied by the tempering of English court supervision of awards have made LCIA arbitration more attractive to commercial parties and given the LCIA a more noticeable presence in the world marketplace of arbitration services.

Also, there are a number of specialized forms of transborder institutional arbitration. The International Centre for the Settlement of Investment Disputes (ICSID) administers arbitrations that involve disputes between private investors and host States. The objective of ICSID or World Bank arbitration is to provide a mechanism by which to reduce the impact of sovereign status upon international investments. ICSID's internal appeal mechanism and other issues, however, rendered the process ineffective for a time. Only a handful of cases (approximately forty) were brought to the ICSID in some thirty-five years of operation. The reference to ICSID arbitration in the NAFTA Treaty and in bilateral trade agreements revitalized the process. The ICSID Secretariat reports that it currently has in excess of sixty pending cases with many more filings. ICSID administrators are aware of the rebirth of their process and are seeking to rival the ICC in terms of transnational prominence. Sovereignty, however, can be an obdurate and uncompromising barrier—even in the arbitration context—that will not necessarily yield to the needs and objectives of international commerce.

During the cold war era, Sweden played a vital role in ICA by acting as the principal center for holding East–West arbitrations. In fact, a sophisticated group of lawyers and other experts eventually assembled in Stockholm to address the special problems associated with these arbitrations. When the cold war ended and China developed CIETAC arbitration, the need for a venue specializing in East–West arbitrations was diminished considerably. In 1999, the Swedish Parliament enacted the Swedish Arbitration Act to modernize the Swedish law of arbitration and to amplify and redirect Sweden's reputation as a venue for international arbitrations. The enactment of the law demonstrated that Sweden was attempting to find its role in the refashioned international commercial order.

The Swedish Arbitration Institute (the Institute) revised its arbitration rules in light of the new law. The Institute was established in 1949 and is part of the Stockholm Chamber of Commerce. It participates in a long tradition of Swedish arbitration. It is a very active arbitral institution, receiving more than 170 new cases in 2008. The revision of the rules was not radical in character; the original rules came into force in 1988 and represented a modern regulation of arbitration. The amendments reinforce the objective of achieving procedural economy and flexibility. For example, the time limit for the rendition of an award has been reduced from one year to six months. The time limit begins to run from the date of the arbitral tribunal's constitution. The Institute can grant extensions. While the shortened time limit is unrealistic for complex arbitrations, it symbolizes the Institute's commitment to expedited dispute resolution through arbitration. The revised rules also authorize arbitrators to issue interim awards for the production of evidence and to secure the enforcement of final awards. While such measures are subject to judicial enforcement, their availability makes clear that Institute rules are meant to foster the effectiveness of arbitration.

The revised rules also emphasize the international character of non-domestic arbitration. For example, when the parties to an international arbitration do not provide for a law governing the merits, the Institute rules state that the arbitral tribunal can choose to apply a specific national law or "rules of law" it finds suitable. The latter category can include transborder laws like The United Nations Convention on Contracts for the International Sale of Goods (CISG), the UNIDROIT "Principles of International Commercial Contracts," or the *lex mercatoria arbitralis*. This is a particularly significant emendation and represents a strong position in favor of arbitral autonomy and arbitrator authority.

Finally, the revised Institute rules have altered the manner in which arbitrator compensation is determined. The prior practice allowed the arbitral tribunal to determine its own fees. In order to promote greater predictability in arbitrator fees, the revised rules provide that the fees will be set by the Institute in accordance with the amount in dispute. The applicable schedule will include minimum and maximum amounts to allow the Institute to take the characteristics of the particular arbitration into account. Arbitrator fees are to be paid at the outset of the proceedings, along with administrative fees.

New rules came into force on January 1, 2007. These emendations seek to incorporate current international standards for transborder arbitration more directly and comprehensively into the SCC Institute Rules. The new rules fill gaps by addressing the issue of consolidation and providing that the SCC Institute can consolidate related arbitral proceedings as long as it consults with the parties and the arbitrators before reaching a decision. They update the regulations by stating a new rule for the appointment of arbitrators in multiple-party arbitrations. If either side fails to appoint an arbitrator because the implicated parties disagree, the SCC Institute names the entire arbitral tribunal. Moreover, the rules of evidence are removed from their foundation in Swedish procedure and aligned with global arbitral practices, meaning that the arbitrators gauge the relevance, admissibility, and weight of evidentiary elements. Arbitral tribunals, however, can order the production of documents or other evidence only upon party request. This rule indicates that the parties control their case and its presentation. Further, interim measures can be delivered or ordered in the form of an award and the SCC Institute is officially charged with an obligation of confidentiality. Finally, the rules authorize a separate award, at the tribunal's discretion, for reimbursement of costs advanced on behalf of another party.

Law and Legitimacy in ICA

Generally, the type of justice that is available in ICA is not the elaborate form of "designer justice" that characterizes U.S. legal proceedings. Rights protection, procedural sophistication, and an uncompromising commitment to due process are not the hallmarks of ICA. In fact, "designer justice" and the complex conflicts that attend the operation of the legal process are some of the principal reasons for the success of non-judicial adjudicatory processes like arbitration. Protracted proceedings and the expense of litigation have made judicial justice inaccessible. In ICA, functionality is the foremost objective along with finality and basic fairness. Rights protection does not supercede these objectives. ICA, however, is neither a simplistic nor an arbitrary process. It is not "justice under a tree." Succinctly stated, ICA (like its domestic counterpart) is a process of adjudication that is accessible, expert, reasonably fair, and professional—the results of which are enforceable. In the international context, it is important to note further that ICA is neutral as to nationality and legal tradition. ICA is the product of party choice, of the parties' exercise of their freedom of contract. In an imperfect and difficult world, it is a realistic and meaningful alternative which provides a remedy where one would not otherwise be available.

What role, if any, does the law play in regard to ICA—its operations and its adjudicatory determinations? At a domestic level, law embodies social and political forces that invest public institutions with authority and legitimacy. It acquires its legitimating function from its origins in democratic processes established by the originating political framework. In the international setting, law does not arise from the same source, have the same content, or perform the same functions. International law is not domestic law and vice versa. The lack of equivalency does not debilitate or detract from either form of law. Domestic law and its foundation in democratic values are not the be-all and end-all of law. International law can stand on its own as law.

In the international arena, no political State in the domestic sense exists; authority vests in a group of "equal" sovereigns. International law often arises from customary practices or the development of a consensus view among States. There is a great deal of fluidity and indefiniteness about international lawmaking. It is more *de lege ferenda* than *lex*. International agreements and treaties often have an aspirational (rather than rule-making) quality. The dictates of sovereignty dilute both the statutory and decisional rule of law. The civilizing influence of law often is secondary to the prospective and actual use of force in State-to-State relations. Acceptance of a practice by powerful States often amounts to the conferral of legitimacy. Majoritarian rule is not the guiding principle. Politics and power are the more usual watchwords of international relations.

National law rules could be used to regulate ICA according to a rigorous domestic policy. The implementation of such a regime would represent a return to a bygone era of legal hostility to arbitration. Statutory provisions and court rulings would become vehicles for imposing restraints on the ICA process. Such restrictions could be selective or comprehensive, and could contain a wide variety of grounds and express numerous policy objectives. The regulations would not exist to consecrate the parties' right to engage in arbitration, but rather to make clear that the provision of adjudicatory services is a State function and prerogative. Only the State can derogate from its own authority and responsibilities in the area. The purpose of legislation on arbitration would be to regulate the limited incursion arbitration can make into the State's privileged domain. Such a regime would probably include a statutory statement on subject-matter inarbitrability, articulate a more aggressive policy on the judicial supervision of awards, and restrict arbitration's scope of application. Domestic law would surrender none of its real authority to the private process. ICA would function through and for the benefit of domestic law.

Present-day realities preclude such a regulatory approach to arbitration. A highly restrictive policy is both impractical and impolitic. A departure from the highly tolerant and liberalist transborder regulation of ICA is unlikely to be achieved simply through a radical reversal of position.

Domestic law does not invest the process of ICA with legitimacy. There is an interface with domestic law for purposes of gaining assistance for arbitral tribunals and proceedings, establishing decisional predicates, and pursuing the coercive enforcement of awards. A national statute on arbitration usually recognizes and upholds ICA and governs a number of other matters that relate to the ICA process: (1) the capacity of the parties to contract (and, relatedly, of arbitrators to act as arbitrators); (2) the validity (and enforceability) of arbitration agreements; (3) the relationship between the court system and the arbitral process (in terms of attachment or other forms of interim relief, the appointment of arbitrators, compelling parties to arbitrate or to cooperate with the process, and the like); and (4) the judicial supervision of awards in the event of noncompliance (grounds for confirmation or vacatur, severance and partial confirmation of awards, resubmission of defective awards to the arbitral tribunal, enforcement and non-enforcement).

Domestic law, therefore, hardly drives ICA. The description of "anational" arbitration makes clear that national law does not provide ICA with its doctrinal anchor. The legal foundation for ICA arises from a universal principle of private law: Freedom of contract (party autonomy for civil law lawyers). According to landmark court decisions, international instruments, statutory provisions, and institutional rules, the contracting parties have a nearly unqualified right to engage in arbitration and to establish the modalities of their arbitration. The United States Supreme Court is fond of stating that courts "enforce arbitration agreements as they are written." It also intones with equal frequency the view that a particular arbitration is a "one-off" event devoid of larger systemic consequences. In other words, there is no need for a rule of law where contract controls and privatizes all aspects of the dispute resolution process. By emphasizing the sovereignty of contract rights and the self-contained character of arbitration, the Court suggests that statutory frameworks, transnational or otherwise, are merely "default" vehicles that fill gaps when party agreement is absent, unclear, or impossible to secure.

Law in ICA, therefore, is the universal law of contract. There also is law-making in arbitration from a *stare decisis* or *jurisprudence étabiie* perspective. Arbitral rulings yield legal principles or rules that can be applied as controlling precedent in subsequent arbitrations. International arbitrators not only adjudicate, but they also make law—a *lex mercatoria arbitralis*. Moreover, practices pertaining to the regulation of arbitration and the conduct of arbitral proceedings have been codified in the UNCITRAL model framework. The Model Law and the Model Rules, as noted earlier, reflect a general world consensus regarding the essential principles of arbitration law and of the rules pertaining to the arbitral trial.

A *laissez-faire* State policy in conjunction with universal contract law principles and the codification of basic regulatory principles through international instruments constitute the legal foundation for the process of ICA. These elements coincide with the development of "anational" arbitration and the law-making function of international arbitrators. The autonomy of the contracting parties is so strong as a controlling proposition that some national courts permit the parties to agree to their own standard of judicial review for awards. The party choice may conflict with an otherwise governing statutory standard, but some courts will enforce it nonetheless. While this position has been criticized and has divided ruling courts, when applied, it makes the governing statute into a default framework. The enforcement of awards nullified at the place of rendition is another illustration of the perfunctory status of national law in ICA. Courts in both France and the United States have enforced awards set aside at the place of rendition. Again, despite its controversial character, this decisional law demonstrates that national law is subservient to the transborder norms that attach to the ICA process. The enforceability of awards trumps the integrity and authority of national legal processes.

Conclusions

There is no doubt that arbitration is serious adjudicatory business: The outcomes are final and binding. Moreover, contract problems are no different if brought before the courts or arbitral tribunals. Contract provisions may be imprecise; oral agreements may have modified the written agreement over time; boilerplate language may not cover the actual characteristics of the transaction; and technical employees may not have understood the business contract. Therefore, the problems treated by arbitration are as serious and as difficult as those brought before the courts of law.

In addition, arbitration often is used in complex business transactions. The arbitral determination can affect the solvency of a commercial enterprise and, thereby, the viability of local economies. It can also extinguish or safeguard individual rights. As the prevailing adjudicatory mechanism, arbitration can establish the basic approach toward consumer claims and other types of grievances. Given the presumptive enforceability of arbitral awards, the rulings of arbitral tribunals generally can affect a wide variety of actors and activities in society.

Lawyers and law firms take the business of litigation through arbitration as seriously as judicial litigation. Arbitral proceedings can become as complicated as complex litigation before the courts. They can involve elaborate pre-hearing conferences, a volume of documentation, a lengthy list and examination of witnesses and various experts, and innumerable motions before the arbitral tribunal and perhaps eventually the courts.

The trial of an action in arbitration can be every bit as time-consuming and painstaking as pursuing the client's interest before a court. The expedition of quality arbitration—having an arbitrator determine on the spot whether the goods delivered conform to specifications—has little relevance to the current, society-wide operation of the arbitral process.

Arbitration is also an enormous service industry. It includes a number of private institutions, each with its own set of rules and practices, as well as private individuals who serve as arbitrators, legal counsel, and administrators, or act as experts and consultants. Moreover, a huge infrastructure of support services is associated with the adjudicatory mechanism. Becoming a venue for arbitration can be a very lucrative business and, especially in the international arena, is seen as a distinctly desirable status. Arbitration has acquired a large share of the volume of adjudication in both the international and domestic areas, and its scope of application has not been constricted. The acceptance of arbitration is a necessary passport to participation in international commerce, and it appears to have become a primary vehicle for dispensing civil justice in the United States. Of necessity, lawyers and business enterprises are developing a substantial acquaintance with, and professional expertise in, arbitration.

The accomplishments of commercial arbitration should not be minimized. In the area of transborder commercial relations, it has established and maintained a procedural, and perhaps a substantive, rule of law that provides for the nonsectarian, expert, and enforceable resolution of international commercial conflicts. International business and globalization would not be possible without arbitration. It even attenuates the effects of sovereignty in trade relations and facilitates the participation of States in international commerce. In domestic matters, the impact of arbitration is less direct and creative, albeit perhaps no less necessary. It functions as a parallel system of adjudication. It long has serviced specialized commercial communities and responded to the needs of labor relations; it now also has the mission of applying regulatory law, supplying consumers and employees with an effective adjudicatory framework, and assisting courts and agencies in their operation. In all these areas, arbitration provides access, expertise, and a means by which to avoid or minimize the harassment and inefficiencies of adversarial trial tactics.

As it has grown, however, arbitration has become increasingly afflicted with traditional complexities. With the possible exception of specialized industry sectors, arbitration is rarely what it was originally:

A simple, informal, and expedient means of resolving conflicts. Arbitral proceedings can be more efficient and economical than a judicial trial, but that advantage is hardly guaranteed in the present state of arbitration practice. Arbitral procedures, especially in international matters but even for consumer or employment claims, can be quite adversarial and akin to the sophisticated trial devices used in court.

In fact, arbitration has lost or abandoned much of its capacity for expedition. In the international area, arbitration maintains its appeal through the neutrality, expertise, and enforceability it proffers. Domestically, recourse to arbitration is commanded by the conventions of the trade, the decisional law of the U.S. Supreme Court, legislative enactments, and the inaccessibility and other disadvantages of the legal system. The onus of arbitration's expanded mission is beginning to weigh upon it. Arbitral adjudication appears to have undergone noticeable modifications in application, structure, and foundational ideology.

Arbitral practice has responded to these changes by supporting the evolution and adaptation of arbitration, on the one hand, and by reintroducing a form of expedition and speed to the existing framework of arbitration, on the other hand. Arbitration service-providers have all embraced an expedited form of arbitration, known generally as Fast–Track Arbitration, for those parties who believe expedited proceedings are an essential part of their dispute resolution needs. The availability of such a mechanism represents a return of the arbitral process to a form of adjudication based upon speed, finality, and basic procedural fairness. Moreover, the contracting parties can always control the arbitration themselves through the arbitral clause by providing, for example, for time-limited arbitral proceedings that exclude some or all of the complex devices of the judicial trial. This contractual response to complex and protracted arbitration is possible in domestic matters as well—provided, of course, that the parties can reach agreement on this matter within the context of their transaction.

In modern society, arbitration has made a trial framework and adjudication available to the greater number. It has made the work of justice possible. In matters international, it has erected bridges between societies divided by culture, mores, values, and traditional practices. It has even provided a workable system for assessing the commercial consequences of political conduct and transborder trade policies.

The true challenge for arbitration and for society in the twenty-first century is not its legitimacy *vis-à-vis* traditional justice and its due process and equal protection values. The U.S. Supreme Court, high courts and justice policies in other countries, and the needs of global commerce have made clear that a suitable accommodation can be, and has been, reached on that score. In many respects, the true challenge to arbitration emanates from the "talking therapy" models of dispute resolution, most particularly, mediation in its multiple formats and manifestations.

The use of mediation is based upon the "empowerment" of the parties and ostensibly minimizes the need for an authority figure who decides. The disputing parties can provide themselves with their own outcomes by subduing unproductive emotions, maintaining their objectivity, and embracing rationality. The promise of mediation is potent because it advances the possibility that human beings can readily transcend the limitations of their aggressive nature. In doing so, it sometimes swells their self-esteem to unsustainable illusory heights.

Mediation is sometimes effective (especially in child custody cases), always opportunistic, and rarely—if ever—completely truthful to clients and respectful of their legal rights. Mediators often wonder aloud why judges and lawyers have a monopoly in dispute resolution. This observation is revealing. It exposes the self-serving ideology that is embedded in the methodology of mediation. Mediation's insatiable range of application now extends to criminal offenses, the most sacrosanct and inviolable area of public law adjudication.

Mediators are not completely trustworthy; they are not beyond manipulation or overreaching to achieve what they believe is right. They employ basic therapeutic techniques to achieve "closure," what they believe to be an "appropriate" resolution of the parties' conflict. Succinctly stated, mediation can be both elitist and paternalistic at its foundation. Clients who lack familiarity and sophistication can be at a distinct disadvantage. Under the guise of humanitarianism, mediation attributes inordinate powers to the mediator.

The practice of mediation is built upon fallacious and incomplete thinking. The use of the designated driver illustrates the point. Selecting a sober driver among a group of drinkers is intended to minimize the dangers associated with social intoxication. In the parlance of mediation, it is a "win-win" situation: Inebriation can take place with much less risk of critical or deadly injury. The "win-win," however, is both fleeting and ultimately self-defeating. In reality, it fosters risky (not to mention illegal) behavior by enabling it. It thereby avoids the fundamental problem: The abuse of alcohol in a public setting in society. It assumes that the identified anti-social conduct is inevitable and cannot otherwise be prevented or effectively corrected. It also underestimates the fragility of the solution and its possibly flawed implementation. Finally, it completely ignores the other, more serious, and long lasting consequence of behavior to advance the "quick fix."

Professing that mediating parties can be "empowered" to reach a resolution of their conflict is similarly short-sighted and counterproductive. There is no real finality in the agreed-upon conclusion. Reflection and whim can alter the commitment. If the parties embrace "healthy" behavior, the mediation methodology has succeeded and the mediator's skills are touted as supremely lucid and effective. If an agreement is not reached or collapses, the parties have simply "chosen" to disregard mediation's benefit. Such evaluations empower no one but the mediator. The prospect of personality growth and emotional insight is momentary and fleeting. If a solution is forthcoming, it is likely to be menial. Trite wisdom provides little, if any, guidance for real difficulties. Thinking "outside the box" is a slogan and devoid of authentic meaning. It lessens the teaching of human experience and distorts the true difficulty of accommodating differences.

The critics of arbitration are apprehensive about the treatment that litigants might receive in arbitral proceedings at the hands of arbitrators. By large and large, that concern has been shown to be unfounded and unjustified. In particular, the recent Searles study on AAA consumer arbitration validates that point. *See* www.searlearbitration.org/report/. Arbitrators are adjudicatory professionals, subject like their proceedings to rules, supervised by the marketplace, arbitral institutions, and the courts.

The likelihood of the mistreatment of "disputants" is much greater in the privileged and confidential nonadjudicatory environment of mediation. Would-be disputants are not suffering from mental illness. They disagree and are in turmoil. In any event, mediators are not trained medical professionals. They do, however, have enormous discretion and control. Confidential sessions and sidebars, like the onus upon the mediating parties, shield mediators from accountability.

Mediation is nothing more than structured negotiation conducted by non-lawyers or by legal professionals who have abandoned the work of adjudication. It does, or should, not exceed the parties' volition or society's willingness to permit self-administered pre-litigation settlement. Because mediation is a framework for settlement, coercive jurisdiction or enforcement does not apply. Mediators' desire to trespass upon the domain of adjudication and the law is based upon their misassessment of their abilities, skills, and the remedy they propound. In many ways, the process is too solipsistic to have an effective systemic impact.

Society needs a dependable and stable form of order and a competent and functional rule-making process—not an occasional individualized remedy. The arbitrator is the modern-day praetor. The lawgiver—the legislature—recognizes that arbitrators can be trusted to apply agreed-upon rules—the law—and to render awards that are capable, and worthy, of legal enforcement. The adjudicatory function of the law is neither a quest for manipulated outcomes nor a form of emotional therapy. It admits its commitment to power and accepts the responsibility of establishing order. It maintains the stability, and therefore the values, of society. It cannot, and does not pretend to, address the emotional consequences of personal disappointments.

By intruding upon adjudication, mediation actually highlights the value of formalization and the need for process—the elements that have made judicial litigation unworkable for most civil cases. These attributes are nonetheless necessary to the legitimacy of the process of dispute resolution. To be viable, the determination of disputes must be grounded in the tradition of the law and respond to recognized social commands. It should not be exempt from external scrutiny.

Like arbitration, mediation arises from contractual choice and operates at the threshold of official justice. At this juncture, the processes separate and follow distinct paths. They assume different characteristics and roles. Mediation endeavors to have the parties agree to a self-imposed solution under the guidance of the mediator in an atmosphere of voluntary communication. Disclosures are not mandated and there is no basis for an objective assessment of the process or its result. Either the parties reach an agreement or they do not. Either the mediator fails or succeeds.

Arbitrators stand in the shoes of a judge for the arbitrating parties. They preside over a privately-created court. In effect, they exercise a surrogate jurisdictional mandate for a single transaction. Arbitrators generally are experts in the relevant business, industry, or area. Proceedings are less formal and more flexible than judicial hearings. Arbitrators can rule in equity, but generally do customary or commercial justice by reference to the law. Arbitration results in an adjudicatory determination that is final and binding. In the event of noncompliance, rulings are enforceable by ordinary judicial means. Once an arbitration agreement is in place, the recourse to arbitration and a final determination are assured.

The choice between arbitration and mediation is more than a mere choice of remedy. It is more than the selection of an approach to dispute resolution or creating additional options by which to reach a solution to conflict. In the end, the two mechanisms are profoundly incompatible. They reflect conflicting ideologies and values. Mediation anchors rectitude in prescribed behavior, while adjudication privileges freedom and fairness in the imposition of societal restraints. Lawyers are not any more equipped to undertake mediation than psychoanalysts are able to perform cardiovascular surgery. Adjudication is more than a social convention held together by the inertia of time. It is how society chooses between competing interests. The choice that is made is not itself as important as how it is made. As a functional form of adjudication, arbitration is instrumental to establishing the rule of law in, and the civilization of, society.

Adjudication recognizes both the potential and limitations of human nature. It pays proper tribute to the need for social order, but acknowledges that the acceptance of authority is dependent upon fairness. The resolution of disputes must respect the essential dignity and freedom of people. Unfortunately, the history of humanity is a story of perpetual warfare. Arbitration eliminates adversarial excesses, provides access and process, and does not trample the human personality. Arbitration promises and delivers justice.

*

INDEX

References are to Pages

ADHESIVE ARBITRATION PROVISIONS
Generally, 171
Challenges, 177
Consumer arbitrations, unilateral nature of, 170
Employment arbitrations, unilateral nature of, 218
Fairness analyses, 172
Jurisdictional authority to resolve adhesion claims, 13
Mutuality of obligation, 176, 227
Public-law/private-law distinctions, 177
Unconscionability, 3, 172, 174

ADVANTAGES OF ARBITRATION
Generally, 18, 26
Consumer and employment disputes, 182
International disputes, 282

AGE DISCRIMINATION IN EMPLOYMENT ACT
Arbitrability of claims, 203, 212

AGREEMENTS TO ARBITRATE
Generally, 11
Adhesive Arbitration Provisions, this index
Ambiguities, resolution in favor of arbitration, 138
Any dispute provisions, 16
Arbitral clauses
    Generally, 11
    Incorporation by reference, 12
    Separability doctrine, 12

343

†